Jobs or Privileges

MENA DEVELOPMENT REPORT

Jobs or Privileges

Unleashing the Employment Potential of the Middle East and North Africa

Marc Schiffbauer
Abdoulaye Sy
Sahar Hussain
Hania Sahnoun
Philip Keefer

 **WORLD BANK GROUP**

ISBN: 978-1-4648-0405-2
eISBN: 978-1-4648-0406-9
DOI: 10.1596/978-1-4648-0405-2

Cover art: © Aladdin El-Gendy. Used with permission. Further permission required for reuse.

Library of Congress Cataloging-in-Publication Data has been requested

Contents

Acknowledgments   xi

About the Authors and Contributors   xiii

Abbreviations   xvii

Overview   xix

Introduction   1
    Notes   7

1 Too Little Too Late: Private Sector Growth and Labor
   Demand   9
    Economic Growth Has Been Moderate and Job Growth Weak   10
    Drivers of Job Growth: Young Firms and Productive Firms
        Create More Jobs   24
    MENA Needs a Larger Pool of Young Firms
        and Productive Firms   33
    Notes   42
    References   45

2 Distorted Dynamics: The Impact of Policies on Firm
   Dynamics and Job Growth   49
    Attracting FDI in Services Sparked Job Growth in Domestic
        Firms in Jordan   51
    Business Regulations Limit Employment Growth among Young
        Firms in Morocco   61
    Energy Subsidies in the Arab Republic of Egypt Discourage
        Growth in Labor-Intensive Industries   64
    Discriminatory Policy Implementation Deters a Level
        Playing Field in MENA   68
    Notes   77
    References   79

3 **Avoiding the Pitfalls of Industrial Policy:**
   Program Design in MENA and East Asia   81

   Industrial Policy in MENA Has Had Limited Success and
      Many Instances of Policy Capture   84
   What Did Successful Countries Do? The Case of the
      Republic of Korea   92
   Lessons from East Asia Are More Difficult to Implement
      than Is Commonly Understood   96
   Notes   98
   References   99

4 **Privileges Instead of Jobs: Political Connections and**
   Private Sector Growth in MENA   101

   Privileges to Politically Connected Firms Undermine
      Competition and Job Creation: Evidence from the
      Arab Republic of Egypt and Tunisia   103
   Available Qualitative Evidence Points to Similar Mechanisms
      of Policy Privileges in Other MENA Countries   131
   What Explains the Different Outcomes in MENA
      and East Asia?   139
   Notes   142
   References   146

Implications for Policy   149

Appendix A Economic Growth and Structural
Transformation   153

Appendix B Firm Censuses and Surveys: Countries,
Time, and Sector Coverage   165

Appendix C Share of Employment in Large Firms among
State-Owned Enterprises and Foreign Firms   169

Appendix D Employment Growth over Firms' Life Cycles:
Manufacturing Sector   171

Appendix E FDI Inflow and Employment in Jordan:
Regression Analysis   173

Appendix F Quality of Business Environment and Jobs
in Morocco: Data, Methods, and Main Findings   175

Appendix G Political Connections and Private Sector
Growth in the Arab Republic of Egypt   179

Boxes

1.1   Is Structural Change in Morocco Gender-Biased?   16
1.2   Who Create More Jobs?   25
1.3   Firm Dynamics and Productivity Growth in Morocco   41
2.1   FDI into Services Sectors Is Often Restricted in MENA
      Countries   54
2.2   Mobility Restrictions Reduces Competition and Job
      Growth in the West Bank   58
2.3   Misallocation of Capital in the Arab Republic of Egypt   67
3.1   Market Failure and Industrial Policy   82
3.2   Are GCC Countries an Exception?   90
4.1   Did Ben Ali Firms Dictate Amendments to the
      Investment Law in the 2000s?   119
4.2   Political Connections and Patronage in the Republic
      of Yemen   129
4.3   The Islamic Republic of Iran: Privatizations without
      the Private Sector   136

Figures

1.1   Decomposition of GDP Per Capita Growth in MENA
        and Other Developing Regions   11
1.2   Structural Change across Regions and among MENA
        Countries, 2000–05   14
1.3   Correlation between Entry and Exit Rates across
        Two-Digit Sectors   15
B1.1.1 Reallocation of Labor across Sectors, by Gender, 2000–11 17
1.4   Demographic Change and Composition of
        Working-Age Population   18
1.5   Employment Share, by Firm Size   19
1.6   Distribution of Employment across Nonagriculture
        Sectors   19
1.7   Percentage Change in Share of Employment in Medium
        and Large Establishments   20
1.8   Employment Transition, by Firm Size   22
1.9   Incidence of Gazelles in All Sectors and Manufacturing   23
1.10   Share of Jobs Created by Gazelles and Nongazelles in
        All Sectors and in the Manufacturing Sector   23
1.11   Net Job Creation, by Firm Size and Age   26
1.12   Net Job Creation, by Firm Size before and after
        Controlling for Firm Age   28
1.13   Net Job Creation, by Firm Age after Controlling for
        Firm Size   29

1.14   Employment Growth Is Strongest in First 4–5 Years
after Firm Entry   30

1.15   Employment Growth over a Firm's Life Cycle
for All Nonfarm Sectors   31

1.16   Characteristics of Gazelles in the Arab Republic of
Egypt, Lebanon, and Morocco   32

1.17   Entry Density of Formal Sector Limited-Liability
Firms across Regions and Countries, 2004–12   34

1.18   Firm Turnover across Countries   35

1.19   Survival Rates Five Years after Entry   36

1.20   Employment Share of Young Medium or Large
Establishments   36

1.21   Distribution of Employment, by Firm Size and Age
across All Nonfarm Establishments: Arab Republic
of Egypt and Turkey, 2006   37

1.22   Labor Productivity Growth over the Life Cycle of
Manufacturing Establishments   38

1.23   Gap between Weighted and Unweighted Labor
Productivity   40

1.24   Productivity, by Firm Size in Tunisia, Lebanon,
and Turkey   40

B1.3.1   Decomposition of Firm Productivity Growth in
Morocco's Manufacturing Sector, 1996–2006   42

2.1   Share of FDI Inflows, by Sector, Selected MENA
Countries, 2003–10   53

B2.1.1   Service Trade Restriction Index, by Sector and Region   54

B2.1.2   Service Trade Restrictions in Transportation Services in
MENA, 2008   55

B2.2.1   Mobility Restrictions Reduce Net Entry, Employment
Growth, and Local Output Growth   60

2.2   Distribution of Employment, by Energy Intensity and
Size and Age   65

2.3   Employment Share, by Sector Factor Intensity in
the Arab Republic of Egypt, 2006, and Turkey, 2010   66

B2.3.1   Productivity, in Manufacturing and Mining, by Size   67

2.4   Regulatory Policy Implementation Uncertainty
in MENA   69

2.5   Variability in Days to Accomplish Various Regulatory
Tasks across Firms, Selected MENA Countries   72

3.1   The Evolution of Average (Weighted) Tariffs and
NTMs on Imports, 1995–2010   87

4.1   The Evolution of Net Profit Differentials between
Connected and Other Firms, 2003–11   110

4.2	Authorization Requirements and FDI Restrictions Protect Politically Connected Firms in Tunisia	112
4.3	Share of Politically Connected Firms in High and Low Energy-Intensive Sectors in the Arab Republic of Egypt	115
4.4	Large Firms in Politically Connected Industries Are More Likely to Be Located in an Industrial Zone	117
4.5	Nontariff Barriers Are Frequently Imposed in MENA	132
4.6	Transparency International: Defence Anti-Corruption Index	133
4.7	Perceptions of Corruption in Government and Business, Middle East and North Africa, 2011	138
4.8	Worldwide Governance Indicators	139
A.1	Real GDP Per Capita Growth Decomposition	154
A.2	Long-Term Structural Change in Four MENA Countries	155
A.3	Structural Change, by Sector, 2000–05	156
A.4	The Product Space	161
A.5	Product Space in Selected Regions, 1976–78 and 2007–09	162
C.1	Number of Firms and Jobs in Foreign, Domestic Private, or Public Establishments	169
D.1	Manufacturing: Employment Growth over the Life Cycle	171

Map

B2.2.1	Mobility Restrictions in the West Bank, 2006 and 2011	59

Tables

1.1	Employment Transition Matrix	21
1.2	Sectors with the Highest Rate of Job Growth across Countries	27
1.3	More Productive Firms Create More Jobs	32
2.1	Averages and Dispersion of Firms' Waiting Days for Regulatory Services	70
2.2	Share of Firms That Disagree with the Statement That Implementation of Rules Is "Consistent and Predictable"	73
2.3	The Extent to Which Firms Take Action to Influence Policy Implementation across Types of Firms in MENA	74
2.4	Higher Policy Implementation Uncertainty Induces Senior Managers to Spend More Time with Government Officials	75

2.5	Policy Implementation Uncertainty Reduces Innovation and Firm Growth in Jordan and the Arab Republic of Egypt	76
3.1	The Cost of Industrial Policy in Morocco, 2010	89
4.1	Number of Politically Connected Firms, by Economic Sectors	107
4.2	Within-Sector Differences, Politically Connected and Other Firms	109
4.3	Politically Connected Firms and All Firms Protected by Nontariff Trade Barriers in the Arab Republic of Egypt	113
4.4	Government Relations and Competition in Sectors with Politically Connected Firms versus Nonconnected Sectors in the Arab Republic of Egypt	116
B4.1.1	Correlation between New Barriers to Entry and the Presence of Ben Ali Firms	120
4.5	Firm Dynamics in Sectors with Politically Connected Firms versus Nonconnected Sectors in the Arab Republic of Egypt	125
4.6	Financial Corruption Risk Subindex: Asset Disposal and Links to Business, MENA Countries	135
A.1	Estimates of Labor's Share and Marginal Productivities Using Harmonized Household Survey Data from the World Bank (I2D2)	158
A.2	Manufacturing Labor Productivity Growth Rates	159
E.1	Employment Spillovers from FDI, by Firm Characteristics	173
F.1	List of Regulatory Policy Variables	177
F.2	Job Growth Regression with Coefficients of the Policy and Environment Variables	177
G.1	Employment Growth Declines after Politically Connected Firms Enter Initially Unconnected Sectors	180
G.2	Entry of Connected Firms into Initially Unconnected Sectors, 1997–2006	180

Acknowledgments

This report was prepared by a team composed of Marc Schiffbauer (task team leader), Abdoulaye Sy, Sahar Hussain, Hania Sahnoun, and Philip Keefer. In addition, the following persons contributed to the individual chapters of the report: Ishac Diwan (Chapter 4), Doerte Doemeland (Chapter 1), Bob Rijkers (Chapters 1 and 4), Dalia Al Kadi (Chapter 1), Izak Atiyas (Chapter 1), Ozan Bakis (Chapter 1), Michael Lamla (Chapter 2), and Michael Gasiorek (Chapter 2). Further inputs were provided by Jamal Haider, Hassen Arouri, Huy Nguyen, Karim Badr, Anna Raggl, Yeon Soo Kim, and Caroline Duclos. Clifton Wiens edited the report. Aladdin El-Gendy produced the cover picture of the report. Muna Abeid Salim, Seraphine Nsabimana, and Faythe Agnes Calandra provided administrative support. The report was prepared under the direction of Bernard Funck.

The report benefited from the overall guidance of Shantayanan Devarajan, Chief Economist of the World Bank Middle East and North Africa region, as well as from Caroline Freund and Manuela Ferro.

The team thanks Najy Benhassine (Practice Manager, Trade and Competitiveness, World Bank), Hafez Ghanem (Senior Fellow, Brookings Institution), and Adeel Malik (Research Fellow in Economics, University of Oxford) for their valuable comments. The report also benefited from comments and guidance from Kevin Carey, Ahmed Kouchouk, Tara Vishwanath, Celestin Monga, Daniel Lederman, Mary Hallward-Driemeier, Jorge Araujo, Nikola Spatafora, Aaditya Mattoo, Ana Fernandes, Peter Mousley, Simon Bell, and Randa Akeel.

The team is grateful to the various statistics and research institutions across the region that facilitated access to data and collaborated with the team, including the Institut National de la Statistique in Tunisia; the Ministry of Planning and International Coordination and the Department of Statistics in Jordan; the Central Agency for Public Mobilization and Statistics in the Arab Republic of Egypt; and the Economic Research

Forum team, in particular Ahmed Galal (Managing Director) and Hoda Selim (Economist).

The team also thanks Antonio Nucifora, Eric Le Borgne, Orhan Niksic, Sibel Kulaksiz, Umar Serajuddin, Nour Jalal Nasser Eddin, Nada Choueiri, Amir Mokhtar Althibah, and the entire Poverty Reduction and Economic Management Department for supporting the country dialogue and for their collaboration during the preparation of various country analytical works undertaken in parallel to this regional report.

About the Authors and Contributors

Marc Schiffbauer is a senior economist and part of the team preparing the World Development Report 2016 on Internet for Development. He joined the World Bank in September 2009, working in the Poverty Reduction and Economic Management unit in the Eastern Europe and Central Asia region as well as in the Middle East and North Africa region. Before that, he worked for the Economic and Social Research Institute in Dublin, Ireland, and as a consultant for the European Central Bank and the International Monetary Fund on issues related to economic growth, firm productivity, and competition. Marc has a PhD in economics from the University of Bonn in Germany and was a one-year visiting scholar at Universidad Pompeu Fabra, Barcelona, and at the University of British Columbia, Vancouver.

Abdoulaye Sy is an economist in the Macro and Fiscal Management Global Practice at the World Bank and currently works in the Middle East and North Africa region where he is the country economist for the Islamic Republic of Iran and Djibouti. Abdoulaye joined the World Bank in September 2011 as a Young Professional, first as an economist in the Sustainable Development Department in the Latin America and Caribbean region, later joining the Poverty Reduction and Economic Management unit in the Middle East and North Africa region. Abdoulaye has a PhD in agricultural and resource economics from the University of California–Berkeley and holds master's degrees in science and economics from the Ecole Polytechnique, the Paris School of Economics (PSE), and the Ecole Nationale de la Statistique et de l'Administration Economique (ENSAE).

Sahar Hussain joined the World Bank as an economist in February 2013 in MENA's Poverty Reduction and Economic Management unit. Prior to that, she worked for the Egyptian Centre for Economic Studies in Cairo as an economist on issues related to the economics of transitions, competition policy, and energy subsidies. She was also an economic consultant for the Planning Commission of Pakistan. Sahar has a master's degree in development economics and policy analysis from the University of Nottingham and a bachelor's degree from the London School of Economics.

Hania Sahnoun is an economist and consultant. She joined the team preparing the World Development Report 2016 on Internet for Development. She has worked with the World Bank as a consultant since 2004. Hania holds a Diploma of Advanced Studies in economics from the University of Pantheon–Paris I in France.

Philip Keefer is a principal advisor of the Institutions for Development Department of the Inter-American Development Bank. He was formerly a lead research economist in the Development Research Group of the World Bank. The focus of his work, based on experience in countries such as Bangladesh, Benin, Brazil, the Dominican Republic, Indonesia, Mexico, Peru, and Pakistan, is the determinants of political incentives to pursue economic development. His research, on issues such as the impact of insecure property rights on growth; the effects of political credibility on policy; and the sources of political credibility in democracies and autocracies; and the influence of political parties on conflict, political budget cycles, and public sector reform, has appeared in journals such as the *Quarterly Journal of Economics* and the *American Political Science Review*.

Ishac Diwan is currently a research fellow at Paris Sciences et Lettres. He taught previously at the Harvard University Kennedy School of Government and at New York University. He has held several positions at the World Bank—in the Research Complex, the Middle East Department, and the World Bank Institute—and in Addis Ababa then in Accra as the country director for countries in East Africa and then in West Africa. His current research interests include growth strategies, the political economy of private sector development, and the analysis of public opinions, with a special interest in Africa and the Middle East. He directs the Economic and Political Transformation program of the Economic Research Forum.

Doerte Doemeland is a senior economist in the Macroeconomics and Fiscal Management Global Practice. Before that, Doerte was a senior economist in the Development Research Group of the World Bank. The focus of her work, based on experience in Albania, Bulgaria, Malawi, Mexico, Nigeria, Senegal, Tunisia, Uganda, and Uruguay, is on the determinants of economic growth and poverty reduction resulting from trade and competitiveness, structural change, or productivity growth.

Dalia Al Kadi is an economist in the Macroeconomics and Fiscal Management Global Practice at the World Bank. She joined the World Bank's Poverty Reduction and Economic Management unit in the Middle East and North Africa Department in February 2013. Before joining the World Bank, Dalia was a project manager at the Executive Council in Abu Dhabi, where she advised the government on economic policy and strategy. She was also a management consultant for McKinsey & Company and advised clients in the banking, telecom, and public sectors in the Middle East and Pakistan. Dalia has an MPA in international development from Harvard University.

Bob Rijkers is an economist in the Trade and International Integration Unit of the Development Research Group at the World Bank. He is interested in political economy, trade and labor market issues. He holds a BA in science and social sciences from University College Utrecht, Utrecht University, and an M.Phil. and D.Phil. in economics from the University of Oxford.

Abbreviations

AISS	Annual Industry and Service Statistics
CAPMAS	Central Agency for Public Mobilization and Statistics
CPI	Corruption Perceptions Index
EAP	East Asia and Pacific
ECA	Europe and Central Asia
EIDS	Egypt Industrial Development Strategy
ES	Enterprise Survey
FDI	foreign direct investment
GCC	Gulf Cooperation Council
GDP	gross domestic product
ICA	Investment Climate Assessment
ICT	information and communications technology
LAC	Latin America and Caribbean
LMIC	lower middle-income country
MENA	Middle East and North Africa
MFTI	Ministry for Trade and Industry
MNE	multinational enterprise
NTM	nontariff measure
OECD	Organisation for Economic Co-operation and Development
PPP	purchasing power parity
SOE	state-owned enterprise
SSO	Social Security Organisation
TFP	total factor productivity
TI	Transparency International
WBES	World Bank Enterprise Survey
WDI	World Development Indicators
WITS	World Integrated Trade Solution

Overview

Middle East and North Africa (MENA) countries face a critical choice as they strive to generate greater private sector growth and more jobs: promote competition, provide equal opportunities for all entrepreneurs, and dismantle the current system of privileges for connected firms or risk perpetuating the current equilibrium of low job creation. This report shows that policies that stifle competition and create an uneven playing field abound in MENA and are a major constraint on private sector growth and job creation. These policies take different forms across countries and sectors but share several common features: they limit free entry in the domestic market, exclude certain firms from government programs, increase the regulatory burden and uncertainty for firms without connections, insulate certain firms and sectors from foreign competition, and create incentives that discourage domestic firms from competing in international markets. The report shows that such policies are often captured by a few privileged firms with deep political connections and that these policies persist despite their apparent cost to society. The millions of workers and consumers and the majority of entrepreneurs who bear the brunt of that cost are often unaware of the adverse impact of these policies on the jobs and economic opportunities to which they aspire. This limits the scope for critical internal debate on the economic future of MENA countries and curtails the policy dialogue necessary for reform.

Labor markets in MENA have underperformed for a long time. This has left large segments of the population on the sidelines of the economy and created a sense of exclusion. MENA has a large reservoir of untapped human resources; it has some of the world's highest unemployment rates among college graduates and youth and the lowest participation of women in the labor force. Strategies focused on increasing employment in the public sector have proved to be unsustainable, and private sector job creation has been too weak to absorb the growing labor force. Desirable private sector jobs—those with high wages, a formal contract, and social

The Impact of Privileges on Policies, Competition, and Jobs

The findings of this report highlight some of the economic impacts of the privileges granted to politically connected firms:

- In the Arab Republic of Egypt, 71 percent of connected firms, but only 4 percent of all firms, sell products that are protected by at least three technical import barriers.

- In Tunisia, 64 percent of politically connected firms operate in sectors subject to restrictions on foreign direct investment (FDI), relative to only 36 percent of nonconnected firms.

- In Egypt, 45 percent of all connected firms operate in energy-intensive industries such as cement or steel, compared with only 8 percent of all firms.

- In Tunisia, 64 percent of politically connected firms are in sectors requiring an exclusive license to operate relative to only 45 percent of nonconnected firms.

- Firms in politically connected industries (that is, with at least one connected firm) are 11–14 percent more likely to have acquired land from the government.

- An additional firm with a politically connected chief executive officer (CEO) reduces the average waiting time for a construction permit in an industry by 51 days.

- Firms in industries with at least one politically connected CEO are inspected by tax officials 4.6 times a year relative to 5.7 times a year for firms in sectors without a connected CEO. In addition, the frequency of inspections by municipalities is about 20 percent higher for firms in nonconnected industries.

- The dispersion of reported inspections across firms is significantly higher within connected sectors. This suggests that politically connected firms receive very few inspections while nonconnected firms are inspected frequently.

- The entry of new firms into politically connected sectors is about 28 percent lower than into nonconnected firms.

- Aggregate employment growth declines by about 1.4 percentage points annually when connected firms enter new, previously unconnected sectors in Egypt.

security benefits—are few, pushing a growing number of workers to seek employment in unproductive subsistence activities, often in the informal economy. This situation has contributed to the widespread frustration with the lack of opportunities, of which Arab Spring uprisings were a powerful expression.

Previous World Bank reports have linked MENA's employment performance to supply-side factors, labor market policies, and qualitative evidence of weak competition as a result of privileges for connected firms. Two past regional World Bank reports provide the starting point to this report. First, the World Bank report *Jobs for Shared Prosperity* (2013a) analyzed how supply-side factors such as education and training, and labor market policies affect employment outcomes in MENA. The report concluded, however, that supply-side factors only partially explain employment outcomes in MENA and highlighted the importance of analyzing demand-side factors to explain the weak private sector job creation record. Second, the World Bank report *From Privilege to Competition: Unlocking the Private-Led Growth in the Middle East and North Africa* (2009) provides rich qualitative evidence that policy capture in MENA countries leads to privileges for a few politically connected firms, which ultimately limits competition and private sector development. The report argued that privileges to politically connected firms in MENA resulted in policies—such as subsidized land acquisitions and directed bank lending—that limited competition and tilted the playing field. The authors of this pre–Arab Spring report used all information available at the time, but did not have access to the full array of data necessary to investigate the possible link between MENA's weak aggregate job creation, the lack of a level playing field, and the absence of competition as a result of prevailing privileges and policy capture in many countries and sectors across the region.

This report fills this gap by analyzing the demand-side factors that constrain faster job creation in MENA countries and how they relate to weak competition and privileges for specific firms. This report aims to answer the following questions: What types of firms create more jobs in MENA? Are they different from job-creating firms in other regions? What policies in MENA prevent the private sector from creating more jobs? How do these policies affect competition? To what extent are these policies associated with privileges to politically connected firms?

This report aims to address these questions by drawing on new data sources that became available after the Arab Spring. First, the report assembles firm census databases for several MENA countries that contain a wide range of firm characteristics and performance measures. This rich source of information is necessary to determine the fundamental drivers of aggregate job creation through the lens of firms. Second, the report combines this information with additional data sources to analyze how certain policies affect competition and the fundamentals of job creation. Third, the report merges these data with new detailed information on state-business relations that surfaced after the Arab Spring. Specifically, the report builds on two novel data sets that identify the first-tier politically connected firms in the Mubarak and Ben Ali regimes in the Arab Republic of Egypt and Tunisia, respectively. These unique data are used to analyze the methods and extent of policy capture by politically connected firms. The report then provides for the first time quantitative evidence that these privileges limit competition, firm dynamics, and job creation. Five main findings of the report stand out.

First, gross domestic product (GDP) per capita growth in MENA over the last two decades was moderate and driven by demographic change, while productivity growth was low. Real GDP per capita growth hovered around 2 percent in the past two decades; about 2–3 percent lower than in South and East Asia, respectively, but comparable to per capita growth rates in other developing regions. Demographic change, leading to an increase in the share of the working age population, accounted for about 50 percent of aggregate real GDP per capita growth over the past 20 years, substantially higher than in any other region. In contrast, aggregate productivity growth was low in MENA compared with other developing regions. Most countries in the region experienced structural change because of a decline of the labor share in agriculture. Aggregate productivity growth was, however, mostly driven by productivity growth within sectors, which still lagged behind all other developing regions. The economic benefits from the ongoing demographic trend could have been much higher had MENA countries been able to absorb their fast-growing labor force into the higher-productivity activities. Instead, job creation was weak and informality, unemployment, and inactivity reached very high levels during this timeframe. Consistent with this trend, analysis of firm census data shows that most workers in MENA are employed in small-scale and low-productivity activities.

Second, the report examines whether the fundamentals of job creation—the types of firms that create more jobs—differ in MENA countries than in fast-growing emerging or even high-income countries in other regions. It shows that they do not: younger firms and more productive firms grow faster and create more jobs in MENA as elsewhere. For example, firm census data show that micro-startups—firms less than five years old and with less than five employees—accounted for 92 percent of net job creation in Tunisia between 1996 and 2010 and 177 percent in Lebanon between 2005 and 2010. In addition, young firms across all size categories contributed positively to net job creation in both countries while employment in older firms tended to contract. However, MENA countries' private sectors have been characterized by low firm turnover (firm entry and exit) and slow productivity growth, which ultimately reduces the pool of young firms and more productive firms. For example, for every 10,000 working-age persons, on average only six limited liability companies were created annually in MENA countries between 2009 and 2012; in contrast, the average across all 91 developing countries with available data was 20 per 10,000 working-age persons, and as high as 40 and 80 in Chile and Bulgaria, respectively. Moreover, we find that productivity growth in MENA is held back by a combination of slow within-firm productivity growth and misallocation of labor and capital across firms. For instance, after 35 years in operation, firms in Tunisia and Egypt barely increase their productivity while firms in India, Mexico, and Turkey increase their productivity about two- or threefold over the same life cycle.

Third, various policies across MENA countries limit competition and undermine the fundamentals of job creation by constraining firm startup and productivity growth. The report presents four case studies that demonstrate how different policies across MENA countries limit competition and result in lower firm turnover, productivity growth, and job creation. The first case study shows how foreign direct investment (FDI) inflow in Jordan led to a partial crowding-out of old and small domestic firms operating in the same sector, but had positive employment spillovers among domestic service providers and young firms. Domestic manufacturing firms (suppliers) did not benefit from FDI spillovers, possibly reflecting a combination of weak competition in the sector and the absence of well-designed and effective technical supplier support programs. Overall, the findings suggest that removing restrictions on FDI into service sectors in Jordan can be expected to generate employment growth among domestic firms. In the second case study, we explore how several dimensions of Morocco's business environment impact employment growth and disproportionately affect young firms. The findings suggest that more competition, equal and predictable treatment by tax administrations, less corruption and fewer obstacles in the judicial system, and lower cost of finance would raise employment growth among young firms. The third case study examines how large energy subsidies targeted to heavy industry in Egypt (equivalent to 2.9 percent of GDP or US$7.4 billion in 2010) affect competition and job creation. A government license is required to legally operate in energy-intensive industries (such as steel and cement), thereby limiting the entry of new firms, equal access for all entrepreneurs, and competition. Moreover, energy subsidies benefit energy-intensive industries thereby discouraging more labor-intensive activities and preventing the economy from fully exploiting its comparative advantage. In the last case study, we show that many firms in MENA identify "policy uncertainty" as a "severe" or "major" obstacle to growth, and that this reflects firms' perception of "policy implementation uncertainty" resulting from discriminatory practices. The large variation in policy implementation leads to reduced competition and innovation in a number of MENA countries. The findings reveal a negative impact of discriminatory policy implementation on productivity growth and private sector dynamism (specifically the entry of new firms) in MENA.

Fourth, past industrial policies in MENA did not reward firms based on performance and did not safeguard or promote competition. Efforts to stimulate private sector growth and jobs in MENA have often taken the form of active industrial policies. But there is limited evidence of success while there are several instances of policy capture by a few insider firms. The report reviews the impact of these policies over the past two decades and compares them with the experience of East Asian countries. This comparison highlights several critical differences in policy design and implementation that underpin the success of industrial policies in East Asian countries when compared with MENA countries. First, East Asian countries seemingly reached broader consensus on a common strategic vision and objectives at the country level, and had a greater focus on new economic activities in sectors where market failures were more likely to constrain industrial development. Second, industrial policy in East Asia was performance oriented, and evaluation systems to assess the performance of policies and public officials were put in place. Third, by linking government support to measurable and verifiable performance, industrial policies in East Asia guaranteed equal access for all firms, while in MENA it often resulted in privileges for a limited number of firms. Fourth, industrial policy in East Asia promoted and safeguarded competition in the domestic market and provided incentives for firms to compete in international markets. East Asian countries invested heavily in human capital and complementary infrastructures improvements, and undertook far-reaching public sector reforms that created a qualified and merit-based public administration.

Fifth, the report provides direct evidence that policies in MENA have often been captured by a few politically connected firms. This has led to a policy environment that created privileges rather than to a level playing field, and has undermined private sector growth and job creation. We show that these privileges insulated firms from domestic and international competition and subsidized their operations via preferential and sometimes exclusive access to cheap inputs (electricity, land, and so forth). Using the theoretical framework proposed by Aghion et al. (2001),[1] we discuss how such policies are likely to reduce competition, undermine equal opportunity for all entrepreneurs, and result in lower efficiency, innovation, and job creation. The report documents how this was the case during the Mubarak and Ben Ali regimes in Egypt and Tunisia, respectively, and provides qualitative evidence for the existence of similar mechanisms in other MENA countries. For example, we find that only a handful of politically connected firms received the bulk of the generous energy subsides to industry in Egypt. Moreover, barriers to entry and trade in Egypt and Tunisia insulated politically connected firms from competition and tilted their incentives towards producing for the domestic market. These policies are typically still in place in both countries; they include exclusive operating licenses that create monopolies in profitable services sectors, unequal access to land, or inconsistent implementation of rules and regulations across firms in the same sector. Furthermore, the report argues that the concentration of connected firms in (nontradable) backbone service sectors in MENA—which lowers the performance of these sectors and increases the relative price of nontradable to tradable goods and services—contributes to the overvaluation of the exchange rate through the phenomenon of *weak links*.[2] The report provides direct quantitative evidence that the preferential treatment of politically connected firms lowers aggregate job growth in Egypt. The available qualitative evidence points to similar mechanisms of policy privileges in other MENA countries. In particular, governance and corruption indicators are higher in MENA than in other regions, especially in corruption in defense as a result of military involvement in business.

The findings of this report have several implications for policy. This report suggests that MENA countries' quest for more jobs should not only include supply-side policies—education, wages, job training—but should also encompass significant policy reforms to stimulate labor demand. The report's findings point to a roadmap for more jobs in MENA in four broad policy areas. Depending on the country context, additional and more specific policy areas also need to be considered:

- First, governments in MENA should reform policies that unduly constrain competition and equality of opportunity for all entrepreneurs. These policies include energy subsidies to industry, exclusive licenses requirements to operate in specific sectors, legal barriers to FDI, and trade barriers—including nontariff measures, administrative barriers to entry and firm growth, and barriers to access the judiciary, land, or industrial zones. Reforms to other policies not analyzed in this report, but potentially equally important in maintaining a level playing field, should also be considered when dealing with specific country cases. These include barriers to firm entry and exit resulting from restrictive hiring and firing laws, cumbersome bankruptcy laws, and so forth. In addition, the findings of this report suggests that if MENA governments want to pursue private sector development programs targeting specific types of firms, they would be well advised to focus on firm age or innovation and not on firm size as a primary targeting criterion, given that startups and more productive firms create most jobs in the region.

- Second, policy makers should reduce the space for discretionary policy implementation and ensure that laws and regulations are enforced equally across firms. This involves ensuring that laws and regulations are clear, that the complexity of policy implementation is reduced, and that policy is designed and implemented by a strong, capable, and accountable administration. The latter can be supported by linking entry into and promotions within the administration to merit, judged on the basis of potential or actual contributions to the legitimate goals of public policy.

- Third, if MENA governments want to pursue state-led development policies, they would be wise to avoid the mistakes of the past and ensure that these new industrial policies—and the administrative structure that implements them—minimize the scope for capture, promote competition, and tightly link support to measurable and verifiable performance.

- One critical aspect of this reform agenda is to create institutions that promote and safeguard competition and equal opportunities for all entrepreneurs. Such institutions include, but are not limited to, a strong, well-organized, and highly competent public administration necessary to implement critical policy changes, such as an effective competition law; an independent competition authority; appropriate procurement laws and implementation; and an independent judiciary.

- Another component, just as important, is to ensure policy making is transparent and open, with a mechanism that facilitates and encourages citizen participation. Citizens should have access to information on proposed and ratified laws and regulations; be able to provide input into policy design and evaluation; be aware of politicians' stakes in firms that benefit from government policies; and have full knowledge of who benefits from subsidies, procurement tenders, public land transactions, privatizations, and so forth.

- This report provides a decision-making guide that summarizes the foregoing, which governments can use as a framework when designing and implementing policies. The decision-making guide is aimed to maximize the likelihood of success given inherent uncertainties and to maximize the positive impact of policies on growth and jobs by minimizing the risk for capture.

Notes

1. The model proposed by Aghion et al. (2001) demonstrates that fair private sector neck-and-neck competition drives economic growth. In this model, competition increases firms' incentives to adopt new technologies in order to reduce costs and escape competition (at least temporarily). However, if a few (colluding) firms have sizeable exogenous cost advantages, which are unbridgeable by competitors in the same sector, then all firms in the sector have fewer incentives to adopt new technologies and sector growth is lower.

In this case, the firms with the cost advantage have little incentive to invest in innovation since they do not face competitive pressures to reduce their costs further; the laggard firms are too far away from the frontier to bridge the cost gap and instead use vintage production technologies, focusing on local market niches to survive. Aggregate growth increases in the number of sectors that are characterized by neck-and-neck competition market structures.

2. See Jones (2011) for a presentation of the concept of *weak links*.

Introduction

This report argues that countries in the Middle East and North Africa (MENA) face a critical choice in their quest for higher private sector growth and more jobs: promote competition, equal opportunities for all entrepreneurs and dismantle existing privileges to specific firms or risk perpetuating the current equilibrium of low job creation. The report shows that policies which lower competition in MENA also constrain private sector development and job creation. These policies take different forms across countries and sectors, but share several common features: they limit free-entry in the domestic market, effectively exclude certain firms from government programs, increase the regulatory burden and uncertainty on nonprivileged firms, insulate certain firms and sectors from foreign competition, and create incentives that discourage domestic firms from competing in international markets. Such policies are often captured by a few privileged firms with deep political connections and persist despite their apparent cost to society. Furthermore, the millions of workers and consumers who bear the brunt of these policies are often unaware of their adverse impacts on the jobs to which they aspire, thereby limiting the scope of debate necessary for internal policy dialogue and reform.

Labor markets in the MENA have been in low equilibrium for a long time. MENA has a large reservoir of untapped human resources with the world's highest youth unemployment rate and the lowest participation of women in the labor force. Desirable private sector jobs, those that are high-paying and attached to a formal contract or social security, are very few. Strategies that consist in increasing employment in the public sector have proven to be unsustainable. On the other hand private sector job creation was too weak to absorb the growing labor force pushing a growing number of workers to seek employment in unproductive, subsistence activities, often in the informal economy. The Arab Spring uprisings were a powerful expression of the lack of employment opportunities and widespread sense exclusion.

A recent Regional Flagship highlights how labor supply factors and labor laws affect employment in MENA. World Bank (2013a) shows that labor force participation is low, especially among women. Unemployment is persistently higher than in other regions and overwhelmingly affects youth. In some countries, such as the Arab Republic of Egypt and Tunisia, the highly educated are more likely to be unemployed (see also World Bank, 2014a). Too often, access to the few desirable jobs depends more on circumstances beyond individual control than on merit. Among those who are employed, the majority are engaged in low-quality jobs—those characterized by low pay and productivity, and without formal labor contracts or social security. The lack of high-quality private sector jobs is also reflected in the small size of formal firms. This report argued that a key challenge for the MENA region to improve the labor market and create more jobs is to "*change the rules of the game to create a dynamic private sector that capitalizes on the full range of theregion's human capital.*" The report highlighted the central role of promoting competition to stimulate private sector growth. However, there is little evidence on the political economy factors that perpetuate and/or accentuate the lack of competition in the region, nor on the type of policy distortions that weaken competition and how those distortions ultimately affect job creation.

This report aims to fill these gaps. It tackles the following questions: What types of firms create more jobs in MENA? Are they different from other regions? What policies in MENA prevent the private sector from creating more jobs? How do these policies affect competition and job creation? To what extent are these policies associated with privileges to politically connected firms?

Previous work has also linked MENA's employment performance to qualitative evidence of privileges to specific firms and weak competition. World Bank (2009) develops the argument that policy privileges captured by a few connected firms limit competition and thus growth in MENA. World Bank (2009) provides rich qualitative empirical evidence describing the lack of competition because of privileges in MENA economies. It used all data available at the time—before the Arab Spring—to characterize the cost of privileges and weak competition. It outlined several relevant policy mechanisms, demonstrating how privileges suppressed competition, ranging from access to credit and land to industrial policy. Building on post-Arab Spring data, this present report broadens the findings of World Bank (2009) by exploring the possible links between privileges and policies limiting competition. Moreover, it provides for the first time direct quantitative evidence that privileges limit competition, firm dynamics, and job creation.

The literature identifies several other prominent explanations for weak private sector job creation in MENA. These explanations often focus on the idea of a natural resource curse. World Bank (2012a) examines how, and the extent to which, overvalued real exchange rates lead to Dutch disease effects that limit diversification and growth in MENA. Overvalued real exchange rates can either originate from natural resource revenues or from *weak links* whereby low performance in nontradable domestic services increase the relative prices of tradable goods (and services). World Bank (2012a) also shows how volatility of commodity prices produces fiscal and real exchange rate volatility in the MENA region. Even oil-poor countries are sensitive to changes in the oil price because a large part of their economies depends on work remittances, aid, tourism revenues, and/or (real estate) investments from oil-rich countries (Dahi and Demir 2008). Previous studies also argue that the adoption of a pegged or fixed exchange rate regime to shelter oil-rich economies from oil price volatility led to a real exchange rate overvaluation, and thus losses in competitiveness in the region (Nabli and Veganzones-Varoudakis 2002; World Bank 2012a). Other explanations include low private investment rates, investments in capital- rather than labor-intensive industries because of energy subsidy distortions (Lin and Monga 2010), cumbersome business and trade regulations (Malik 2013), or the lack of access to finance (World Bank 2011b).

This report provides evidence that privileges granted to politically connected firms are associated with many of the policy distortions that the literature identifies to weaken private sector growth and job creation. The report follows the argumentation of World Bank (2009) and Malik (2013), and provides new data supporting this thesis. We provide direct quantitative evidence that the generous energy subsides to industry in Egypt profited a handful of politically connected firms. Moreover, we provide evidence that cumbersome business regulations, including barriers to entry and trade, protect a few politically connected firms in Egypt and Tunisia. Similarly, this report puts forth data that connects the unequal access to credit and land, and inconsistent implementation of business rules and regulations, to the presence of politically connected firms in Egypt. Furthermore, we argue that overvalued real exchange rates caused by weak links, at least in part, originate from the concentration of politically connected firms in (nontradable) backbone service sectors in MENA. This report also highlights the dynamic interactions between shortcomings in the design of well-intentioned industrial policy and policy capture in MENA.

We employ a rich set of techniques and newly available data to examine the fundamentals of job creation in MENA, and how privileges may impede job growth. This report assembles the most comprehensive firm census database ever put together for the MENA region. This allows us to measure accurate characteristics of and trends in firms' demand for labor, and provides reliable representative estimates of both aggregate private sector job creation and productivity growth determinants.[1] Recent academic contributions, based on comparable firm census data from other regions, provide the basis for benchmarking and give important new insights on specific firm characteristics and dynamics driving job creation (see, among others, Haltiwanger et al. 2011; Hsieh and Klenow 2012; Bartelsman et al. 2014). These latest state-of-the-art techniques are applied to provide novel empirical stylized facts on the fundamentals of job creation in MENA, based on the newly available firm census data. Moreover, following the Arab Spring and the regime changes in Egypt and Tunisia, two novel data sets were constructed that identify firms politically connected to the Mubarak and Ben Ali regimes or their close collaborators.[2] These two unique data sets enable us to quantify how political connections lead to policy privileges that distort both competition and the firm dynamics associated with job creation. Several findings stand out:

- First, GDP growth in MENA over the past two decades was moderate and mostly driven by demographic and structural change, while within sectors productivity growth was slow, lagging behind all other developing regions (chapter 1). While demographic change (an increase in the working-age population) contributed positively to growth, MENA did not fully harness the growth benefits of this trend, as unemployment and inactivity remained high. In addition, most workers are employed in small-scale and low productivity activities.

- Second, job growth in MENA is weak because there are not enough startups and productive firms (chapter 1). We test whether the fundamentals of job creation in MENA countries are different from fast-growing emerging and high-income countries in other regions. They are not: young firms and more productive firms are the engines of private sector job creation in MENA as elsewhere. However, in MENA the pool of young firms is too low and productivity growth too slow to accelerate job creation. The low number of young firms is due to weak entry and growth of new firms. Productivity growth is held back by slow within-firm productivity growth and by misallocation of labor and capital across firms within sectors.

- Third, many existing policies lower competition, create an uneven playing field and reduce the emergence and development of young firms and productive firms (chapter 2). We illustrate how different policies—ranging from energy subsidies and barriers to foreign direct investment (FDI) into services sectors, to the regulatory environment and its implementation—shape and in most cases reduce private sector growth and job creation. The chapter shows how these policies systematically led to reduced competition, created unequal opportunities between entrepreneurs, resulted in low entry or growth of new firms, and weakened productivity growth.

- Fourth, shortcomings in the design and implementation of past industrial policies in MENA resulted in firm-specific policies and did not promote performance and competition (chapter 3). The chapter reviews industrial policies in a number of MENA countries over the past two decades and compares them with the experiences of East Asian countries, analyzing differences in policy design and implementation. The chapter shows how the success of industrial policies in East Asian countries is related to several factors. The most critical include: a focus on *new* economic activities in sectors where market failures are more likely to have a binding influence on industrial development; the implementation of more performance-oriented policies; an evaluation system in which both the performance of policies and officials can be assessed; the promotion and safeguarding of competition; and equal access to all firms based on their performance.

- Last, the report shows how many of these policies have benefitted a handful of politically connected firms, while reducing competition, tilting the level playing field, and impeding aggregate job growth (chapter 4). Novel data sets on first-tier politically connected firms in Egypt and Tunisia that became available after the Arab Spring allow us, for the first time, to provide quantitative evidence on how firm privileges distort regulations, competition, and job growth in the region. Together these findings shed light on the entire microeconomic transmission channels from political privileges to distorted competition and firm dynamics that slow aggregate job growth. Moreover, the report provides direct quantitative evidence that the presence of politically connected firms reduces aggregate job growth by lowering the growth opportunities of the majority of nonconnected firms in Egypt. The available qualitative evidence points to similar mechanisms of policy privileges in other MENA countries.

The empirical findings and mechanisms of this report are rooted in the theoretical framework of Aghion et al. (2001), who demonstrate that fair private sector neck-and-neck competition drives economic growth. The authors show that competition increases firms' incentives to invest in the adoption of new technologies to reduce their costs and escape competition (at least temporarily).[3] However, if a few (colluding) market leaders have sizeable exogenous cost advantages, which are unbridgeable by competitors in the same sector, then all firms in the sector have reduced incentives to adopt new technologies and sector growth is lower. The market leaders have little incentive to invest in innovation since they do not face competitive pressures to reduce their costs; the laggard firms are too far away from the frontier to bridge the cost gap and instead use vintage production technologies, focusing on local market niches to survive. In contrast, aggregate growth increases in the number of sectors that are characterized by neck-and-neck competition market structures. Put together our empirical findings demonstrate that more market competition and a level playing field are required to boost employment growth in MENA.

This report is closely related to a parallel report providing firm level evidence for export and import dynamics and performances in MENA (World Bank, 2014b). Taken together, both reports provide a comprehensive picture of macroeconomic trends and their underlying empirical microeconomic causes in MENA countries ranging from exports and imports to productivity growth and job creation.

This report focuses on oil-importing developing countries in MENA. Most of the analysis excludes Gulf countries and other major oil and gas exporting countries in the region. This is not to say that the issues tackled in this report are not relevant in these countries. However, it is important to keep in mind when reading this report that the patterns of firm dynamics and job creation, and the specific policies that distort these dynamics in oil-exporting MENA countries could potentially be different. Nevertheless, privileges and capture of policies by firms connected to political leaders or monarchs are a major concern as they lead to policies distorting a level playing field in all countries in the region. As such, the main findings and policy implications of this report are relevant for the region as a whole.

The report is organized in four chapters and proceeds as follows:

- Chapter 1 analyzes the dynamics and determinants of job creation and tests whether the fundamentals of job creation in MENA are similar to those in fast-growing developing and high-income countries in other regions.

- Chapter 2 shows how different policies in MENA countries shaped private sector competition and thus the firm dynamics associated with job creation identified in chapter 1. The report analyzes the effect of various policy distortions on firm dynamics and job creation across the MENA region, ranging from energy subsidies to industry in Egypt; FDI restriction and FDI domestic in Jordan; (mobility) restrictions to market access in the West Bank; the relation between red tape and job growth in Morocco; and the impact of inconsistent implementation of regulations across the region.

- Chapter 3 documents past industrial policies in MENA and compares the experiences with the experiences of East Asian countries, highlighting how the differences are linked to policy objective, design, and implementation.

- Chapter 4 analyzes how privileges to politically connected firms result in these policy distortions that undermine competition and constrain private sector growth and jobs in MENA. It uses novel data sets that identify first-tier politically connected firms in Egypt and Tunisia to quantify for the first time not only their impact on regulatory and policy distortions, but also how they impact on job growth. The chapter also presents and discusses qualitative evidence on state-business relations from other countries.

- The report concludes by laying out the implications for policy of the various findings and highlights the specific areas for policy reform to create a roadmap for more private sector growth and jobs in MENA.

Notes

1. Most of the analysis on job creation in MENA is based on survey data with small samples that cover only part of the economy; often merely including selected larger formal sector establishments. For example, the World Bank Enterprise Survey (WBES) data only survey a few formal firms. Apart from sampling issues, which are particularly severe for MENA countries, the largest survey for the Arab Republic of Egypt, for example, includes only about 1,100 out of 2.4 million establishments in 2006. Moreover, all of the surveyed 1,100 establishments have at least five employees while 91 percent of all establishments in Egypt in 2006 had less than five employees.
2. To the best of our knowledge, comparably rich data on politically connected firms across various economic sectors have only been employed for Indonesia in the academic literature so far.
3. The framework is closely related to Parente and Prescott (2002). Its validity has been tested empirically by estimating the impact of increased product market competition on growth (Aghion et al., 2006, 2009) as well as entry deregulation in India (Aghion et al., 2008).

CHAPTER 1

Too Little Too Late: Private Sector Growth and Labor Demand

Over the past two decades, moderate GDP per capita growth in MENA was driven by demographic change rather than labor productivity and did not create enough formal private sector jobs. The economic benefits from the ongoing demographic trend could have been higher if MENA countries were able to absorb the fast increasing labor force into their formal economy. Instead, weak formal private sector job creation has resulted in a large portion of the labor force being inactive. Why has private sector job creation been so weak? We first examine whether the fundamentals of job creation in MENA countries are different from fast-growing emerging or high-income countries in other regions. They are not: young firms and more productive firms are the engines of private sector job creation in MENA as elsewhere. However, MENA countries' private sector has been characterized by low firm turnover—firm entry and exit—and slow productivity growth, limiting the pool of both young and productive firms.

This chapter examines the nature of labor demand in MENA countries' private sectors, and discusses possible determinants of private sector growth and job creation. First, the chapter briefly examines MENA's performance in aggregate growth and the drivers of economic growth. Growth in MENA over the last two decades appears to have been moderate and driven by demographic change, while productivity growth was low compared with other developing countries. Job creation was too weak over this period to absorb the growing working-age population. This resulted in high unemployment, inactivity, and informal jobs. The chapter then turns to the reasons why private sector job creation in MENA over the last two decades was weak. The analysis shows that the determinants of job growth in MENA countries do not differ from those in high-income or fast-growing emerging economies in other regions: in MENA, as elsewhere, it is young firms and more productive firms that create more jobs. The chapter contends that low firm turnover and slow productivity growth limit the pool of young firms and productive firms, and undermine faster job creation.

The analysis is based on newly available firm census data from MENA, which are crucial to identify the fundamentals of job creation. The determinants of job creation are analyzed through the lens of the firm, using unique firm census data collected in six MENA countries (Egypt, Tunisia, Morocco, Jordan, Lebanon, West Bank and Gaza), and Turkey, which is used as the benchmark country.[1] To the best of our knowledge, this is the first time that these census data, apart from Morocco, are being used for research purposes.[2] There are, however, important differences in the type of census, coverage of variables, and years across countries. For example, the census data in Egypt cover over 2,000,000 establishments across all sectors in 1996 and 2006, and a smaller annual manufacturing panel that includes all establishments with at least 10 employees between 2007 and 2011. The Turkish census comprises more than 2,400,000 establishments between 2005 and 2010. In Tunisia, Jordan, Lebanon, and West Bank and Gaza, the census data are also in panel format and cover all sectors, including between 100,000 and 600,000 economic establishments, depending on the country and year. In Morocco, the data is a panel of manufacturing firms covering all firms with at least 10 employees and some smaller firms between 1996 and 2006. These differences in data coverage across countries are carefully taken into account, and are highlighted when presenting the analysis. Moreover, the same methodologies and definitions are used in each country to compute firm entry and exit, firm productivity, and so forth. A detailed summary of the available census data is provided in appendix B.

The chapter is organized as follows. The first section examines the growth and job performance of MENA countries. The second section provides evidence that the fundamental mechanisms of job creation are the same in MENA as in other regions: young and more productive firms create jobs. The third section shows that low firm turnover and slow productivity growth limit the pool of young firms and productive firms and thus impede job growth in MENA.[3]

Economic Growth Has Been Moderate and Job Growth Weak

MENA grew moderately during the last two decades. Growth was driven by demographic change (increased working-age population), while aggregate productivity growth was low.

Real GDP per capita growth hovered around 2 percent in the last two decades; about 2–3 percent lower than in East and South Asia, but comparable to per capita growth rates in the other developing regions. After prolonged economic stagnation during the 1980s, growth in MENA recovered in the 1990s as governments shifted away from state-led economic models towards more private sector-led growth and trade integration. Between 1991 and 2012, real GDP growth per capita averaged 2.2 percent in constant terms (figure 1.1). Thus, it was about 2 to 3 percent lower than real GDP per capita growth in South and East Asia. Nevertheless, it was comparable or even slightly exceeded per capita growth in Latin America and Caribbean, Eastern Europe and Central Asia, and Sub-Saharan Africa. This decent growth performance was not driven solely by MENA's oil-exporting high-income countries. Real GDP per capita growth was comparable among MENA's developing

FIGURE 1.1

Decomposition of GDP Per Capita Growth in MENA and Other Developing Regions

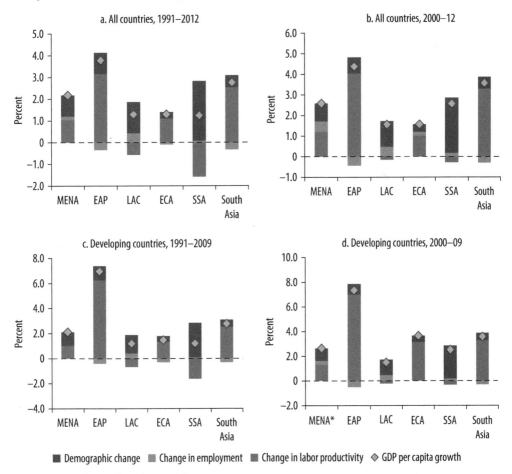

Source: Calculations based on World Development Indicators.
Note: Developing MENA effectively excludes the GCC (data missing for Qatar).

countries, averaging 2.1 percent from 1991–2009 and accelerating to 2.6 percent from 2000–2009.

Demographic change accounted for about 50 percent of aggregate real GDP per capita growth over the past 20 years, substantially higher than in any other region. Demographic change is measured by the change in working-age population as a share of total population. The MENA region has the second highest population growth rate in the world. Its population growth rate between 1990 and 2012 averaged 2 percent and was only surpassed by population growth in Sub-Saharan Africa (2.7 percent). High fertility rates combined with rapidly declining mortality contributed to a sharp increase in MENA's working-age population as a share of total population (figure 1.1, left), rapidly increasing MENA's potential labor supply. Though its demographic profile is often blamed for MENA's high youth unemployment, the relative size of the labor force is a key determinant of the region's recent economic growth performance.

Aggregate productivity growth was low in MENA compared with other developing regions. Figure 1.1 demonstrates that the change in labor productivity explained about 50 percent of GDP growth among MENA's developing countries over the past two decades, generating 1 percent real GDP per capita growth annually in that period. Productivity growth was significantly lower than in other developing regions: it generated about 4.5 percent real GDP per capita growth annually in East Asia, 4 percent in South Asia, and about 2 percent in Europe and Central Asia and Sub-Saharan Africa. For the MENA region as a whole, per capita growth increased between 1995–2000 and 2000–2005 when demographic change accelerated. Among GCC countries, labor productivity did not contribute to economic growth over the past fifteen years. Among MENA's developing countries, however, productivity growth averaged 1.3 percent over the past decade, primarily based on growth in non–oil-exporting countries.

MENA experienced significant productivity growth through reallocation across sectors, but within-sector productivity growth was the lowest among all regions

The reallocation of workers from sectors with lower (marginal) productivity to sectors with higher productivity can be an important driver of aggregate productivity growth. One key insight of development economics is that growth is driven by a structural shift from agriculture to manufacturing and services. This sectoral shift tends to be mirrored in the pattern of employment, so that over time the labor force in the nonagricultural sector increases while employment in the agricultural sector declines (Kuznets 1996). As labor moves to the usually higher-productivity industrial sector, overall productivity rises and incomes expand (Duarte and Restuccia 2010; Herrendorf, Rogerson, and Valentinyi 2013).[4] As incomes rise, the demand for services increases. In many countries the share of the service sector in GDP rises almost linearly with the income level. Moreover, Eichengreen and Gupta (2011) reveal that in OECD countries service sector labor productivity as a share of average labor productivity tends first to rise at lower-income levels, then decline over an intermediate range, before increasing again. The second surge is most likely caused by the rise of modern services (business services, tele-communication, finance, and so forth). In many fast-growing developing countries, especially in Asia, the reallocation of workers from low productivity to high productivity sectors has contributed positively to growth during the last twenty years (Duarte and Restuccia 2010; Rodrik and McMillan 2012).

All MENA countries in the sample, with the exception of Saudi Arabia, experienced aggregate productivity gains because of labor real-locations between sectors from 2000 to 2005. Labor productivity growth expressed as the change in output per worker can be decom-posed into within-sector change and reallocations "across" sectors or structural change (figure A.3 in appendix A). We note that the follow-ing results are based on measurements of average, not marginal labor productivity.[5] However, as a robustness check, we also approximate marginal sector productivities based on wage data from harmonized household surveys for Egypt and Tunisia (World Bank, I2D2 data-base). The results show that the gaps in marginal productivities mea-sured by average wages across sectors are smaller than gaps measured by value added per worker, but sectoral differences remain significant (see table A.1 in appendix A). The contribution of labor reallocations (that is, structural change) to aggregate productivity growth was stron-gest in the Syrian Arab Republic and Egypt (figure 1.2a). In Syria, the country with the fastest structural change in the MENA region, real-location of labor contributed about 1.8 percentage points to aggregate productivity growth (which was 2.7 percent). In Egypt, it contributed one percentage point to aggregate productivity growth, which was negative (–2.2 percent) because of low within-sector productivity growth. The negative contribution in Saudi Arabia is a result of the influx of non-Saudi workers, many of whom were hired for low value added service activities. In Tunisia, the contribution of labor realloca-tion to growth (i.e., structural change) slowed after a wave of privatiza-tion came to an end in 2005.

However, within-sector productivity growth was the lowest among all regions. Figure 1.2a illustrates that aggregate productivity growth among the seven MENA countries was the lowest among developing regions,

FIGURE 1.2

Structural Change across Regions and among MENA Countries, 2000–05

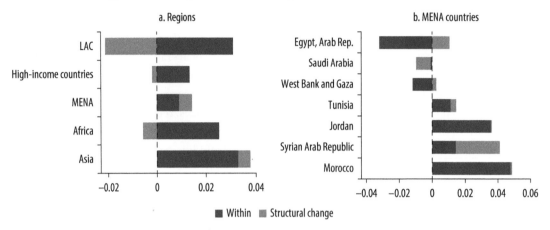

Source: World Bank calculations; data source see appendix A.

because of low within-sector productivity growth. Figure 1.2b demonstrates that the regional average hides substantial variations across the seven MENA countries. Within-sector productivity growth has been negative in Egypt since 1982, primarily driven by declining labor productivity in mining, manufacturing, and wholesale and retail trade. Within-sector productivity growth was also negative in Saudi Arabia and West Bank and Gaza between 2000 and 2005. In West Bank and Gaza, labor productivity fell steeply in agriculture, wholesale and retail trade, and transport and communication. Within-sector productivity growth was high in Jordan and Morocco. In Jordan, it was driven by manufacturing (through labor shedding), transport and communication, and finance (by attracting new workers); in Morocco, by agriculture, mining, and community, social, personal, and government services.

In Tunisia, human capital accounted for a significant share of labor productivity, but the analysis also reveals important misallocation of human capital. The lack of data prevented accounting for human capital in the growth decomposition for other countries in the region. Several countries in the MENA region have undergone a steep increase in educational attainment during the last two decades. To understand better how recent increases in Tunisia's educational attainment have affected the reallocation of human capital across sectors, we replicate the structural change analysis for the years 2005–10, using data on output per unit of human capital.[6] Accounting for improvement in education of the labor force nuances some of the previous findings. For example, while both agriculture and the public sector employed

18 percent of the total working population in 2005, the share of imputed human capital was 12 percent for agriculture but 27 percent for the public sector. Human capital productivity growth within the agricultural sector was even negative, implying that growth of human capital exceeded overall employment growth. Overall, human capital exceeded employment growth by about 50 percent, accounting for a significant share of the labor productivity increase. Moreover, the adjusted productivity measure also reveals significant misallocation of human capital. In 2009, 75 percent of Tunisia's human capital augmented labor was employed in sectors with below-average productivity, 24 percent in public administration alone, with 12 percent in the public works program.

Consistently, firm census data suggest that firm turnover in MENA is driven by structural change rather than creative destruction. Bartelsman, Haltiwanger, and Scarpetta (2004) suggest a way to assess if firm churning is driven by structural change (resource reallocations between sectors) or creative destruction (resource reallocations among firms within a sector). In the former case, the correlation between entry and exit rates across sectors should be negative; in the latter, positive

FIGURE 1.3

Correlation between Entry and Exit Rates across Two-Digit Sectors

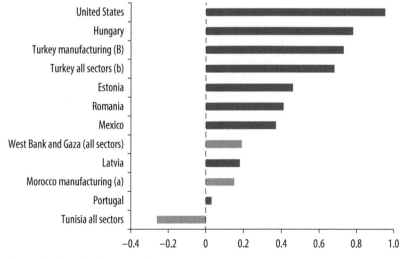

Source: Calculations based on census data.
Note: The entry/exit rates are weighted by employment; correlation coefficients are significantly different from 0 at the 10% level in Tunisia, Estonia, Turkey, Hungary, and the United States; a) entry in /exit out 10+ employees; b) Entry in /exit out 20+ employees. Correlations are measured between 2005 and 2010 in Turkey, 1996–2006 in Morocco, 2004–2012 in West Bank and Gaza, and the 1990s for all other countries.

(i.e., new firms enter and old firms exit the same two-digit sector). Figure 1.3 reveals that countries at a later stage of development have higher positive within-sector correlations, indicating that the sectoral structures in these countries have converged so that the main force behind firm turnover is creative destruction. In contrast, in less developed countries the correlations tend to be lower. Morocco, Tunisia, and West Bank and Gaza are among the lowest, suggesting that sectoral adjustment resulting from structural change is still ongoing.

BOX 1.1

Is Structural Change in Morocco Gender-Biased?

In the following, we disaggregate the relative changes in sectors' employment shares by gender to examine if structural change in Morocco increased the probability of female and/or male employment in higher productivity sectors. The analysis is based on World Bank (2014d). Figure B1.1.1 plots the relative labor productivity of different sectors on changes in the employment share in these sectors. The sizes of the circles represent the size of the sector. Sectors above the (horizontal) dashed line have above-average labor productivity, while sectors to the left of the (vertical) dashed line increased their employment share. The left panel shows the changes in the labor share among women (on the x axis), while the right panel illustrates the changes in the labor share among men (on the x axis).

The results show that structural change did not benefit women and men equally. Figure B1.1.1 compares the reallocation (changes in labor shares) of women and men across the different sectors. There are some important similarities. The high productivity communications and finance and real estate sectors increased their employment shares for both women and men, but the numbers of new jobs in these sectors are very small in proportion. These benefitted mostly educated women and men in cities. The overall number of jobs provided in these two sectors is small, so relatively few employees benefitted from this trend. In contrast, employment trends are very different for the majority of uneducated women living in rural areas. About 60 percent of women in the labor force work in agriculture; more than 77 percent of them worked as family helpers, and 44 percent work part-time. The share even slightly increased from 59 percent in 2000 to 61 percent in 2011 (figure B1.1.1, left). Conversely, it declined for men (figure B1.1.1, right). Given that the agriculture sector is by far the largest employer in Morocco (39 percent of the total labor force in 2011), this employment trend outweighs any other. Note that the aggregate labor share in agriculture still declined since the overall labor force participation of men is 2.8 times that of women.

(continued on next page)

BOX 1.1 *Continued*

FIGURE B1.1.1

Reallocation of Labor across Sectors, by Gender, 2000–11

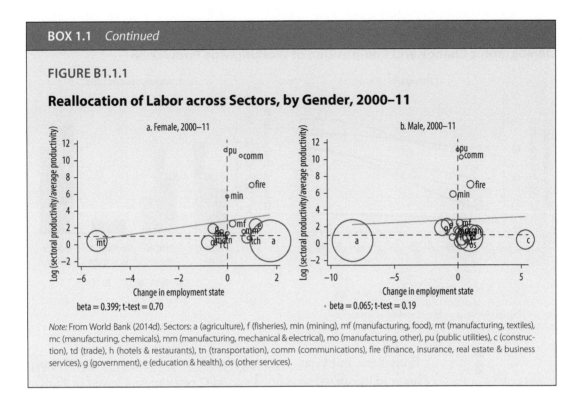

Note: From World Bank (2014d). Sectors: a (agriculture), f (fisheries), min (mining), mf (manufacturing, food), mt (manufacturing, textiles), mc (manufacturing, chemicals), mm (manufacturing, mechanical & electrical), mo (manufacturing, other), pu (public utilities), c (construction), td (trade), h (hotels & restaurants), tn (transportation), comm (communications), fire (finance, insurance, real estate & business services), g (government), e (education & health), os (other services).

The analysis showed that aggregate productivity growth was low in MENA compared with other developing region in the past 20 years. How did labor markets and in particular labor demand evolve during this period?

MENA has had weak job performance. Most workers are employed in small-scale low productivity activities; this employment structure persisted and increased somewhat over the past decade

MENA's labor market failed to absorb the fast growing labor force. Formal sector workers as a share of working-age population in MENA is much lower than in other middle-income regions such as Latin America and Caribbean (LAC), or Eastern Europe and Central Asia (ECA); figure 1.4. While the measured share of informal labor is lower than in LAC, the share of the working-age population dropping out of the labor force is much higher, especially among women. Less than a quarter of all working-age women in the MENA region participated in the labor force in 2012 (see also World Bank 2014a).

Small-scale activities provide the majority of jobs in MENA, albeit with some noteworthy differences across countries. Figure 1.5 illustrates the distribution of employment across firm size categories in the different MENA countries. The share of employment in micro establishments with less than five employees dominates the private sector in Egypt and

FIGURE 1.4

Demographic Change and Composition of Working-Age Population

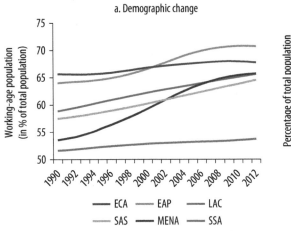

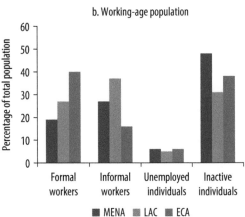

Source: a. Calculations based on World Development Indicators.
b. World Bank 2013, based on ILO-KILM database.

West Bank and Gaza, reaching almost 60 percent. It is significantly lower in Jordan (40 percent), Tunisia (37 percent), and lowest in Turkey (34 percent). In contrast, Tunisia (36 percent)[7] and Jordan (33 percent) have the highest concentration of workers in large establishments,[8] while Turkey has the highest share of workers in medium-size establishments (29 percent), also exceeding its share of workers in large ones (26 percent). The share of jobs in firms with at least 1,000 employees is less than 10 percent in all five countries, which starkly contrasts with the employment situation in high-income countries. For example, in the U.S., 48 percent of all employees work in firms with more than 10,000 employees. Overall, figure 1.5 highlights that small scale activities in micro enterprises are an important source of employment in MENA countries. The high share of jobs in micro establishments is alarming given that businesses with fewer than 10 employees are much more likely to be informal in MENA (World Bank 2011a). Moreover, informality in MENA is associated with a lower level of productivity relative to other regions at comparable stages of development.

The concentration of jobs in micro establishments is also a reflection of MENA's sectoral structure; low productivity services provide the most jobs. Most of these services are likely to represent subsistence activities rather than a vibrant informal sector. Figure 1.6 illustrates the distribution of employment by sectors; economic sectors are approximately sorted by their share of formal sector employees. The majority of domestic private sector jobs are small scale; they are often low-productivity service sector activities. In Egypt and West Bank and Gaza, around 40 percent of

FIGURE 1.5

Employment Share, by Firm Size

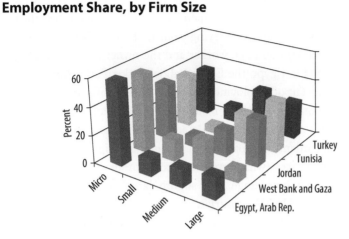

Source: Calculations based on census data.
Note: The graph shows the share of employment by firm size according to the following classification: micro firms have less than 5 employees, small firms have between 5 and 9 employees, medium firms have between 10 and 99 employees, large firms have 100 employees or more. Periods covered by country: Turkey (2006), Tunisia (1996–2010), Jordan (2006), Egypt (2006), Palestine (2004, 2007, 2012). The employment shares in Tunisia are based on firm data while it is establishment data for the other countries. Lebanon is not included as the nature of the census data is different; its coverage limited to firms with a tax ID.

FIGURE 1.6

Distribution of Employment across Nonagriculture Sectors

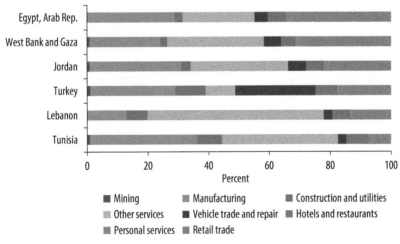

Source: Calculations based on census data.

all jobs are in these sectors. All three sectors hold primarily what are often informal one- or two-person firms in MENA (see World Bank 2011a). For example, the average establishment size in retail trade is less than 2 percent in all of the countries, varying from 1.2 in Tunisia to 1.9 percent in Egypt (including one wage worker and the owner). Moreover, labor force survey data in Egypt (the Egypt Labor Market Panel Survey) indicate that 70 percent of employment in retail trade is informal: jobs without a formal contract or social insurance (World Bank 2014a). Retail trade, personal services, and hotels and restaurants still account for 28 percent in Jordan. In Lebanon and Tunisia, the highest share of jobs is in business services (which are included in other services). Business service firms have, on average, only slightly larger firm sizes than retail service firms in all MENA countries.

The concentration of employment in small and micro-firms decreased slightly in recent years, but it is still higher than in the late 1990s in certain countries. The share of jobs in medium and large establishments increased somewhat in the oil-importing middle-income MENA countries (apart from Egypt) between 2005 and 2012, albeit at a much slower pace than in Turkey. Figure 1.7 shows that the share increased by almost 10 percent in Turkey at the end of the 2000s, compared with less than 5 percent in

FIGURE 1.7

Percentage Change in Share of Employment in Medium and Large Establishments

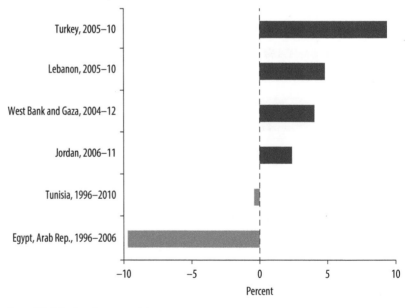

Source: Calculation based on census data.
Note: Medium and large establishments are defined as having more than 10 employees.

MENA countries. In Egypt and Tunisia, the share of employment in large establishments declined over the longer time horizon, reflecting stagnation in formal sector job growth preceding the recent crisis. Figure 1.7 highlights that employment declined in Egypt by 7 percentage points (from 23 to 16 percent) between 1996 and 2006. In contrast, the dominance of small-scale activities in micro establishments with fewer than 10 employees increased over time (from 62 percent in 1996 to 72 percent in 2006).[9]

Most firms in MENA had weak employment growth; a few fast-growing firms account for a large share of job creation

Small firms did not grow. Micro firms with fewer than 10 employees almost never enter larger size categories. This finding is illustrated in the case of Tunisia in table 1.1 which summarizes the probabilities that firms transitioned among different size categories (or exited them) in 2007–11. For example, of all one-person firms in Tunisia in 2007, 22 percent exited by 2011, 76 percent remained one-person firms, and only 2 percent hired at least one more worker. Overall, table 1.1 highlights that micro firms with fewer than 10 employees almost never grow beyond 10 employees over time. In particular, table 1.1 reveals that the probability of all nonfarm micro firms to grow beyond 10 employees four to five years later is 2 percent in the West Bank and Gaza (6 percent in the West Bank alone), 3 percent in Tunisia, and 12 percent in Lebanon. The very low probability that micro firms will transition to larger size categories is striking. This finding is consistent with those of the World Bank (2014a), which showed that most micro firms are informal, and that informal firms have a very low chance to formalize in MENA.

The probability that medium-size manufacturing establishments grow to become large establishments four years later is low across

TABLE 1.1

Employment Transition Matrix
Percent

Status in 2007	Tunisia Transitions 2007–11 Status in 2011				
	Exited	1-Person	Micro	SME	Large
1-person	22	**76**	2	0	0
Micro	9	21	**67**	3	0
SME	6	11	16	**64**	4
Large	6	11	3	15	**65**

Source: Calculation based on census data.
Note: Micro: 2–9 employees, SME: 10–99 employees, Large: ≥100 employees. Bold signifies stagnation (no growth in jobs), red signifies shrinkage (jobs or exit), and orange signifies expansion (growth in jobs).

FIGURE 1.8

Employment Transition, by Firm Size

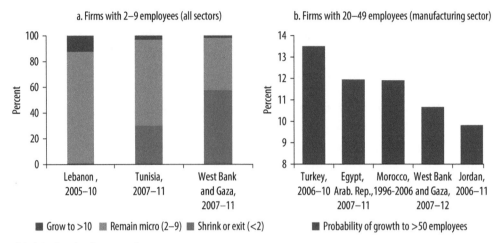

Source: Calculation based on firm census data.

Note: Because of data constraints, the transition probability for Jordan is for incumbents only; excluding entrants and exiters.

MENA countries. Figure 1.8 (right panel) shows that this probability for firms with 20–49 employees is 13.5 percent in Turkey, 11.9 percent in Egypt and Morocco, 10.7 percent in West Bank and Gaza, and 9.8 percent in Jordan.

A few fast-growing firms (the *gazelles*) account for a high share of job creation in MENA. Gazelles are defined as firms that double their employment over a four-year period.[10] The analysis is restricted to firms with more than 10 employees in the base year.[11] Figure 1.9 shows the incidence of gazelles across MENA countries, the U.S., and Turkey. Lebanon has the highest share of gazelles (5.6 percent) out of the MENA countries. The shares are only slightly lower in Tunisia and Turkey. Jordan has the lowest incidence of gazelles (1.4 percent). However, gazelles accounted for a high share of employment growth in MENA. Figure 1.10 shows the share of jobs created by gazelles and non-gazelles. Gazelles accounted respectively for about 64 and 42 percent of total net job creation in Jordan and Tunisia. In contrast, Turkey's job creation was broader-based across all firms, as gazelles only contributed 15 percent to job growth. Gazelles accounted for all net job creation in the manufacturing sector in Morocco, offsetting job destruction by all other formal manufacturing firms. In Egypt, manufacturing net job creation was negative between 2007 and 2011, driven by substantial job destruction among nongazelle establishments, while in Jordan manufacturing net job creation was positive, whereby nongazelles created more jobs (60 percent) than gazelles (40 percent).

FIGURE 1.9

Incidence of Gazelles in All Sectors and Manufacturing

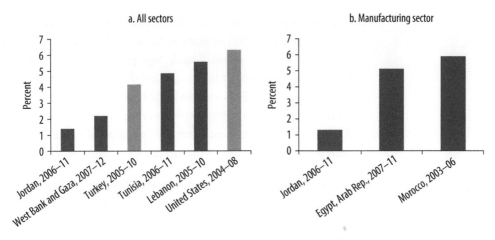

Source: Calculation based on census data.
Note: Gazelles are defined as firms with at least 10 employees in the base year that double employment over any four-year period. Data for Turkey includes only firms with at least 20 employees.

FIGURE 1.10

Share of Jobs Created by Gazelles and Nongazelles in All Sectors and in the Manufacturing Sector

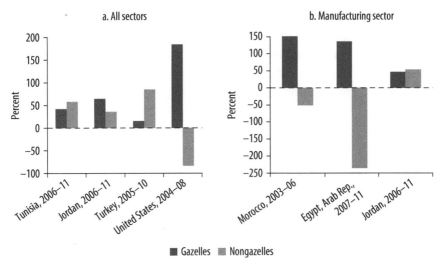

Source: Calculation based on census data.
Note: Gazelles are defined as firms with at least 10 employees in the base year that double employment over any four-year period. Data for Turkey includes only firms with at least 20 employees.

Drivers of Job Growth: Young Firms and Productive Firms Create More Jobs

The previous section showed that MENA has had a weak jobs as well as aggregate productivity performance in the last 20 years. Moreover, most workers are employed in small-scale low productivity activities. It is important to understand the factors behind this weak performance at the microeconomic level. This section aims to shed light on this issue by answering the following questions: what types of firms drive job growth in MENA countries? Are these micro fundamentals of job creation different from those found in (fast-growing) countries outside of the region?

Analysis of firm census data shows that it is younger firms and more productive firms that create more jobs in MENA, as in fast-growing and high-income countries

Evidence from other regions suggests that younger and more productive firms create more jobs. Age, size, and productivity are fundamental determinants of firm employment growth. Understanding their relative importance in explaining job creation is critical to determine the policy mix for stimulating private sector growth. There is growing literature analyzing these questions (Box 1.2). For example, Haltiwanger, Jarmin, and Miranda (2010) find that in the Unites States, net employment growth is associated with firm age and not firm size. The literature also identifies productivity as an important determinant of firm growth in developing countries (e.g., Berman and Machin 2004; Vivarelli 2012). Another strand of the literature highlights the importance of firm growth over their life cycle; Hsieh and Klenow (2012) show that U.S. firms increase their size (number of employees) and productivity by a factor of 8 over their life cycle (within the first 35 years). In contrast, Mexican firms double and Indian firms do not increase their employees over the same period (both approximately double their productivity).

Are the firm characteristics associated with job growth different in MENA countries?

Job creation in MENA is dominated by young firms. Micro-startups create most jobs. These findings are illustrated in figure 1.11, which shows net job creation by firm size and firm age in Tunisia and Lebanon. Almost all net job creation in Lebanon and Tunisia was generated by young firms at their start-up period; i.e., in the first four years after they were established. In both countries, it was primarily micro-startups with between one and four employees that created most jobs. For example, micro-startups generated about 66,000 jobs in Lebanon between 2005 and 2010, accounting for 177 percent of net job creation. The second largest number of jobs (12,000) was created by young large firms with 200–999 employees.

BOX 1.2

Who Create More Jobs?

Young firms are an engine of job creation. There is a large and growing literature linking employment growth to firm dynamics. Studies typically find that younger and smaller firms have higher employment growth rates than older and larger firms (e.g., Mansfield 1962; Hall 1987; Hart and Oulton 1996; Ayyagari, Demirguc-Kunt, and Maksimovic 2011). Likewise, Davidsson and Delmar (2006) show that most of the growth of younger and smaller firms is organic, while for larger and older firms, job growth primarily comes through acquisitions. Hsieh and Olken (2014) contribute to the debate on firm size and job creation, showing that large firms have higher average products of capital and labor, which suggests that large (not small) firms are growth constrained. Haltiwanger, Jarmin, and Miranda (2010) nuance these findings, showing that net employment growth is associated with firm age and not firm size in the United States, implying that young firms, especially start-ups, are the drivers of job creation. However, as young firms tend to be small, there is also a positive bivariate correlation between firm size and net job growth in the data. Furthermore, Hsieh and Klenow (2012) corroborate the importance of firm age growth. The authors show that U.S. firms increase their number of employees and productivity by a factor of 8 over their life cycle (within the first 35 years). In contrast, Mexican firms double and Indian firms do not increase their employees over the same period (both approximately double their productivity).[a] Again, the study highlights the importance of firm age as a determinant of firms' potential to create jobs.

Among the pool of young firms, a small number of fast-growing firms appear to create most new aggregate jobs in high-income countries. A recent stream of the literature linking employment growth to firm dynamics suggests that a small group of fast-growing firms, often referred to as gazelles, are the main drivers of aggregate job creation (e.g., Bottazzi and Secchi 2007). In other words, a handful of firms experience a period of accelerated employment growth while most other firms hardly grow at all. Empirical studies for various developed countries find that 5–10 percent of the firms deliver 50–80 percent of aggregate employment creation (e.g., Acs, Parsons, and Tracy 2008; Coad and Hoelzl 2010). These fast-growing firms can be found in all industries and are usually young firms that are more innovative and take more risks (Bars et al. 2006; Goedhuys and Sleuwaegen 2009; Henrekson and Johansson 2010).

Most microeconomic studies find a positive relationship between productivity and employment creation (van Reenen 1997; Blanchflower and Burgess 1998; Piva and Vivarelli 2004; Coad and Hoelzl 2010; Vivarelli 2012). In this regard, it is useful to distinguish between product and process innovation. Product innovation is generally found to increase labor demand and hence firm-level employment growth. Process innovation is associated with productivity growth which might, however, compensate labor. Indeed, the findings for process

(continued on next page)

BOX 1.2   *Continued*

innovation are less clear-cut and also indicate job destruction in some cases, especially in the short run (e.g., Hall, Lotti, and Mairesse 2008; Harrison et al. 2008).

Among developing countries, studies suggest that the adoption of foreign technologies increases firms' demand for labor, especially for skilled labor. Product and process innovation in developing countries take the form of diversification into new products and the adoption of foreign technologies (or organizational structures), respectively. Both processes have been found to increase the demand for labor in developing countries. Foreign technology adoption has been found to increase the demand for skilled labor, referred to as "skill-biased technological

change" in the literature (e.g., Berman and Machin 2004). Conte and Vivarelli (2010), Hanson and Harrison (1999), and Fuentes and Gilchrist (2005) find that imported skill-biased technological change is an important determinant of the recent increase in the relative demand for skilled labor in developing countries.

Thus, these findings highlight a positive relation between productivity and employment in developing countries. Innovation, which takes the form of diversification into new products and the adoption of foreign technologies in developing countries, is found to increase the demand for labor, leading to a positive relation between productivity and job growth in developing countries.

Note:
a. The fact that older plants in India and Mexico are small may not have a large effect on aggregate outcomes if there are fewer surviving old plants. The authors show, however, that exit rates in India and Mexico are generally not higher than in the United States.

FIGURE 1.11

Net Job Creation, by Firm Size and Age

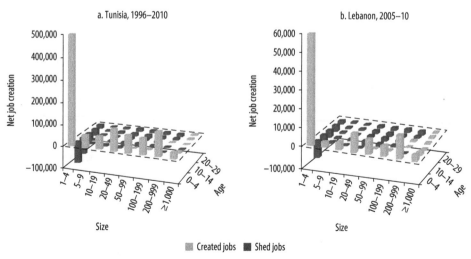

a. Tunisia, 1996–2010   b. Lebanon, 2005–10

Created jobs   Shed jobs

Source: Calculation based on census data.

In Tunisia, micro-startups created 580,000 jobs between 1996 and 2010, accounting for 92 percent of all net job creation.

However, the aggregate performance masks important differences in the sectoral patterns of job creation across countries. In all MENA countries with available data, job creation was driven by retail trade, business services, or personal and community services. World Bank (2011a) shows that job creation in micro-firms in these sectors is often part of the informal economy, which is less productive in MENA than in other developing regions. In particular, table 1.2 reports that many new jobs in micro establishments are in retail trade and personal services, which are dominated by informal firms. In these sectors, the average firm size is below one worker. In Egypt, these two sectors generated more than 700,000 and 400,000 new jobs from 1996 to 2006, respectively, accounting for over 80 percent of total net job creation. Labor force survey data from the Egypt Labor Market Panel Survey show that this trend continued between 2006 and 2012.

Certain higher productivity activities such as real estate and finance, tourism, ICT, and manufacturing also contributed to job creation. In Jordan, potentially higher productivity real estate and finance, chemicals and pharmaceuticals, and the food sector accounted for 28 percent of total net job creation between 2006 and 2011, counterbalancing somewhat the trend towards jobs in the informal sector (table 1.2). In Tunisia, 46 percent of total net job creation between 2006 and 2012 was concentrated in real estate and transport services, manufacturing of machinery and electrical equipment (mostly electric cables and switches), food products, and transport vehicles. The sectoral pattern of job growth in Turkey is different; there 77 percent of job growth between 2005 and 2010 was in real estate business services and construction, and other manufacturing.

TABLE 1.2

Sectors with the Highest Rate of Job Growth across Countries

Egypt, Arab Rep., 1996–2006		West Bank and Gaza, 2004–12		Jordan, 2006–11		Tunisia, 1996–12		Turkey, 2005–10	
Sector	Δ Jobs (%)	Sector	Δ Jobs (%)	Sector	Δ Jobs (%)	Sector	Δ Jobs (%)	Sector	Δ Jobs (%)
Retail trade	39	Retail trade	26	Retail trade	18	Real estate, business service	16	Real estate, business service	37
Business service	17	Personal service	9	Hotels and restaurants	18	Machinery, electrical equipment	12	Construction	25
Other manufacturing	12	Hotels and restaurants	7	Health, social	17	Retail trade	12	Other manufacturing	15
Hotels and restaurants	9	Business service	7	Education	13	Transports	10	Hotels and restaurants	10
Personal service	6	Finance	6	Business service	12	Textiles	9	Food and beverages	6

Source: Calculation based on census data.

The ICT sector is an example of an emerging and dynamic sector that has experienced the entry and growth of new firms in several MENA countries. Consider the story of Eskadenia (World Bank 2009) founded by a Jordanian couple who worked for Ericsson in China, Dubai, Lebanon, and Sweden and decided to return to Jordan in 2000 to launch what grew into one of the largest and fastest-growing software firms in the Middle East. Their network of worldwide industry contacts from 30 years abroad helped them penetrate foreign markets quickly. Unable to tap startup capital from banks demanding high collateral, the partners self-financed the startup investment. By 2008 Eskadenia employed about 100 engineers and exports 80 percent of its products to countries in the Middle East, Eastern Europe, and North Africa.

Even after controlling for sectoral heterogeneity, young firms are still the engine of job creation in MENA countries. We follow the methodology of Haltiwanger, Jarmin, and Miranda (2010) for the United States to test whether, after controlling for sector effects, young firms create more jobs regardless of their size. Figure 1.12 illustrates the rate of aggregate net job creation by firm size categories. The figure shows the coefficient estimate from a regression of firm employment growth on the various firm size categories (controlling for sector and year dummies). The dashed-blue lines

FIGURE 1.12

Net Job Creation, by Firm Size before and after Controlling for Firm Age

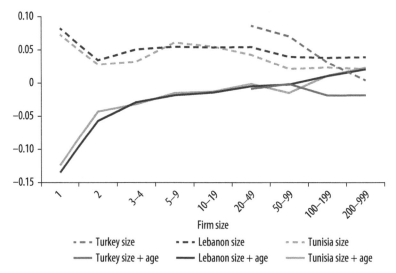

Note: Calculation based on census data. The figure shows the results of a weighted regression of net job creation, measured by the Davis-Haltiwanger-Schuh growth rate, on firm size dummies, controlling for sector and year effects. The figure plots the coefficients on the dummy variables representing the different firm size categories before (dashed line) and after (solid line) controlling for firm age. The omitted category is firms with at least 1,000 employees.

show the impact of the different firm size categories on job growth when neglecting the joint distribution of firm size and age.[12] It suggests that smaller firms create the majority of jobs in Lebanon and Tunisia.[13] However, once the joint distribution of firm size and age is accounted for, the results change dramatically: smaller firms create fewer jobs than large firms. This indicates that the association between firm size and employment growth depends critically on firm age. A similar pattern can be observed among firms in Turkey (it is only possible to identify the same firms over time when they have at least 20 employees). Considering this finding, is it the case that young firms systematically create jobs regardless of their size? Figure 1.13 plots the relation between aggregate job creation and firm age (when accounting for the joint distribution of firm size and age). The findings shows that independent of firm size, young firms grow faster and create more jobs, particularly during their first four years of activity.

The analysis is extended to additional MENA countries figure 1.14 by plotting the employment growth of entry cohorts in the first 10 years after they started operating. It confirms that employment growth is strongest in the first four to five years after firm entry and tends to level off thereafter. In Jordan, establishments from all nonagriculture economic sectors double their size in the first five years after entry, while manufacturing firms in Morocco are 1.7 times larger. The effects are comparable to growth rates of entrants in manufacturing and all other sectors in the first four years of operation.

FIGURE 1.13

Net Job Creation, by Firm Age after Controlling for Firm Size

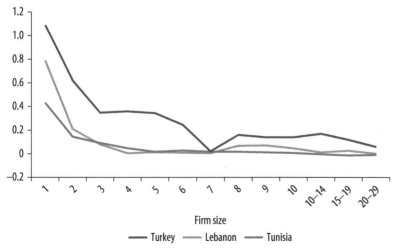

Source: Calculation based on census data.
Note: The figure shows the results of a weighted regression of net job creation, measured by the Davis-Haltiwanger-Schuh growth rate, on firm size and age dummies, controlling for sector and year. The omitted category is firms older than 30 years.

FIGURE 1.14

Employment Growth Is Strongest in First 4–5 Years after Firm Entry

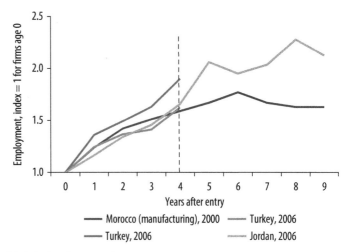

Source: Calculation based on census data.
Note: Employment is normalized to one for the entry year (age equal to zero). a) For Morocco (manufacturing), firm size exceeds 10 employees; for Turkey (manufacturing) and Tunisia, firm size exceeds 20 employees.

If MENA governments want to pursue private sector development programs targeting specific types of firms, they would be well advised to include firm age as a targeting criterion. SMEs have often been considered as the main source of employment growth, which explains the large volumes of access-to-finance support programs focused on small firms in developing countries in the past. The evidence for MENA countries, however, highlights the critical role of firm age rather than size; i.e., young firms are in fact the engine of job creation. Thus, there is room for improving existing SME support programs in MENA countries by targeting such programs to young firms, including startups and potential entrepreneurs.

Average employment growth over firm's life cycle in MENA is relatively weak. The analysis follows Hsieh and Klenow (2012), which shows the relationship between employment and establishment age among surviving firms based on cross-section census data (figure 1.15).[14] The average weighted number of employees for the youngest age cohort (0–4 years after entry) is normalized to one. In contrast to Hsieh and Klenow (2012), the data allows the illustration of this relation among private establishments based on all economic (nonfarm) sectors, instead of the manufacturing sector only. Figure 1.15 shows that after 25 years in operation, surviving firms approximately doubled their number of employees in the Arab Republic of Egypt, Jordan, Tunisia, and Turkey, with typically higher growth for younger age cohorts. Thereafter, employment for older age cohorts (founded before 1980) declined in Egypt, but increased in the other

FIGURE 1.15

Employment Growth over a Firm's Life Cycle for All Nonfarm Sectors

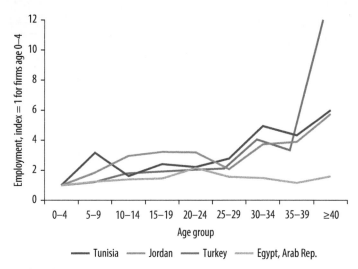

Source: Calculation based on census data.

Note: The figure shows the average number of employees for different age-cohorts across establishments in all private nonfarm sectors (weighted by employment share of four-digit sectors following Hsieh and Klenow 2012). The average number of employees in each age cohort has been normalized to 1 for the youngest age category (age 0–4). The analysis for Turkey and the Arab Republic of Egypt is based on census data in 2006, for Tunisia in 2012, and for Jordan in 2011. Results for Jordan and Tunisia are similar for other years (e.g., 2006, 2010, or 2012).

countries, most strongly in Turkey. For all MENA countries, the relation between employment and age is strongest in manufacturing, which also has the highest share of formal firms (figure D.1 in appendix D).

More productive firms create more jobs. Apart from firm age, firm productivity is identified as an important determinant of job growth in fast-growing middle-income and high-income countries. We show this is also the case in MENA countries. Table 1.3 summarizes the results from regressions of job creation rates on base period (log) productivity levels, after controlling for firm size, age, and two-digit sector dummies.[15] Using (log) value added per worker as a measure of productivity, we find that firms with higher labor productivity experience higher subsequent job growth.[16] The result also provides some partial evidence of creative destruction in MENA economies, in the sense that establishments with higher productivity levels create more jobs.

Consistent with the previous analysis, gazelles (fast-growing firms) are more productive and younger than nongazelles in MENA. The left panel of figure 1.16 shows the results of regressions of (log) labor productivity and age on a dummy variable equal to one for gazelle firms. For the two countries with available data, Lebanon and Egypt, gazelles are significantly more productive than nongazelles. Moreover, gazelles are found to be about

TABLE 1.3

More Productive Firms Create More Jobs

	Lebanon, 2005–10	Tunisia, 1997–2012	Turkey, 2005–10	West Bank and Gaza, 2004–12	Egypt, Arab Rep., 2007–11	Egypt, Arab Rep., 2007–11
	(all sectors)	(all sectors)	(all sectors, 20+)	(all sectors)	(manufacturing 10+)	(manufacturing 10+)
Labor productivity	0.039***	0.029***	0.007***	0.022	0.007	
Total factor productivity						0.019***
Controlling for firm size and age	Yes	Yes	Yes	Yes	Yes	Yes
No. of observations	141,061	129,516	176,665	3,075	7,925	7,988
R^2	0.40	0.34	0.03	0.41	0.10	0.09

Source: Calculation based on census data.
Note: The dependent variable is the Davis-Haltiwanger-Schuh growth rate. Regressions are weighted by the average size of firms over the growth period. Job growth is measured annually, and productivity is measured at the beginning of the period. In Egypt, data include manufacturing and mining establishments with at least 10 employees; in Turkey, firms with at least 20 employees in all sectors are considered. Labor productivity in Egypt is significant at the 1 percent level when the job creation rate measured over the four-year period (2007–11) is regressed on initial labor productivity in 2007.
Significance level: *** = 1%.

FIGURE 1.16

Characteristics of Gazelles in the Arab Republic of Egypt, Lebanon, and Morocco

a. Labor Productivity and Age in the Arab Republic of Egypt and Lebanon

Country	Labor productivity (log)	Age
Egypt, Arab Rep., 2007–11	0.880***	–5.619**
Lebanon, 2005–10	0.261***	–4.723***

$**p < 0.05.$ $***p < 0.01.$

b. Firms that are gazelles in Morocco, 2003–06

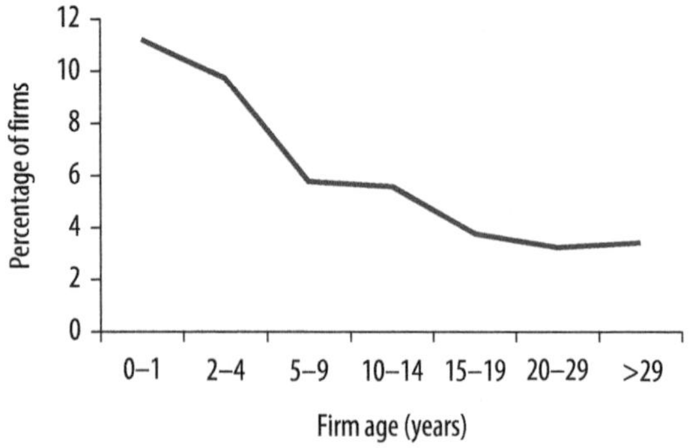

Source: Calculation based on census data.
Note: Gazelles are defined as firms with at least 10 employees in the base year that double employment over any four-year period. Data for Turkey includes only firms with at least 20 employees.

4.7 and 5.6 years younger than other firms in Lebanon and Egypt, respectively. The right panel figure 1.16 shows that young manufacturing firms are more likely to be gazelles in Morocco than older firms; about 34 percent of all gazelles are at most four years old, and about 55 percent are less than 10 years old. Moreover, we find that gazelles emerge across all sectors of the economy. For example, the largest numbers of gazelles in Tunisia are in textiles, construction, and real estate. In Jordan, the highest incidence is in the construction sector. Nevertheless, gazelles also emerge in most other manufacturing or service sectors in both countries.

MENA Needs a Larger Pool of Young Firms and Productive Firms

The previous section showed that job creation in MENA countries is weak, but that the fundamentals of job creation in the region are similar to the fundamentals in fast-growing and high-income countries: younger firms and more productive firms create more jobs. Given the fundamentals of private sector job creation are the same as elsewhere, why has job creation been so weak?

Low firm turnover (firm entry and exit) and weak productivity growth in MENA countries reduce the pool of young firms and productive firms

Non-GCC MENA countries have the lowest formal sector entry rates, reducing the pool of young firms that grow and create jobs. MENA countries have some of the lowest entry densities across all regions (figure 1.17, left panel). Entry density is defined as the number of newly registered limited liability firms per 1,000 working-age people, and thus captures entry (of specific) formal sector firms. Formal sector entry in GCC countries is higher than in non-GCC MENA countries, but still relatively low by international comparison. Moreover, it declined somewhat between 2004 and 2012.

Firm entry densities are particularly low in Algeria, Iraq, Egypt, and Syria, with less than 0.5 newly registered limited liability firms per 1,000 working-age people. Among MENA countries, Oman had the highest rate of limited liability firm creation per capita (figure 1.17, right panel) between 2009 and 2012. The entry density in Oman was, however, still lower than the average across all 91 (nonfinancial offshore) developing countries with available data. Among non-GCC countries, Tunisia and Morocco had the highest formal sector entry rates per capita; Algeria, Iraq, Egypt, and Syria had the lowest. The entry densities in many fast-growing developing countries such as Serbia, Brazil, Croatia, Chile, and Bulgaria are between two and eight times higher than in Morocco and Tunisia (the two non-GCC MENA countries with the highest entry densities).

FIGURE 1.17

Entry Density of Formal Sector Limited-Liability Firms across Regions and Countries, 2004–12

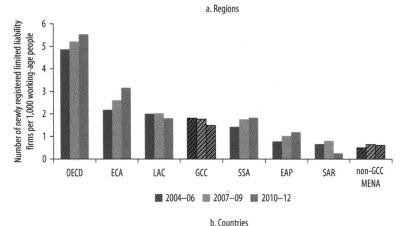

a. Regions

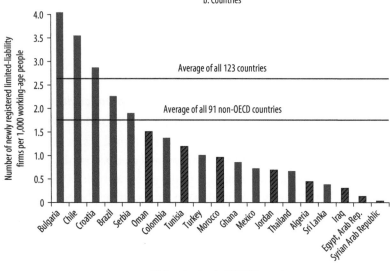

b. Countries

Countries of study   ▨ MENA countries

Source: Calculation and Klapper and Love (2010).
Note: The average of 123 (91 non-OECD) countries represents the average entry density in all (nonfinancial offshore) countries with available data.

Firm turnover rates (entry and exit rates) among MENA countries are low by international standards. High firm entry rates spur experimentation, but also increase the likelihood of the marginal firm's failure. Thus, one should expect a positive association between firm entry and exit rates in the data. Figure 1.18 plots the entry and exit rates in manufacturing and service sectors across MENA countries and developing countries from other regions. Overall, gross entry and exit rates in MENA countries are remarkably low by international standards. For example, entry and exit rates in manufacturing in Colombia are about 11 and 12 percent,

FIGURE 1.18

Firm Turnover across Countries

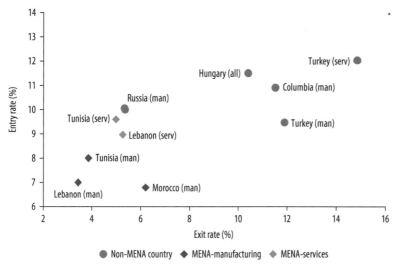

Source: Calculation based on census data.
Note: Entry (exit) in Turkey implies that firm size exceeds (falls below) 20 employees; in Morocco and Colombia it means exceeding (or falling below) 10 employees. man = manufacturing; serv = services.

respectively, almost twice as high as in Morocco. Moreover, firm turnover in the services sector is higher than in the manufacturing sector; this reflects the higher dynamism of services, and also the smaller size and lower productivity firms found in the sector.

Even after controlling for cohort effects, firm exit rates among MENA countries are low compared with a benchmark country like Turkey. Firm cohorts that entered in the manufacturing sector in Tunisia and Morocco in the early 2000s have high survival, and hence low exit rates, in the first five years after entry. Figure 1.19 shows the survival rates across MENA countries and Turkey. Apart from the different periods for entry cohorts across countries, it is important to note that firm exit definitions in Morocco and Turkey are somewhat different. Figure 1.19 reveals substantially higher survival rates in Tunisia than in West Bank and Gaza and Jordan. In other words, fewer entrants are forced to exit after the first five years in operation, indicating low firm turnover in Tunisia. In contrast, about 60 percent of firms that exceeded 20 employees in Turkey in 2006 are projected to have fallen to fewer than 20 employees again by 2011.

The low share of jobs in younger medium or large establishments highlights MENA's challenge of missing young firms. Figure 1.20 shows the employment distribution by establishment size and age in Egypt, Jordan, Tunisia, and Turkey. It reveals that the share of employment in younger medium or large establishments (i.e., firms with at least 10 employees and created less than 15 years ago) is highest in Turkey,

FIGURE 1.19

Survival Rates Five Years after Entry

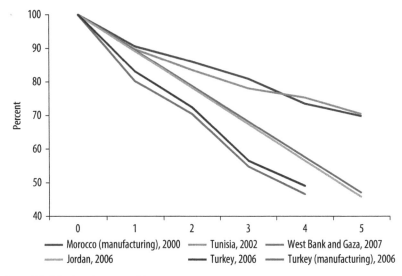

Source: Calculation based on census data.
Note: For Morocco-manu, exit implies firm size falls below 10 employees; for Tunisia and Turkey-manu, exit implies firm size falls below 20 employees. The survival rates for Jordan and West Bank and Gaza were only available for the fifth year after entry. The rates for years one through four were estimated assuming that the same fraction of firms exited every year.

FIGURE 1.20

Employment Share of Young Medium or Large Establishments

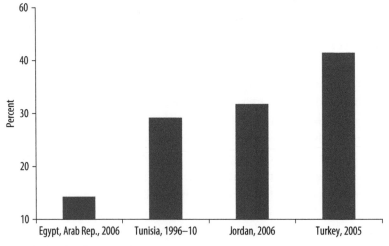

Source: Calculation based on census data.
Note: Medium and large: at least 10 employees; young: created less than 15 years ago.

significantly lower in Jordan and Tunisia, and particularly low in Egypt. These findings reflect a combination of low firm entry and overall weak employment growth among most young firms and point to severe constraints on business creation and startup growth in MENA.

The shortage of medium- and large-size young establishments in Egypt is particularly noteworthy. Figure 1.21 illustrates the distribution of the total number of employees by detailed establishment size and age categories in Egypt and Turkey in 2006. It reveals that employment in Egypt is concentrated in micro establishments independent of their age,

FIGURE 1.21

Distribution of Employment, by Firm Size and Age across All Nonfarm Establishments: Arab Republic of Egypt and Turkey, 2006

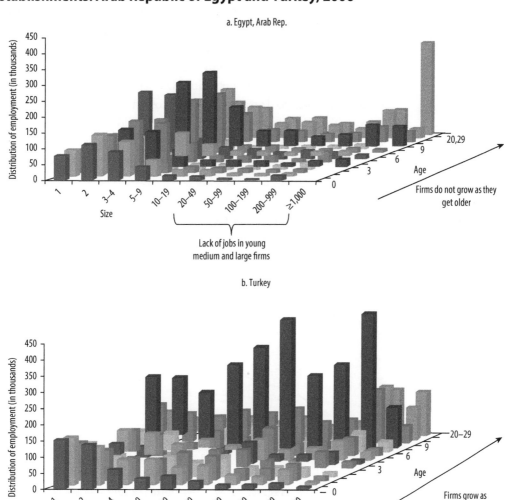

Source: Calculation based on census data.

and in the few very old and very large establishments; the latter accounted for less than 300,000 jobs out of more than 7 million in Egyptian economic establishments in 2006. The concentration of jobs in small, old establishments suggests that, in contrast to Turkey, small Egyptian establishments do not grow over time. Furthermore, the high share of jobs in old establishments in Egypt is cause for concern. Either they remain small on purpose (to stay below the radar of scrutiny by public officials and large competitors), or they are unproductive and might be forced to exit in a more competitive environment (up-or-out dynamics).

Firm productivity growth in MENA countries has been low

Productivity growth over firms' life cycle is weak in MENA countries and relatively stronger for the youngest cohorts.[17] Figure 1.22 plots the evolution of firm productivity over establishments' life cycle. The productivity of the youngest cohort is normalized to one so that figure 1.14 effectively depicts life cycle productivity. It illustrates that average productivity of establishments in the U.S., and to a lesser extent also in Turkey, increases with age. After 35 years in operation, U.S. establishments increase their productivity eight-fold on average, while those in Mexico, India, and Turkey increase their productivity about two-or three-fold. In contrast, in Tunisia and Egypt establishments barely increase their productivity over their life cycle on average. Notably, firms are more productive at the beginning of

FIGURE 1.22

Labor Productivity Growth over the Life Cycle of Manufacturing Establishments

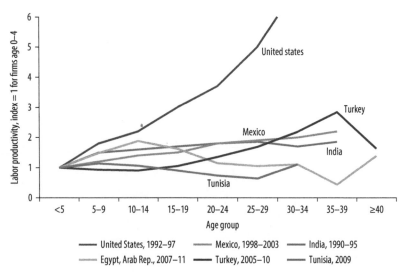

Source: Calculation based on census data; India, Mexico, and United States from Hsieh and Klenow 2012.
Note: The figure shows the average labor productivity over different age cohorts across establishments in manufacturing (weighted by the employment share of four-digit sectors, following Hsieh and Klenow 2012).

their life cycle in both countries, but initial productivity gains disappear for older cohorts.[18] For example, establishment productivity in Egypt increases two-fold, peaking at the age of 10 years; in contrast, productivity of the surviving cohort 40 years after entry is, on average, only 1.4 times higher than the productivity of the youngest cohort. Similarly, Tunisian firms do not increase their productivity beyond 1.1 times the size of the youngest cohort.

Productivity growth can ensue from within-firm growth or from the reallocation of resources across firms. We calculated the contribution of both sources of labor productivity growth in MENA countries with the latest available data. Olley and Pakes (1996), among others, show that the way resources are allocated in an economy has implications for productivity growth. In the following, the analysis shows how the divergence in establishment dynamics between MENA and more competitive economies is suggestive of a misallocation of resources.

Low efficiency in resource allocation has limited productivity and employment growth. In the previous sections, we have highlighted that there is some evidence for creative destruction in that establishments with higher productivity create more jobs. This finding points to the existence of dynamics involving resource allocation to more productive firms. We quantify the resource misallocation across firms in MENA countries following the productivity decomposition approach of Olley and Pakes (1996); these results are then compared with emerging economies from other regions. Figure 1.23 shows the Olley-Pakes covariance term, calculated as the difference between the weighted and un-weighted labor productivity across manufacturing firms.[19] The term is a summary measure of the *within-industry* cross sectional covariance between size and productivity and indicates to what extent more productive firms within industries hire more employees.[20] Figure 1.23 shows that the allocative efficiency is lower in Morocco and Egypt than in Chile, Colombia, or Indonesia.[21] The results indicate higher resource misallocation (weaker creative destruction) across firms in MENA countries than in other developing regions.

In contrast to fast-growing developing countries, large firms in the MENA region are not necessarily more productive. This low allocative efficiency is also reflected in the finding that large firms do not necessarily have higher labor productivity. If large firms are growth constrained (face higher marginal costs of labor and capital), we would expect that they would have higher average levels of value added per worker (and capital), to the extent that average and marginal products of labor (or capital) move together.[22] In turn, small firms would be expected to have higher average labor productivity if they are more growth constrained relative to large firms (for given levels of value added per capital).[23] The left panel in figure 1.24 shows the average log labor productivity for different firm size categories in Lebanon and Tunisia. Labor productivity hardly varies among firms size categories in Lebanon. In contrast, firm productivity is lower for larger size categories in Tunisia, suggesting that small firms are more growth constrained (for given values of capital).[24] These findings starkly contrast with Turkey (figure 1.24b) where large firms are much more productive (in terms of labor productivity and TFP). They also contrast with the findings of Hsieh and Olken (2014), who argue that large firms are (more) growth constrained in India, Indonesia, and Mexico on the basis that the average value added per labor and capital is higher among large firms in these countries.

FIGURE 1.23

Gap between Weighted and Unweighted Labor Productivity

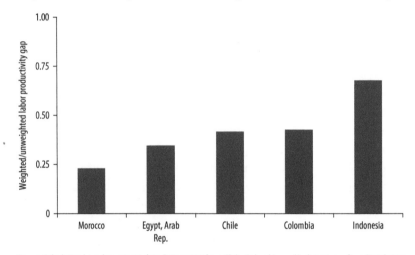

Source: Calculation based on census data. Data points from Chile, Colombia, and Indonesia are from Bartelsman, Haltiwanger, and Scarpetta 2004.
Note: Labor productivity gaps are the weighted (by employment shares) average of two-digit industries. Data cover firms with more than 10 employees in all countries.

FIGURE 1.24

Productivity, by Firm Size in Tunisia, Lebanon, and Turkey

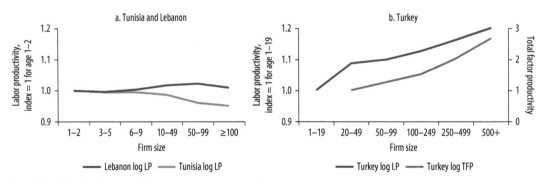

Source: Calculation based on census data.
Note: Labor productivity is the average value added per employee and average TFP is weighted by value added.

BOX 1.3

Firm Dynamics and Productivity Growth in Morocco

Productivity decomposition shows that net firm entry and improvements in allocative efficiency contributed largely to aggregate productivity growth in the Morocco's manufacturing sector between 1996 and 2006. However, the contribution of surviving firms (incumbents) to aggregate productivity growth was close to zero. The methodology proposed in Foster et al. (2001) was used to decompose productivity growth according to the following equation[a]:

$$\Delta p_{st} = \sum_{i \in C} \theta_{is,\,t-1} \Delta p_{is} + \sum_{i \in C} \Delta \theta_{is,\,t}(p_{i,\,t-1} - p_{s,\,t-1}) + \sum_{i \in C} \Delta \theta_{is,\,t} \Delta p_{it} + \sum_{i \in C} \theta_{is,\,t}(p_{i,\,t} - p_{s,\,t-1})$$

$$- \sum_{i \in S} \theta_{is,\,t-1}(p_{i,\,t-1} - p_{s,\,t-1})$$

where p refers to productivity; θ refers to a firm's share of total sector output (thought of in terms of revenues); and the subscripts t, s, i, C, N, and S refer to time, sector, firm, continuing (surviving) firms, new entrants and exiting firms, respectively. The first term on the right-hand side of equation (1) refers to the within effect. It represents internal restructuring effects stemming from changes in productivity of surviving firms. The second term shows the between effect for surviving firms. This is positive when the market shares increase for those survivors with above-average productivity in the previous period (t–1). The third term is an additional covariance term that is positive when market share increases (falls) for establishments with growing (falling) productivity. The BHC decomposition combines these two terms together by calculating the between effect as the sum of changes in market share weighted by ending period productivity (period t). The final two terms represent the contributions of firm entry and exit, respectively. These will be positive when there is entry (exit) of above (below) average productivity firms.

The results are summarized in figure B1.3.1.[b] The within effect is quite unstable, with large oscillation around a mean of zero suggesting that surviving firms do not make a systematic contribution to aggregate productive growth. Moreover, the lack of upward trends in the within effect point to the fact that surviving firms did not systematically improve their technical efficiency (through the adoption of better technologies, management practices, worker training, and so forth) between 1996 and 2006. The between effect is negative over the entire sample period, but increased in later years suggesting that the allocative efficiency has improved in the Moroccan manufacturing sector while that scope for improvements remains. Between 1998 and 2004, the average productivity growth resulting from net entry was .03, or about 43 percent of average growth in the same period. Moreover, the contribution of net-entry to aggregate productivity growth seems to have accelerated

(continued on next page)

BOX 1.3 *Continued*

between 2000 and 2002. The contribution of net entry to productivity growth was largest in the electrical machinery sector, where the entry rate of large startups was highest in the sample period.

FIGURE B1.3.1

Decomposition of Firm Productivity Growth in Morocco's Manufacturing Sector, 1996–2006

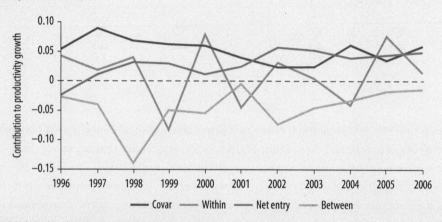

Source: Calculation based on Morocco manufacturing census.
Note: The methodology is explained in detail in the appendix and in Sy (2014).

Notes:
a. The decomposition is done using a window of three years to the contribution of entry to aggregate productivity growth. See Sy (2014) for details.
b. The productivity decomposition cannot be conducted for Egypt, Jordan, West Bank and Gaza as data on firm exit or output are missing. See the data section in Appendix B for more details.

Notes

1. To the best of our knowledge firm census data, including informal firms (below 5 employees), from all nonagriculture economic sectors has only been applied in research for very few other developing countries from other regions including India, Indonesia, and Mexico.
2. The data were collected over the course of more than a year. In the Arab Republic of Egypt, Tunisia, and Turkey the entire data sets were only accessible in the offices of the corresponding statistical departments in Cairo, Tunis, and Istanbul, respectively.
3. The different methodologies used and additional country specific analysis are described in detail in the corresponding companion papers of this report, including Sy (2014) for Morocco; Rijkers, et al. (2013) for Tunisia; Al Kadi (2014) for Jordan; Hussain and Schiffbauer (2014) for Egypt; and Atiyas and Bakis (2014) for Turkey.

4. Under perfect competition in input and output markets labor should move to the sector with the highest marginal productivity (i.e., wage) equalizing marginal rates across sectors over time. In the presence of market failures, distortions, and rigidities (e.g., because of product or labor market regulations) wages and labor flows do not fully adjust driving a wedge between marginal productivities across sectors. While the impact of these distortions is difficult to measure, it is likely that they are more severe in developing countries. For example, Herrendorf and Valentinyi (2012) find large sectoral TFP differences relative to the United States in agriculture, manufacturing, and services. Moreover, the sectoral TFP gaps relative to the United States are larger in agriculture and services than in manufacturing.

5. In fact, under a Cobb-Douglas production function specification, the marginal productivity of labor is the average productivity multiplied by the share of labor in GDP. Thus, large differences in labor shares, i.e., in capital intensities across sectors, drive a wedge between marginal and average labor productivity levels. For example, among the aforementioned sectors, public utilities and mining are likely to have higher capital intensities potentially overstating their measured marginal productivities when approximated with averages. McMillan and Rodrik (2011) argue, however, that in the case of the other sectors, which employ most labor, it is not clear that there is a significant bias. Thus, we assume in the following that large gaps in average productivity across sectors within a country are positively correlated with the underlying unobservable gaps in marginal productivities across sectors. See also Hsieh and Olken (2014) for a detailed discussion under which conditions the average and the marginal products of capital and labor move together.

6. For the years 2005–10, we have data on the amount of employees by sector with a primary, secondary, or post-secondary degrees. We assign 0, 6, 12 and 16 years of education to employees with no degree, primary degree, secondary degree, and post-secondary degrees, respectively. Using a standard Mincerian technique and assuming a 10% return to each year of schooling, we assign each employee a human capital equal to $e^{(1\text{*}years)}$.

7. For more details, see World Bank (2014d). In contrast to all other countries, the employment distribution in Tunisia is based on firms instead of establishments; hence the share of jobs in large establishments is potentially slightly overstated. We note, however, that this bias is expected to be small since, for example, in Egypt only 1 percent of establishments were not firms, but part of larger entities in 2006.

8. Jordan's, and to a lesser extent Tunisia's, relatively high concentration of employment in large firms is in part explained by higher inflows of foreign direct investment (FDI). That is, 19 percent of all large firms in Jordan and Tunisia are foreign owned. These firms account for 30 and 19 percent of employment generated by large establishment in each countries, respectively (figure C.1 in appendix C).

9. These trends are consistent with survey data from the Egypt Labor Market Panel Survey showing an increase in the share of Egyptians working in the informal economy between 1998 and 2006 as well as between 2006 and 2012, respectively: jobs that provide neither social insurance nor a formal labor contract increased from 53 percent in 1998 to 61 percent in 2012. See World Bank (2014a). The report also shows that the trend to more informal work

   materialized in all sectors. In addition, there has been a shift towards irregular work in the second half of the 2000s.

10. US gazelles are based on a somewhat stricter definition: firms whose sales and employment have at least doubled over the same four-year period (Spencer 2011).

11. This definition avoids considering micro businesses as gazelles that increased employment, for example, from two to four over a four-year period by hiring two more family members.

12. The results are based on regressions of the (Davis-Haltiwanger-Schuh) job growth rate following the methodology of Haltiwanger, Jarmin, and Miranda (2010) for the United States. All regressions control for two-digit sector and year dummies. The census data include all firms and economic sectors apart from agriculture (as in the US data). Thus, the results measure the aggregate job creation rate. The graph plots the coefficient estimates of the firm size dummies of two regressions. First, job growth is regressed on firm size dummies and controls only (blue-dashed line). Second, job growth is regressed on firm size dummies and controls as well as firm age dummies (red solid line).

13. The census data from the other MENA countries are not appropriate to apply the Haltiwanger methodology. Firm age in West Bank and Gaza is not included, while in Egypt the census data are not in panel format. In Jordan and Morocco the census data are only in a panel format for a subset of firms (e.g., manufacturing sectors).

14. Note that the analysis shows the relationship between average plant employment and age based on cross-section census data, which conflates size differences between cohorts at birth and employment growth of a cohort over its life cycle. Thus, when interpreting the results as reflecting dynamics over time, it is implicitly assumed that the relative size differences between different age cohorts are time-invariant.

15. The order of magnitudes of the coefficients are not directly comparable in Turkey and Egypt. The analysis tracks the same firms over time if they have at least 20 employees or 10 employees, respectively.

16. The corresponding coefficients are all statistically significant (at the 1 percent level) apart from Egypt. However, in Egypt, capital stocks of establishments are also taken into account, allowing for calculation of the preferred measure of total factor productivity (TFP) following the method of Caves, Christensen, and Diwert (1982).

17. Again, the analysis is based on cross section census data so that we have to assume that cohorts' life cycle characteristics are time invariant.

18. Results are similar for manufacturing firms in Morocco, which increase their average productivity almost three-fold five years after entry, while average productivity is lower in the following five years. The results for Morocco are not reported here as the Moroccan (cross section) data only include firms above a certain size threshold (e.g., more than 10 employees). Note that in Turkey only firms exceeding 20 employees in panel format are included in yearly cross sections.

19. See also Bartelsman, Haltiwanger, and Scarpetta 2004 and 2013 or Hsieh and Klenow (2014).

20. Labor productivity gaps are the weighted average of two-digit industries (weighted by employment shares).

21. The data covers firms with more than 10 employees in all countries.

22. For example, Hsieh and Olken (2014) analyze differences in average labor productivity by firm size across countries and discuss the conditions under which the average and marginal products of labor move together.

23. In an efficient economy, competitive forces lead to a reallocation of resources to more productive firms equating (marginal) productivities across different categories of firms over time. In developing countries, firms are more likely to be growth constrained because of high growth opportunities (from adopting new foreign technologies) paired with market failures (for example, access to finance, markets) preventing firms from harnessing these investment opportunities.

24. The same analysis is performed for manufacturing firms in Morocco and Egypt. However, there is no reliable data on firms with fewer than 10 employees. The findings suggest that larger firms in Morocco are more productive while in Egypt labor productivity is higher and TFP is lower for larger size categories.

References

Acs, Z., J., W. Parsons, and S. Tracy. 2008. "High-Impact Firms: Gazelles Revisited." Working Paper 328, SBA Office of Advocacy, Washington, DC.

Aghion, P., R. Blundell, R. Griffith, P. Howitt, and S. Prantl. 2009. "The Effects of Entry on Incumbent Innovation and Productivity." *The Review of Economics and Statistics* 91 (1): 20–32.

Aghion, P., R. Burgess, S. Redding, and F. Zilibotti. 2008. "The Unequal Effects of Liberalization: Evidence from Dismantling the License Raj in India." *American Economic Review* 98(4): 1397–412.

Aghion, P., R. Burgess, S. Redding, and F. Zilibotti. 2006. "Entry Liberalization and Inequality in Industrial Performance." *Journal of the European Economic Association* 3 (2–3): 291–302.

Aghion, P., C. Harris, P. Howitt, and J. Vickers. 2001. "Competition, Imitation and Growth with Step-by-Step Innovation." *The Review of Economic Studies* 68 (3): 467–92.

Al-Kadi, Dalia. 2014. "Firm dynamics in Jordan." Mimeo, World Bank, Washington, DC.

Atiyas, Izak and Ozan Bakis. 2014. "Firm Dynamics and Job Creation in Turkey." Mimeo, Sabanci University, Istanbul, Turkey.

Ayyagari, M., A. Demirguc-Kunt, and V. Maksimovic. 2011. "Small vs. Young Firms across the World: Contribution to Employment, Job Creation, and Growth." Policy Research Working Paper 5631, World Bank, Washington, DC.

Bars, F., S. Boiteux, M.-F. Clerc-Girard, and S. Janczak. 2006. "Entrepreneurship and the High Growth Companies: The Evolution of the Gazelles and Their Ties to the Territory." Business School Working Paper 2006–02, ICN, Nancy, France.

Berman, E., and S. Machin. 2004. "Skill-Biased Technology Transfer around the World." *Oxford Review of Economic Policy* 16: 12–22.

Bartelsman, Eric, J. Haltiwanger, and S. Scarpetta. 2004. "Microeconomic Evidence on Creative Destruction in Industrial and Developing Countries." World Bank Policy Research Paper 3464, World Bank, Washington, DC.

Bartelsman, Eric, John Haltiwanger, and Stefano Scarpetta. 2013. "Cross-Country Differences in Productivity: The Role of Allocation and Selection." *American Economic Review* 103 (1): 305–34.

Blanchflower, D., and S. M. Burgess. 1998. "New Technology and Jobs: Comparative Evidence from a Two-Country Study." *Economics of Innovation and New Technology* 5: 109–38.

Bottazzi, G., E. Cefis, G. Dosi, and A. Secchi. 2007. "Invariances and Diversities in the Patterns of Industrial Evolution: Some Evidence from Italian Manufacturing Industries." *Small Business Economics* 29: 137–59.

Caves, D.W., Christensen, L.R., and Diwert, W.E. 1982. "The Economic Theory of Index Numbers and the Measurement of Input, Output, and Productivity." *Econometrica* 50: 1393–414.

Coad, A., and W. Hoelzl. 2010. "Firm Growth: Empirical Analysis." Paper on Economics and Evolution 1002, Max Planck Institute of Economics, Jena, Germany.

Conte, A., and M. Vivarelli. 2010. "Imported Skill Biased Technological Change in Developing Countries." *Developing Economies* 49: 36–65.

Dahi, Omar and Firat Demir. 2008. "The Middle East and North Africa." In *International Handbook of Development Economics*, edited by A.K. Dutt and J. Ros, Vol. 2, 522–535. London: Edward Elgar Publishing.

Davidsson, P. and F. Delmar. 2006. "High-Growth Firms and Their Contribution to Employment: The Case of Sweden 1987–96." In *Entrepreneurship and the Growth of the Firm*, edited by P. Davidsson, F. Delmar, and J. Wiklund. Cheltenham, U.K.: Edward Elgar.

Davis, Steven J., John C. Haltiwanger, and Scott Schuh. 1996. *Job Creation and Destruction*. MIT Press.

Doemeland, Doerte and Marc Schiffbauer. 2014. "Structural Change in the Middle East and North Africa." Mimeo, World Bank, Washington, DC.

Duarte, Margarida and Diego Restuccia. 2010. "The Role of the Structural Transformation in Aggregate Productivity." *Quarterly Journal of Economics* 125: 129–73.

Eichengreen, Barry, and Poonam Gupta. 2011. "The Service Sector as India's Road to Economic Growth." Working Paper 16757, NBER, Cambridge, MA.

Foster, L., J. Haltiwanger, and C. J. Krizan. "Aggregate Productivity Growth: Lessons from Microeconomic Evidence." In *New Developments in Productivity Analysis*, edited by C. R. Hulten, E. R. Dean, and M. J. Harper. Chicago: University of Chicago Press, 2001, 303–63.

Fuentes, O., and S. Gilchrist. 2005. "Trade Orientation and Labor Market Evolution: Evidence from Chilean Plant-Level Data." In *Labor Markets and Institutions*, edited by J. Restrepo and A. Tokman. Santiago: Central Bank of Chile.

Goedhuys, M., and L. Sleuwaegen. 2009. "High-Growth Entrepreneurial Firms in Africa: A Quantile Regression Approach." *Small Business Economics* 34(1): 31–51.

Hall, B. H. 1987. "The Relationship between Firm Size and Firm Growth in the U.S. Manufacturing Sector." *Journal of Industrial Economics* 35: 583–600.

Hall, B. H., F. Lotti, and J. Mairesse. 2008. "Employment, Innovation, and Productivity: Evidence from Italian Microdata." *Industrial and Corporate Change* 17: 813–39.

Haltiwanger, John, Ron S. Jarmin, and Javier Miranda. 2010. "Who Creates Jobs? Small versus Large versus Young." *Review of Economics and Statistics* 95 (2): 347–61.

Hanson, G., and A. Harrison. 1999. "Trade and Wage Inequality in Mexico." *Industrial and Labor Relations Review* 52: 271–88.

Harrison, R., J. Jaumandreu, J. Mairesse, and B. Peters. 2008. "Does Innovation Stimulate Employment? A Firm-Level Analysis Using Comparable Microdata from Four European Countries." Working Paper 14216, NBER, Cambridge, MA.

Hart, P. E., and N. Oulton. 1996. "The Growth and Size of Firms." *Economic Journal* 106 (3): 1242–52.

Henrekson, M., and D. Johansson. 2010. "Gazelles as Job Creators: A Survey and Interpretation of the Evidence." *Small Business Economics* 35 (2): 227–44.

Herrendorf, Berthold, Richard Rogerson, and Akos Valentinyi. 2013b. "Growth and Structural Transformation." In *Handbook of Economic Growth*, edited by Philippe Aghion and Steven N. Durlauf. Philadelphia, PA: Elsevier.

Herrendorf, Berthold, and Akos Valentinyi. 2012. "Which Sectors Make Poor Countries so Unproductive?" *Journal of the European Economic Association* 10: 323–41.

Hidalgo, C. A., B. Klinger, A. L. Barabasi, and R. Hausman. 2007. "The Product Space Conditions and the Development of Nations." *Science* 317: 482.

Hsieh, Chang-Tai, and Peter J. Klenow. 2012. "The Life Cycle of Plants in India and Mexico." Working Paper 18133, NBER, Cambridge, MA.

Hsieh, Chang-Tai, and Benjamin Olken. 2014. "The Missing 'Missing Middle'." Working Paper 19966, NBER, Cambridge, MA.

Hussain, Sahar, and Marc Schiffbauer. 2014. "Struggling for Growth: Labor Demand and Job Creation in Egypt." Mimeo, World Bank, Washington, DC.

Klapper, L., and I. Love. 2010. "The Impact of the Financial Crisis on New Firm Registration." Policy Research Working Paper 5444, World Bank, Washington, DC.

Kuznets, Simon. 1996. *Modern Economic Growth*. New Haven: Yale University Press.

Mansfield, E. 1962. "Entry, Gibrat's Law, Innovation, and the Growth of Firms." *American Economic Review* 52 (5): 1023–51.

McMillan, M., and D. Rodrik. 2011. "Globalization, Structural Change and Productivity Growth." Working Paper 17143, NBER, Cambridge, MA.

Nabli, Mustafa, and M. A. Veganzones-Varoudakis. 2002. "Exchange Rate Regime and Competiveness of Manufactured Exports. The Case of MENA Countries." MENA Working Paper 27, World Bank, Washington, DC.

Olley, G., and A. Pakes. 1996. "The Dynamics of Productivity in the Telecommunications Equipment Industry." *Econometrica* 64: 1263–79.

Parente, S., and E. Prescott. 1999. "Monopoly Rights: A Barrier to Riches." *American Economic Review* 89: 1216–33.

Piva, M., and M. Vivarelli. 2004. "The Skill Bias in Italy: A First Report." *Economics Bulletin* 15: 1–8.

Rijkers, Bob, Hassan Arrouri, Caroline Freund, and Antonio Nucifora. 2013. "Which Firms Create the Most Jobs in Developing Countries." Working Paper, World Bank, Washington, DC.

Rodrik, Dani. 2013. "Unconditional Convergence in Manufacturing." *The Quarterly Journal of Economics* 128 (1): 165–204.

Sahnoun, Hania, and Marc Schiffbauer. 2014. "Mapping MENA's Manufacturing—The Export Performance and Prospects of MENA Countries since the First Structural Reforms." Mimeo, World Bank, Washington, DC.

Sy, Abdoulaye. 2014. "Firm Dynamics, Employment and Productivity Growth in Morocco." Working Paper, World Bank, Washington, DC.

Tracy Jr., Spencer L. 2011. "Accelerating Job Creation in America: The Promise of High-Impact Companies." Corporate Research Board, LLC, Washington, DC.

Van Reenen, J. 1997. "Employment and Technological Innovation: Evidence from U.K. Manufacturing Firms." *Journal of Labor Economics* 15: 255–84.

Vivarelli, M. 2012. "Innovation, Employment and Skills in Advanced and Developing Countries: A Survey of the Literature." IZA Discussion Paper Series 6291, Institute for the Study of Labour (IZA), Bonn.

World Bank. 2009. *From Privilege to Competition: Unlocking the Private-Led Growth in the Middle East and North Africa.* MENA Development Report. Washington, DC: World Bank.

———. 2011a. "Informality in the Middle East and North Africa." Working Paper, World Bank, Washington, DC.

———. 2011b. "Financial Access and Stability: A Road Map for the Middle East and North Africa." Working Paper, World Bank, Washington, DC.

———. 2012. "Natural Resource Abundance, Growth, and Diversification." Mimeo, World Bank, Washington, DC.

———. 2013. "Jobs for Shared Prosperity: Time for Action in the Middle East and North Africa." Mimeo, World Bank, Washington, DC.

———. 2014a. "More Jobs, Better Jobs: A Priority for Egypt." Mimeo, World Bank, Washington, DC.

———. 2014b. "Why Doesn't MENA Export More? A Firm-Level Perspective." Mimeo, World Bank, Washington, DC.

———. 2014c. "Structural Change and Gender in Morocco." Mimeo, World Bank, Washington, DC.

———. 2014d. "Tunisia Development Policy Review." Mimeo, World Bank, Washington, DC.

CHAPTER 2

Distorted Dynamics: The Impact of Policies on Firm Dynamics and Job Growth

The previous chapter established that, in MENA, employment growth is limited by the small pool of younger firms and more productive firms. This chapter presents several case studies that show how various policies across MENA countries tend to lower competition and create unequal opportunities between entrepreneurs, thereby limiting the number of young firms and productivity growth. The case studies cover several policies ranging from energy subsidies to industry, cumbersome business regulations, uneven implementation of these regulations, to barriers to foreign direct investment.

The Schumpeterian growth model predicts that fast-growing economies are characterized by specific firm dynamics echoing neck-and-neck competition market structures. Aghion et al. (2001) predict that the majority of sectors in fast-growing economies will exhibit high firm turnover, higher within-firm productivity growth, and low resource misallocations.

In contrast, the firm dynamics in MENA identified in chapter 1 resemble market structures in which a few leading firms have large (exogenous) cost advantages, while potentially large numbers of informal micro-firms use unproductive vintage technologies to serve local market niches. The Schumpeterian growth framework predicts that sectors in which leading firms enjoy large, exogenous cost advantages because of policy distortions should display a number of traits that distinguish them from sectors in which leading firms do not enjoy such privileges. That is, Aghion et al. (2001) predict that sectors dominated by firms with large and exclusive cost advantages should face less competition and exhibit less entry and exit. Likewise, sectors dominated by these firms should have a more skewed firm distribution, characterized by a large privileged market leader, and a potentially large number of small and/or informal micro-firms using vintage technologies to serve local market niches.

Low firm turnover, productivity growth, and resource misallocation, which hold back job growth in MENA, point to lack of competition. The lack of both entering and growing young firms also reduces the pool of firms that can put competitive pressure on incumbent firms. Thus, incumbents face less pressure to become more cost-effective over time or exit. Moreover, in the process of creative destruction, resources are reallocated to more productive firms, either through the higher growth of more productive firms, or through firm churning, whereby the least productive firms are forced to exit. Chapter 1 contends that this process is undermined by various policies in MENA.

Competition is a catalyst in the process of creative destruction, which has been identified in chapter 1 as the main driver of long-term employment growth in MENA. Bartelsman, Haltiwanger, and Scarpetta (2004) demonstrate that for several Eastern European countries the *threat of entry* serves as a disciplining device, forcing incumbents to innovate more rapidly. For the MENA countries with available data, we also find a positive correlation between net entry and incumbents' productivity growth in four-digit industrial sectors. In other words, sectors that are more *contestable*—that have more competition from entering firms— tend to exhibit rapider productivity improvements among existing firms.

This chapter offers several case studies that demonstrate how policies in MENA shape (distort) private sector competition and thus firm dynamics associated with higher job growth. Thus, while chapter 1 documented that firm dynamics in MENA are consistent with weak *neck-and-neck* competition in the sense of Aghion et al. (2001), this section highlights specific policies in MENA countries that lower competition by providing large exogenous cost advantages, in the form of policy privileges to a few leading firms.

Increasing the pool of younger firms and more productive firms—the engines of job creation—requires more competition and equal opportunities for all entrepreneurs; in other words, it requires the removal of policies that undermine competition by tilting the level playing field. Increasing private sector competition requires a comprehensive approach to competition policy since a level playing field for all firms can be distorted in many different ways. For instance, the literature identifies several potential distortions to fair competition in MENA countries including energy subsidies, access to finance, and access to land (World Bank 2009, 2011).

The following sections summarize the main results from case studies evaluating: (a) the employment spillovers from FDI in Jordan ("Attracting FDI in Services Sparked Job Growth in Domestic Firms in Jordan" section); (b) the impact of mobility restrictions on firm dynamics in the West Bank; (c) the link between job growth and the quality of the business environment in Morocco ("Business Regulations Limit Employment Growth among

Young Firms in Morocco" section); (d) the impact of energy subsidies on employment and resource misallocation in the Arab Republic Egypt ("Energy Subsidies in the Arab Republic of Discourage Growth in Labor-Intensive Industries" section); (e) and how discretionary policy implementation by public officials affect competition and innovation ("Discriminatory Policy Implementation Deters a Level Playing Field in MENA" section).

Attracting FDI in Services Sparked Job Growth in Domestic Firms in Jordan

We show that FDI inflow in Jordan led to a partial crowding-out of domestic firms in the same sector, but had positive spillovers on firms in supplying or using sectors. The analysis shows that FDI spillovers depend on specific characteristics of the domestic suppliers—domestic suppliers only benefit if they provide services, not goods, or if they are young. In turn, the employment contraction among firms in the same industry is concentrated in old and small firms. The results show that FDI benefits primarily the type of domestic firms that have been identified in chapter 1 to drive job growth. Moreover, domestic manufacturing firms (suppliers) did not benefit from FDI spillovers, possibly reflecting a combination of weak competition in the sector and the absence of larger scale technical supplier support programs. Overall, the findings suggest that removing the remaining restrictions to FDI into service sectors in Jordan is expected to generate employment growth among domestic firms.

Technology transfers through FDI to domestic suppliers, downstream sectors, or competitors are considered to have played a major role in the process of technology adoption, structural change and job creation of many East Asian economies including China, India, and Malaysia (Rodrik 2004, 2008; Sutton 2005). Policymakers in many developing economies provide incentives to attract FDI in the expectation that FDI inflows bring capital, new technologies, marketing techniques, and management skills. In fact, FDI is considered as one of the major channels for fostering technology transfers to developing countries (Keller 2004). Technology spillovers may take place when local firms copy technologies either through observation or by hiring workers trained by foreign affiliates. Moreover, entries of foreign firms change the market structure in the domestic economy typically increasing competition. In particular, it has been shown that FDI in backbone service sectors can increase the quality of services benefitting using firms (Arnold et al. 2012).

This section aims to quantify the effects of FDI inflow on jobs in Jordan by accounting both on direct as well as spillover effects. Following the methodology of Javorcik (2004),[1] the information on foreign ownership used is based on the establishment census data in 2006 and 2011 covering both manufacturing and service sectors. The census includes panel information (and sample weights) for a subset of 15,500 establishment covering 53 percent of total employment in the economy (relative to labor force survey data). Firms with a share of foreign ownership of more than 10 percent account for 19 percent of all large firms in 2006 as well as 30 percent of total employment among large firms (see figure C.1 in appendix C). Data from the establishment census are combined with detailed data on input-output tables for about 80 two-digit sectors in 2006. This allows for approximating the linkages between foreign firms and the domestic suppliers and users of foreign intermediates and services. Lamla and Schiffbauer (2014) provide more details on data and methodology, and additional results and robustness tests.[2]

The approach allows us to distinguish between horizontal spillovers to firms in the same sector and vertical spillovers to domestic suppliers (backward linkages) and downstream users (forward linkages). The distinction is important, as vertical spillovers are more likely: while foreign firms have an incentive to prevent technology leakages to local competitors in the same industry, they benefit from technology diffusion to suppliers through improved input quality. In Lithuania and Romania, Javorcik (2004) and Javorcik and Spatareanu (2011) find positive spillovers from manufacturing FDI only for domestic suppliers in manufacturing (backward linkages).

Jordanian firms appear to be relatively well placed to benefit from FDI spillovers in the form of foreign technology transfers that increase productivity and ultimately job growth. Jordan has some of the highest shares of foreign investment in its total investments: almost half of total investment in Jordan is of foreign origin, according to the WDI in 2009. Likewise, FDI in Jordan accounted on average for about 11 percent of GDP from 2000 to 2009, which is among the highest shares in emerging economies. Figure 2.1 provides the breakdown of FDI inflows into Jordan from 2003 to 2010 by sector. More than half of all FDI is in real estate; FDI in manufacturing accounts for another 30 percent; foreign investments in all other sectors are negligible, at only around 10 percent of total FDI combined. This pattern is comparable with other MENA countries (apart from FDI in the oil sector), but contrasts with the high shares of FDI inflows into manufacturing and ICT services in India, Indonesia, China, and Brazil.

Foreign firms crowd out both small and old domestic firms in the same industry. Job creation declines among domestic firms producing the same product or service as foreign firms which operate in the same four-digit industry. These domestic firms are directly competing with foreign firms, which are often more productive at introducing superior technologies.

FIGURE 2.1

Share of FDI Inflows, by Sector, Selected MENA Countries, 2003–10

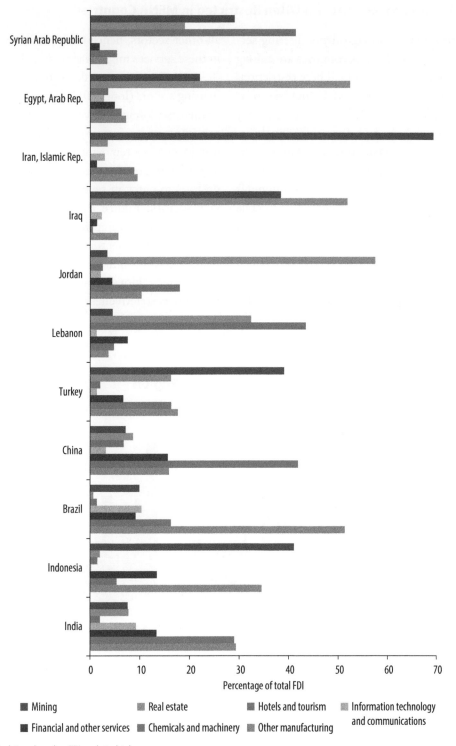

Source: Calculations based on FDI markets database.

BOX 2.1

FDI into Services Sectors Is Often Restricted in MENA Countries

Restrictions on foreign firms entering service sectors in MENA countries are among the highest in the world. These restrictions are generally larger in GCC countries relative to non-GCC MENA countries.[a] They are particularly high for professional services (such as accounting, consulting, judiciary), transport, and finance; some service trade restrictions also exist in telecommunications and retail trade (figure B2.1.1). The partial protection from foreign competition in domestic service sectors has potentially led to lower productivity growth of services. Backbone services (banking, telecommunication, transport) are important inputs for

all other sectors, hence weak performance in these services might lead to weak links in the economy dragging down productivity in using sectors (Jones 2011; Kremer 1993). In this case, foreign entry into these services can improve performance and growth in using sectors by removing weak links.[b]

Jordan imposed some major restrictions on foreign entry in several backbone service sectors. Figure B2.1.2 summarizes restrictions on foreign firms to entry into different service sectors in MENA countries, and (unweighted regional) averages from other regions. Countries are ranked by their restrictiveness to foreign entry

FIGURE B2.1.1

Service Trade Restriction Index, by Sector and Region

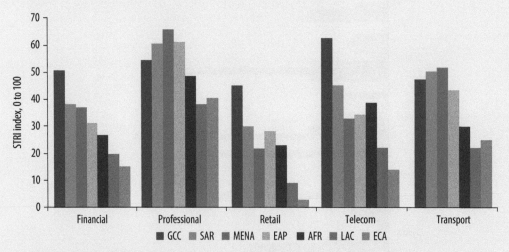

Source: Calculation based on World Bank Service Trade Restriction Database (Borchert, Gootiiz, and Mattoo 2012).
Note: STRI reflects simple country averages. The higher the index, the more restrictions are imposed on foreign firm entry: zero implies no restrictions on foreign owners, 100 implies foreigners are not allowed to operate in the sector at all. The Service Trade Restriction Index ranges from 0 (least restrictive) to 100 (most restrictive).

(continued on next page)

BOX 2.1 *Continued*

FIGURE B2.1.2

Service Trade Restrictions in Transportation Services in MENA, 2008

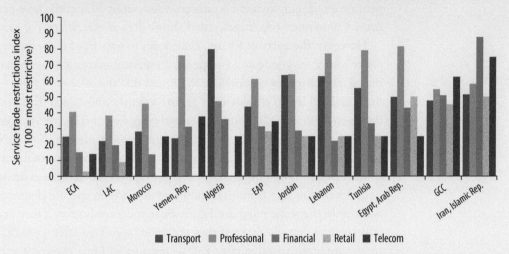

Source: Calculation based on World Bank Service Trade Restriction Database (Mattoo et al. 2012).
Note: The higher the index, the more restrictions are imposed on foreign firm entry: zero implies no restrictions on foreign owners, 100 implies foreigners are not allowed to operate in the sector at all.

across all service sectors (from lowest to highest). In 2008, Jordan imposed higher restrictions than the average country in Latin America and Caribbean (LAC), Eastern Europe and Central Asia (ECA), or East Asia and Pacific (EAP). Professional and transport services were the most restricted in Jordan. The transport sector comprises air, land, maritime, and auxiliary

transport services. The index reveals that some transport sectors are virtually closed to foreign competition in Jordan. For example, in contrast to the majority of the 81 coastal countries in the sample, Jordan restricts foreign investors' access to all auxiliary port services (cargo handling, storage, maritime agency services, and freight forwarding).

Notes:
a. A new (2008) World Bank database allows comparison of service trade restrictions in five key service sectors across 103 countries, including 13 MENA countries. The database on service trade restrictions provides comparable information across countries for the following five service sectors: telecommunications, finance, transportation, retail, and professional services. The indicators focus on policies and regulations discriminating against foreign service providers. Information on the de facto implementation of policies is captured in some cases, such as the extent to which the process of granting licenses is transparent and accountable. See Borchert, Gootiiz, and Mattoo (2012) for a detailed description of the data and sampling.
b. Marotta, Ugarte, and Baghdadi (2014) analyze the extent to which weak links reduce productivity in the Tunisian economy. They show that weak links are consistently associated with lower levels of productivity per worker. Moreover, the authors identify an important spatial dimension in that the probability of facing weak links in intermediate inputs is higher in inland regions. In addition, economic sectors exposed to more international trade are less likely to be affected by the weak links.

Thus, the results suggest at least a partial crowding-out effect of jobs in domestic firms to jobs in foreign firms.[3] This crowding-out effect, however, is limited to small (less than 30 employees) or old (created before 1990) domestic establishments. Supposing that small and old establishments are less productive, the finding is consistent with a competition effect: employment is only crowded out by FDI in the least productive domestic firms, which either shrink (lose market shares) or exit.

However, the entry of foreign firms leads to growth of domestic suppliers which are young and/or operate in service sectors. On aggregate, the analysis provides no evidence to suggest that the presence of foreign firms in 2006 led to employment growth over the subsequent five years (between 2006 and 2011) among domestic suppliers (backward linkages). Domestic suppliers do not have a stronger growth pattern if goods or services are supplied to sectors with a high initial concentration of foreign firms (that is, FDI). The analysis does show, however, that the existence of backward linkages from FDI spillovers depends on specific characteristics of the domestic suppliers. Domestic suppliers only grow if they provide services, not goods, or if they are young—created after 1990. The results are summarized in table E.1 in appendix E. Thus, those domestic establishments supplying services to sectors with a high initial share of foreign firms experience higher subsequent employment growth. Thus, job creation among domestic service suppliers is strong in the medium term after the entry of foreign firms. Moreover, the findings suggest that young establishments, which started operations after 1990, created more jobs from 2006 to 2011 when they supplied their good or services to sectors with a larger presence of foreign firms in 2006. While the age of supplying firms matters—i.e., only young firms create more jobs—the size of domestic suppliers does not.

Removing the remaining restrictions to FDI into service sectors in Jordan is expected to generate employment growth among domestic firms. The type of FDI also matters for jobs spillovers. FDI into services creates jobs among domestic firms in other service sectors. Domestic firms providing services to as well as using services from foreign firms experience significantly higher subsequent medium term growth (columns 8–10 in table E.1 in appendix E). In contrast, FDI into manufacturing does not lead to growth among domestic firms in upstream or downstream sectors. The positive growth effect of services FDI on downstream firms in Jordan using these services is consistent with the theory of weak links. In fact, figure B2.1.2 shows that FDI in some service sectors such as transport or professional service is restricted in Jordan. Our findings suggest that removing these restrictions would increase growth among domestic firms using these services or providing themselves services to these multinational companies.

The positive growth spillovers from FDI into service sectors to domestic service providers and young suppliers are permanent, lasting even after foreign firms exit. In contrast, the crowding-out effect of domestic firms operating in the same sector is only temporary, as domestic firm growth picks up again after the exit of the foreign competitor. Note that the time periods provided in the data allow for a clear empirical identification to test for asymmetric effects of foreign entry (FDI) versus foreign exit (sudden stops). That is, FDI to developing countries declined substantially when many foreign firms exited in 2009 and 2010, when multinationals adjusted their portfolios to reduce exposure to high-risk investments after the global financial crisis. The data show that the average weighted share of foreign establishments, relative to all establishments, declined from 2.3 percent in 2006 to 1 percent in 2011. (The number of foreign-owned establishments declined from 338 to 142.) If initial employment spillovers from FDI before 2006 are truly technology spillovers, the growth effect for domestic suppliers is expected to endure. In contrast, if it is due to a temporary demand effect, job growth among domestic suppliers should disappear after the exit of the foreign firm. The results show the positive backward spillovers from foreign firms to domestic suppliers endure even after the exit of foreign firms. In contrast, the initial decline in employment among domestic competitors in the same sectors after foreign entry is reversed after the exit of the foreign firm (crowding in). The findings suggest that job creation among domestic suppliers is due to permanent technology spillovers and not temporary demand effects. Furthermore, after the domestic supplier is able to supply goods or services to the foreign firms, the firm is well positioned to supply its services also to other firms afterwards, in Jordan or abroad.

Attracting FDI can be a powerful tool to enhance private sector competition and growth. The results show that FDI benefits primarily the type of domestic firms that have been identified in chapter 1 to drive job growth. In Jordan, FDI led to permanent growth spillovers to young firms supplying to foreign-owned firms. In line with previous contributions, these spillovers emerge from vertical rather than horizontal foreign presence. While FDI spurs employment growth among young and service firms, it temporarily crowds out employment growth in small or old domestic competitors in the same sector. The absence of positive spillovers to domestic suppliers in Jordan's manufacturing sector, however, raises questions.

The absence of linkages with domestic manufacturing suppliers rationalizes an evaluation of targeted policy interventions in other developing countries. The results for Jordan contrast with evidence from other developing countries, where findings typically identify spillovers to domestic manufacturing suppliers as the main growth channel of FDI (Javorcik 2004; Javorcik and Spatareanu 2011; Rodrik 2008; Sutton 2005).

The lack of spillovers to domestic manufacturing suppliers in Jordan also corroborates the findings of industry case studies. For example, the pharmaceutical sector hosts several large foreign multinationals and large domestic producers. Still, the sector appears to be only weakly linked to domestic suppliers: 90 percent of all chemicals used as inputs in the sector are imported. Only HIKMA Pharmaceuticals, the largest domestic producer, has a small spin-off supplying chemicals. The main reasons are said to be the high requested quality standards; the small economies of scale relative to East Asian suppliers such as India; and the relatively low transportation costs for chemicals. Similarly, other less-sophisticated inputs such as glass containers or packaging material are often imported rather than being supplied domestically.

Government policies in Turkey, Malaysia, India, and China actively supported linkages between foreign multinationals and domestic suppliers by subsidizing technical training programs. For example, the government in Turkey supported producers of domestic car components by promoting joint ventures and providing training programs to bridge the initial technology gap and enabling them to supply to foreign multinational automobile enterprises (MNEs) in the country. Once domestic producers satisfied MNEs' quality standards in Turkey, they also automatically obtained the quality accreditation to export to factories of the MNEs in other countries. As a result, Turkey developed a domestic car parts industry supplying intermediate goods ranging from tires to motor parts to foreign MNEs such as Ford, Mercedes, Peugeot, and Isuzu.

BOX 2.2

Mobility Restrictions Reduces Competition and Job Growth in the West Bank

Competition among firms is distorted by restrictions in their access to markets. Market fragmentation increases the local market power of firms, shielding them from potential competitors. Higher transport costs increase market fragmentation and thus the degree of competition between firms operating in these markets. Transport costs are often determined by geographical distances between markets. However, what matters for the degree of competition between firms are not physical, but economic distances. In the West Bank, economic distances can be large because of restrictions on the mobility of firms. They distort firms' market access and hence the level playing field and firm dynamics associated with job growth.

Political constraints on firms' market access, in the form of mobility restrictions imposed by Israel in the West Bank, distort the firm dynamics associated with

(continued on next page)

BOX 2.2   *Continued*

job growth. Figure C.1 highlights that the contribution of large domestic private sector firms to total employment in the West Bank & Gaza is marginal (about 5 percent) even by regional standards. Establishments in the West Bank also have low survival probabilities and low growth: the probability that micro establishments in 2007 grow beyond 10 employees in 2012 is only 6 percent. These stagnant firm dynamics are determined by firms' playing field, which is not only shaped by domestic policies, but also by mobility restrictions on firms' access to customers, suppliers, and so forth. Mobility restrictions were installed in the West Bank as part of the broader 'closure' regime, initially instituted by Israel in response to the first Palestinian uprising. They include roadblocks, checkpoints, earth mounds, trenches, and a separation barrier wall.

In this section, we evaluate the extent to which these restrictions in access to markets in the West Bank shaped firms' playing field and thus their dynamics. The analysis is based on an index of mobility restrictions measuring the effective physical constraints faced by firms in accessing customers, suppliers, and so forth. The index compares the population that can be reached within a specific amount of time in a world with and without the mobility restriction. Map B2.2.1 reveals that restrictions in market access for firms in the West Bank declined between 2006 and 2012. This section in based on the analysis of Blankespoor, van der Weide, and Rijkers (2014) in World Bank (2014b).

MAP B2.2.1

Mobility Restrictions in the West Bank, 2006 and 2011

a. 2006

b. 2011

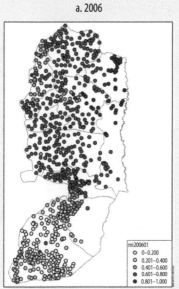
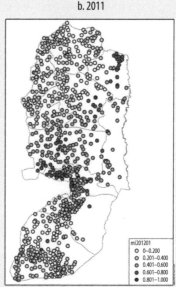

Mobility index calculated with the negative potential accessibility index with a = 40 and b = 2   Mobility index calculated with the negative potential accessibility index with a = 40 and b = 2

(continued on next page)

BOX 2.2   *Continued*

Mobility restrictions reduce net firm entry. The relatively high gross entry and exit rates in West Bank and Gaza might be related to changes in restrictions to market access over time, leading to a more frequent reshuffling of economic activity; for example, the closure and reopening of establishments in different locations. Figure B2.2.1 plots the variations in entry and exit rates between 2007 and 2012 among different subregions within the West Bank against the average mobility restriction index for these locations over the same time period. It shows that gross entry and exit rates tend to be higher in locations that suffer from greater constraints to market access. Figure B2.2.1 also reveals that the net effect of these constraints on firm entry is negative. Lower net entry rates, in turn, translate into lower competition from entry, hence reducing incumbents firms' incentives to increase their efficiency. The lower net entry resulting from mobility restrictions is

also associated with lower firm productivity growth of incumbents.

Mobility restrictions tilt the level playing field reducing employment growth in the affected local economic centers. Figure B2.2.1 illustrates the impact of higher mobility restriction on job growth in the affected locations within the West Bank. It shows that job growth declines with an intensification in mobility restrictions providing evidence that distortions in firms' exposure to competition (i.e., markets access) reduces job growth.

The weaker firm dynamics resulting from distortions to market access also translate into lower output growth. Local economic activity is measured by night time lights (Henderson et al. 2012) for the West Bank in total as well as among four major economic centers affected by the restrictions. The strong decline in mobility restrictions around 2009 coincides with an increase in local output.

FIGURE B2.2.1

Mobility Restrictions Reduce Net Entry, Employment Growth, and Local Output Growth

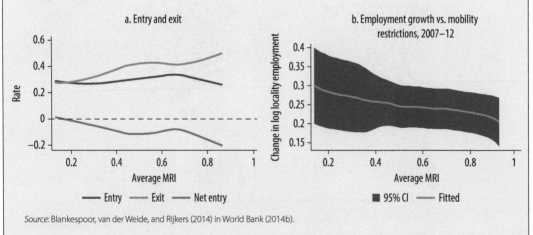

Source: Blankespoor, van der Weide, and Rijkers (2014) in World Bank (2014b).

In Malaysia, the government subsidized training programs of foreign MNEs to domestic suppliers, while China and India used domestic content requirements for foreign MNEs in the electronics and automobile sectors (Rodrik 2004, 2008; Sutton 2005).

Technical support programs targeting potential domestic suppliers to foreign firms have shown some success in Jordan. Jordan implemented a technical support program operated by JEDCO targeting potential domestic suppliers to foreign firms in the mid-2000s. The program generated some success stories despite small-scale funding, but was later abandoned. In one example, the program provided technical support for a local packaging firm so it could supply Kentucky Fried Chicken (KFC) after KFC entered the Jordan market. A few years later KFC began using this firm as its main supplier of packaging material for all stores in the Middle East region.

Business Regulations Limit Employment Growth among Young Firms in Morocco

We show how various dimensions of the business environment in Morocco impact employment growth and disproportionately affect young firms. The findings indicate that more competition, equivalent treatment by tax authorities, less corruption and fewer obstacles in the judicial system, and lower cost of finance would raise employment growth among young firms.

This section evaluates the extent to which red tape in the regulatory environment distorts manufacturing job growth in Morocco. Since the early 1990s Morocco has undertaken a range of macroeconomic, regulatory, and social reforms to improve the functioning of the market economy. Yet, GDP growth over the last decade was accompanied by stagnation in job creation. Figures 1.17, 1.18, 1.19, or 1.23 asserted that the firm dynamics driving job growth are limited in the Moroccan manufacturing sector. In this section, we relate these dynamics to cumbersome business regulations that distort private sector competition in Morocco. We empirically investigate how certain firm characteristics interact with constraints in the regulatory environment, finance, and competition, thus inhibiting job creation among Morocco's manufacturing firms. Detailed data from the analysis presented here are found in the companion paper by Gasiorek, Bottini, and Lai Tong (2014).[4]

Our approach allows for testing this hypothesis: do young firms with high growth potential suffer more than other firms in a less competitive business environment? We combine manufacturing census data with firm-level information from the World Bank Enterprise Surveys in

Morocco.[5] A unique feature of this version of the WBES is that it contains the same unique firm identifiers as the census. This allows us to use much more detailed firm-level information on job growth and regulatory policy variables (for competition and finance) by combining the census and the WBES data at the firm level. Cleaning the data set results in an unbalanced panel containing 35,534 observations covering 6,119 firms over nine years (1997–2006). The list of regulatory policy, finance, and competition variables is reported in detail in table F.1.

Startups and small firms create more jobs if they face more domestic competition. We measure three different components of competition: number of domestic competitors, unfair informal sector competition, and the extent of foreign competition. The informal sector accounts for a significant share of manufacturing firms. Since firms operating in the black market are not subject to government control or taxation, they could create a degree of "unfair competition" for other firms, which could negatively impact firm dynamics. We find that higher domestic competition (more competitors) is positively correlated with employment growth for startups (those less than four years old), and small firms (those with less than 15 employees). The correlation between employment growth and domestic competition is statistically zero for all other types of firms (larger and older ones). Similarly, startups and small firms create more jobs if they report higher domestic competition from the informal sector; medium-age and large firms tend to create less jobs when in competition with informal firms. Firms have lower employment growth when they report higher foreign competition. This effect is particularly strong among old and large domestic firms.

Startups grow faster when they face more transparent and predictable tax authorities. "Equivalent Fiscal Treatment" measures the percentage of firms stating their view as to whether all firms in their sector face equivalent treatment by authorities. Hence, it indicates that the firm perceives a more transparent and predictable fiscal regime in its sector and subregion.

After their startup phase, younger firms create fewer jobs when they report more corruption in their industries, or face greater obstacles in their district's judiciary. The *judiciary* indicators are dummy variables reflecting firms' responses to whether the judicial system and dispute resolution dynamics constitute an obstacle to growth, respectively. These variables are aggregated to the sector level so that they reflect the share of firms considering the judiciary as a barrier. We find that large firms and startups have higher employment growth when they operate in sectors and locations with stronger constraints from the judiciary. This result could be reflecting the privileged position of some large firms resulting from their superior access to legal services; the positive correlation with startup employment growth might be due to self-selection because politically connected firms that can circumvent judiciary constraints through personal contacts enter districts and sectors where the judiciary is a constraint. In contrast, after their startup period, young firms (older than 4 years of age but younger than 10 years) have significantly lower employment growth when they face judiciary obstacles in courts or dispute resolution processes in their district and/or sector. In addition, we find that after their startup period, small and young firms have lower growth when they report more *corruption* in their industries. In contrast, large firms grow faster in these sectors, potentially pointing to the privileged positions of some large firms.

Younger firms that operate in sectors or locations with a higher administrative burden have lower employment growth. We consider the following variables, which all reflect *red tape* in procedures of starting and conducting business: (a) number of days needed to obtain a construction permit (wait permit); (b) number of permits needed each year to continue to operate (administrative constraints); and (c) total number of permits required to create a new firm. We find that longer waiting periods for construction permits have a negative impact on employment growth for all types of firms. Young firms, after their startup period, and old firms both have lower employment growth when their sector (and subregion) has more barriers to entry—when a larger number of permits are required to start a business. Startup firms have higher job growth when they operate in sectors with higher entry barriers, a finding which suggests that only the most promising potential entrepreneurs enter these sector or locations. In contrast, startups have lower job growth when they face higher administrative burdens in conducting their business.

High administrative burden is frequently raised as a major constraint to firm growth by entrepreneurs across the region. The experience of a hotel manager in the capital city of the region exemplifies these constraints. The hotel, a small operation of 40 rooms, with excellent quality service, had no restaurant. Here is the owner's account of trying to set one up (World Bank 2009):

> *To attract more clients, especially foreign visitors, I really needed a restaurant. The problem is that according to our laws, I needed a separate license for the restaurant. The hotel one was not enough. I eventually got it. I invested $200,000 in furniture and equipment. When I was ready to start, the whole venture collapsed: a representative of one of the four government agencies regulating the tourism industry visited the hotel, claimed that the license for the restaurant was not enough, and requested a large bribe for another license. I refused and decided to go out of the hotel business. I am now leasing my property on a long-term contract—a line of business that is regulated by only one government agency.*

Apart from startups, all types of firms that report higher costs of finance create fewer jobs. The results show that a high *cost of external borrowing* reduces the growth of firms of all sizes. Only startups grow when cost of external borrowing is higher, suggesting that they rely on other sources of finance (self-financing or informal sources). Moreover, older and large firms create fewer jobs when they report that access to bank finance is a growth constraint. These findings are consistent with Augier et al. (2012), who show that limited access to external finance reduces productivity growth among larger and older manufacturing firms in Morocco.

Overall, the results suggest that cumbersome business regulations in Morocco constrain primarily the type of firms that have been identified in chapter 1 to drive job growth; i.e., startups and young firms. The analysis indicates that greater administrative burdens, less transparent and predictable tax authorities, more obstacles in the judicial system, and higher corruption levels and less domestic competition reduce the growth opportunities for younger and, to a lesser extent, smaller manufacturing firms in Morocco. Morocco's period of jobless growth over the past decade appears related to the growth constraints faced by young firms, which we identified as having a higher growth potential in chapter 1.

Energy Subsidies in the Arab Republic of Egypt Discourage Growth in Labor-Intensive Industries

Energy subsidies targeted to heavy industry in Egypt are large; in 2010, subsidies to energy-intensive sectors accounted for 2.9 percent of GDP, or US$7.4 billion (equal to nearly half of total public investments in 2010). A government license is required to legally operate in energy-intensive industries, such as steel and cement, thereby limiting the prospect for free-entry and competition. Moreover, energy subsidies affect the price of labor relative to capital, thereby dis-incentivizing more labor-intensive activities, and drifting the economy away from its core areas of comparative advantage.

Implementation of the subsidies reduced the prospect for free-entry and competition. A few large and old firms disproportionally benefitted from the energy subsidies. Entry into energy-intensive industries typically requires large upfront fixed investments, which in turn demand access to land and credit. In addition, a government license is required to legally operate in energy-intensive heavy industries, such as steel and cement, thereby limiting free entry and competition. This license previously was issued by either the Ministry of Industry and Trade or the Ministry of Investment and had to be renewed annually, which meant that some firms could be excluded from the energy subsidies. Figure 2.2 illustrates the distribution of employment classified by firm size or age and the intensity of industries' consumption of energy.[6] Note that this sample covers all establishments in the 2006 census. Large establishments accounted for half of the employment in high energy-intensive industries. In contrast, large establishments accounted for only about 24 and 23 percent of employment in moderate and low energy-intensive industries, respectively. In contrast, employment in these industries is concentrated in small establishments which employ 57 and 63 percent of all workers in moderate and low energy-intensive industries, respectively. The difference in the employment distribution across energy intensive industries is even more striking when we distinguish establishments by their age. That is, old establishments accounted for 73 percent of the employment in high energy-intensive industries while young establishments accounted for only 27 percent. The implied higher cost of labor—relative to capital—also helps to explain why old and large establishments failed to contribute significantly to job creation.

FIGURE 2.2

Distribution of Employment, by Energy Intensity and Size and Age

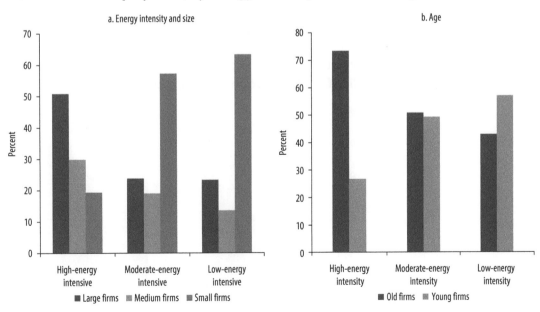

Source: Calculations based on establishment census.
Note: Large: at least 200 employees, medium: at least 10 but less than 200, small: less than 10. Young establishments are less than 10 years in operation and old establishments at least 10 years.

These distortions come at a significant cost to labor; the industrial sector in Egypt generates 1.4 million fewer jobs than in Turkey. Turkey serves as a good benchmark, as both countries have a comparable population (74 million in Turkey relative to 81 million in Egypt in 2012) while total GDP (in US$) is about three times lower in Egypt. Moreover, Turkey's manufacturing sector grew strongly in the past 20 years, benefitting from integration into European value chains. This performance difference between manufacturing sectors in the two countries is reflected in the total number of jobs: the industrial sector in Turkey employed 4.8 million workers in 2012, compared with 3.4 million in Egypt.[7]

Despite Egypt's relative comparative advantage in labor, the share of jobs in labor-intensive manufacturing sectors among industrial establishments is lower than in Turkey. Figure 2.3 plots the number of jobs by factor intensity based on the 2006 establishment census for Egypt. The figure shows that approximately 562,000 people work in labor-intensive manufacturing establishments in Egypt relative to about 886,000 in Turkey.[8] The lower share in Egypt is striking given that Egypt's lower stage of development (GDP per capita is about 3.2 times lower than in Turkey) entails a relative comparative advantage in labor-intensive sectors such as manufacture of textiles, garments, leather products, footwear, paper products, and publishing and printing.

FIGURE 2.3

Employment Share, by Sector Factor Intensity in the Arab Republic of Egypt, 2006, and Turkey, 2010

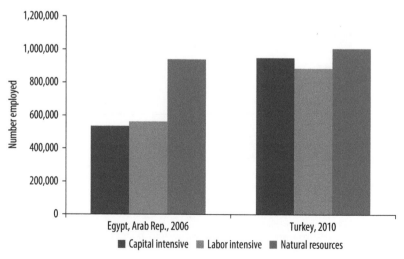

Source: Calculation based on establishment census data; Hussain and Schiffbauer (2014).

Misallocation of Capital in the Arab Republic of Egypt

Larger industrial establishments in Egypt are more capital-intensive but less productive. Small firms in MENA have less access to credit (World Bank 2011). Thus, there is good reason to expect that small firms are more growth constrained than large firms because they cannot finance all profitable investment projects. Similarly, small firms might have less access to land, industrial zones, or subsidies, also suggesting that they face higher marginal costs of capital than large firms. As discussed in Chapter 1, if small firms face higher growth constraints (higher marginal costs of labor or capital), they should have higher average levels of value added per worker and capital, to the extent that average and marginal products of labor and capital move together (Hsieh and Olken 2014). Figure B2.3.1 shows that this is the case in Egypt. Larger establishments in manufacturing and mining have higher labor productivity and higher capital intensities, but lower value added per capital. Larger establishments also have lower total factor productivity (TFP) which is the preferred productivity measure, as it controls for differences in capital intensities across establishments.[a] Thus, the significantly higher capital-to-labor ratios' of large firms over-compensate for their lower TFP and helps push their labor productivity.

FIGURE B2.3.1

Productivity, in Manufacturing and Mining, by Size

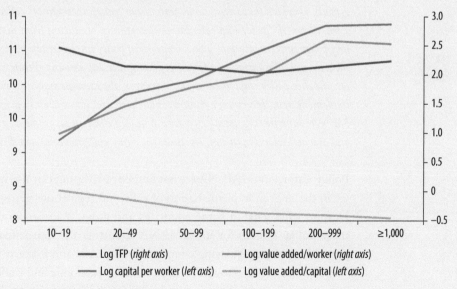

Source: Calculation based on industrial census.

(continued on next page)

BOX 2.3   *Continued*

The results suggest that smaller firms in Egypt are capital constrained; in other words, capital in the industrial sector is misallocated towards a few large old firms. In an efficient economy, competitive forces lead to a reallocation of resources to more productive firms, equating marginal productivities across different categories of firms over time. Thus, reallocating capital from large to smaller industrial establishments would raise aggregate productivity in Egypt. This type of resource misallocation across firm size is striking since large establishments are typically found to be more productive in other countries, potentially reflecting past convergence because more productive firms grow before marginal productivities equate. For example, Hsieh and Olken (2014) argue that large, rather than small firms, are potentially growth constrained, based on manufacturing census data in India, Indonesia, and Mexico.

Note:
a. Higher labor productivity accompanied by lower TFP implies higher capital intensity, at least for conventional production functions. For example, in the case of a Cobb-Douglas production function, log labor productivity is the weighted sum of log TFP and log capital intensity; i.e.,: $\log\left(\frac{Y}{L}\right) = \log(\text{TFP}) + (1-\alpha)\log\left(\frac{K}{L}\right)$, where Y is output, L labor, K capital, and α the share of labor in output.

Discriminatory Policy Implementation Deters a Level Playing Field in MENA

Firms in MENA identify policy uncertainty as a "severe" or "major" obstacle to growth. We show that firms' complaints about "policy uncertainty" reflect largely a perception of "policy implementation uncertainty" resulting from discriminatory policy implementation. The variations in policy implementation observed in the data are substantial, and firms spend a significant amount of time and effort to influence policy implementation. Moreover, the analysis indicates that policy implementation uncertainty reduces competition and innovation in a number of MENA countries, suggesting its potential negative impact on productivity growth and private sector dynamism, especially the entry and growth of new firms.

Policy distortions in MENA are not limited to laws, but can also materialize in the uneven implementation of rules and regulations across firms.[9] Despite wide gaps in some countries and areas, macroeconomic and trade policy indices for most MENA countries are approximately on par with other fast-growing countries in East Asia and Eastern Europe. World Bank (2009) shows that gaps in macroeconomic and trade policy indicators are too small to explain the differences in performance between MENA and fast-growing countries in other regions. It concludes that, apart from a few exceptions, the region's rank is as "average" as that of China, Malaysia, Poland, Thailand, and Turkey. Moreover, apart from a few very restrictive countries (Iraq, the Islamic Republic of Iran, Djibouti, and to a lesser degree, the Syrian Arab Republic and West Bank and Gaza), the *Doing Business* indicators[10] suggest that the legal business environment in most MENA countries is comparable to those in fast-growing dynamic emerging economies in other regions, especially if one abstracts from the restrictions in access to finance and judiciary contract enforcement.[11]

In MENA, an overwhelming majority of firms surveyed identify policy uncertainty as a "severe" or "major" obstacle to firm growth. Over 50 percent of surveyed firms regard economic and regulatory policy uncertainty as an obstacle to their firms' growth, and almost 35 percent regard it as a "severe" or "major" obstacle (figure 2.4). Though there is some variation across countries, regulatory policy uncertainty remains one of the biggest obstacles to growth in MENA, along with competition from the informal sector, access to finance, and macroeconomic uncertainty. For example, the biggest obstacle to growth in Egypt was competition from the informal sector (over 19 percent of firms surveyed), with macroeconomic uncertainty and regulatory policy uncertainty close seconds (13.5 percent and 12.5 percent, respectively). While most other

FIGURE 2.4

Regulatory Policy Implementation Uncertainty in MENA

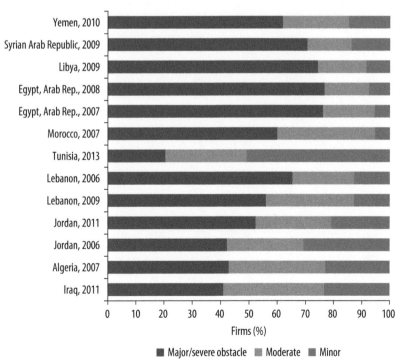

Firms (%)

■ Major/severe obstacle ■ Moderate ■ Minor

Source: Calculations using Enterprise Surveys in 2006–13.

obstacles, such as infrastructure, macroeconomic uncertainty, or access to finance, are linked to the literature on economic growth, the interpretation of what "regulatory uncertainty" is and how it impacts firm growth, is less obvious. In the following, we present evidence that MENA firms' aversion to regulatory uncertainty is predominantly about discriminatory policy implementation that benefits selected firms with specific characteristics and thus hinders a level playing field among all firms.

The variation in the outcomes of policy implementation across firms in MENA countries is considerable. One approach to understanding regulatory uncertainty is to look at firm-level variability in MENA. We examine the evidence provided by surveys of 8,120 firms in eleven countries in MENA.[12] The Enterprise surveys carried out by the World Bank cover qualitative and quantitative assessments by firms concerning numerous obstacles to their growth. The analysis looks at evidence of variation in policy implementation outcomes reported by firms, such as the time they had to wait to obtain an operating license, get a construction permit, or clear goods through customs. That is, table 2.1 summarizes the

TABLE 2.1

Averages and Dispersion of Firms' Waiting Days for Regulatory Services

Country name	Average number of days					Coefficient of variation				
	Operating license	Clear customs imports	Clear customs exports	Import license	Construction permit	Operating license	Clear customs imports	Clear customs exports	Import license	Construction permit
Jordan	—	—	2	—	—	—	—	1.43	—	—
Egypt, Arab Rep.	—	9	7	33	200		1.21	1.55	2.26	2.37
Egypt, Arab Rep.	282	9	6	59	346	2.89	1.22	1.05	1.47	1.93
Yemen, Rep.	13	—	8	24	48	2.84	—	1.43	2.51	1.54
Jordan	10	9	4	5	37	2.59	1.50	0.94	2.14	1.75
West Bank and Gaza	30	22	6	24	50	2.46	1.40	1.25	1.15	0.72
Tunisia	19	9	5	19	158	2.20	1.46	1.36	1.55	2.65
Morocco	4	4	2	2	61	1.87	1.46	1.32	0.61	1.72
Algeria	19	17	14	33	112	1.39	0.91	0.91	1.04	1.46
Lebanon	151	10	7	109	150	1.28	1.40	1.39	1.33	0.92
Syrian Arab Republic	184	10	5	39	245	1.26	1.13	1.13	1.81	1.08
Libya	50	13	6	—	90	1.22	0.87	0.22	—	1.24
Lebanon	81	7	7	30	218	0.87	1.27	1.32	0.52	1.53
Iraq	30	21	11	21	36	0.72	0.89	0.41	0.98	0.56
Turkey	37	10	—	21	42	2.88	1.34	—	1.67	1.65
Chile	84	17	—	17	143	2.62	1.39	—	1.59	1.94
Croatia	26	2	—	12	182	1.69	1.25	—	1.27	1.25
Bulgaria	62	3	—	21	94	1.59	1.1	—	1.17	1.04
Indonesia	21	3	—	11	32	1.43	1.09	—	0.94	1.93
India	29	14	—	15	28	1.4	1.02	—	1.82	1.33
Brazil	83	15	—	43	139	1.14	1.1	—	1.25	1.31

Source: World Bank Enterprise Surveys, various years between 2006 and 2011.

Note: — = cells where not enough data are available because very few firms responded to the question or the information was not collected.

averages and dispersion of the number of days that firms in MENA countries had to wait for different regulatory services in various years between 2006 and 2013. Although the results suggest that there are some differences across countries in MENA, variations reported within-countries are larger than variations across countries. These large within-country variations are linked to *actions* undertaken by firms to control policy outcomes, such as spending time with government officials or paying bribes.

Qualitative evidence supports the argument that *policy implementation uncertainty* is a severe constraint to firm growth. In 1998 a large and diversified family conglomerate in a country of the region opened the first supermarket of a new chain; in 2005 it had 18 stores across the country. When asked about their business constraints, an executive from this chain replied (World Bank 2009):

> *We would have opened more than 50 stores by now to meet the growing demand if opening branches was not so cumbersome. This is by far our biggest challenge. We have to deal with 11 different authorities at the local level to get approval. Typically, you get only a temporary approval that allows you to start operating, but final approval may be delayed for months and sometimes for years. Their temporary licenses must be renewed every six months. Many of the laws we are subject to date back to more than five decades, when there were no supermarkets, so the actual application is almost entirely discretionary.*

Firm survey results reveal large variations in government officials' implementation of regulations across firms in MENA, relative to most other emerging countries. The average waiting time to obtain an operating license, a construction permit, and an import license is the longest in Egypt, Syria, and Lebanon. The firm survey results are consistent with the Doing Business indicators confirming that legal business regulations are, on average, relatively restrictive in Syria and Egypt, and more competitive in Tunisia or Jordan.[13] However, table 2.1 shows that there are large variations in the implementation of regulations across firms in all MENA countries: the coefficient of variation in waiting times for different regulatory services is typically higher in MENA countries, especially in Egypt, Jordan, Tunisia, the Republic of Yemen, and Morocco, than in emerging economies from other regions.[14]

The large variations in policy implementation persist among firms operating in the same sector. Figure 2.5 shows the 90th, 50th, and 10th percentiles of the distribution of the number of days to get an operating license, a construction permit, or to clear customs from the most recent Enterprise Survey data for each MENA country. Again, the findings confirm that the variation across firms within a country is, in many instances,

FIGURE 2.5

Variability in Days to Accomplish Various Regulatory Tasks across Firms, Selected MENA Countries

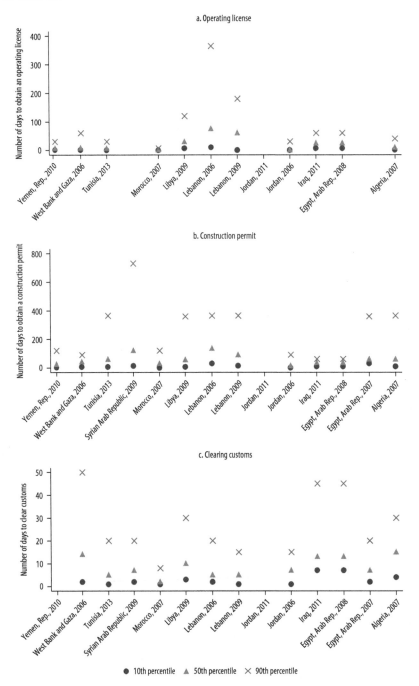

Source: Calculations using various World Bank Enterprise Surveys 2006–13.

larger than the differences across countries. Among the eleven MENA countries, the country with the lowest median time to obtain an operating license is Jordan—one day. Some others report low median times—the median time in Tunisia and the Republic of Yemen is seven days. While sector specific characteristics might explain part of the variations, the large variations in policy implementation persist among firms operating in the same sector. For example, in the textile and garment sector in Jordan, 10 percent of firms waited only five days to obtain a construction permit, while the next 80 percent waited between 5 and 120 days. In other manufacturing, the median firm waited seven days for imports to clear customs, while the next 40 percent of firms waited between 7 and 21 days. At least part of the variations in policy implementation across firms within the same sector appears to reflect firm-level variations in *deals*. That is, the variations reflect differences in the way firms are treated based on their characteristics such as ownership (e.g., politically versus non–politically connected firms—see chapter 4). The outcomes of such deals are conditional on firms' activities to influence public officials implementing the policies so that some of the firm-level variations could reflect firms' uncertainty about the influence function; i.e., some obtained a good deal and some a bad deal (Hallward-Driemeier, Khun-Jush, and Pritchett 2010).

The perceptions of firms that the implementation of policies is consistent and predictable vary by firm size and location. Table 2.2 shows the share of firms that disagree with the statement that implementation is *consistent and predictable*. In Egypt and Jordan there is a large difference in policy implementation perceptions between firms located in the capital

TABLE 2.2

Share of Firms That Disagree with the Statement That Implementation of Rules Is "Consistent and Predictable"

	Egypt, Arab Rep., 2008	Lebanon, 2006	Jordan, 2006	Morocco, 2007	Tunisia, 2013	Algeria, 2007	Yemen, Rep., 2010	Syrian Arab Republic, 2009	Iraq, 2011	West Bank and Gaza, 2006
Small (5 to 19 employees)	47	42	34	53	23	66	65	45	70	68
Medium (20 to 99 employees)	50	49	50	57	28	52	55	42	62	66
Large (100 or more employees)	45	39	43	67	27	51	67	44	54	55
Food sector	53	49	40	56	25	59	45	44	62	56
Textiles and garments	48	56	51	68	26	62	59	46	86	75
Chemicals	41	44	67	63	18	48	88	35	54	67
Other manufacturing	47	39	39	60	32	53	59	46	70	68
Services	na	43	33	51	25	na	67	43	67	68
Construction and transport	na	na	44	59	na	68	50	27	69	64
Capital city (or major city)	51	41	62	54	21	60	58	59	34	60
Outside capital city	46	50	24	73	30	57	63	63	67	74

Source: Calculations using various World Bank Enterprise Surveys, 2006–13.

city areas of Cairo and Amman and firms in the periphery. In the greater Amman area 62 percent of firms report inconsistent and unpredictable policy implementations, as compared with only 24 percent in peripheral areas. In the greater Cairo area 51 percent of firms report inconsistent and unpredictable policy implementations, compared with 46 percent in peripheral regions. These regional differences in policy implementation perceptions are not observable in the other MENA countries, where on average policy implementation perceptions show opposite perceptions, except in the case of Algeria. Geographical differences partly reflect different attitudes or access to the government (municipal administrations). In many cases, most of the relevant business regulatory administrations are located within the capital city, reflecting an ease of access for firms in that area. A possible explanation for Jordan is that firms outside of Amman face lower competition, implying that higher costs resulting from variations in regulatory services are less important. Firms outside of Amman are on average smaller, less likely to export, and operate more often in the service sector. The same may be inferred for Egypt. SMEs are more likely to complain about unpredictability of policy actions in Algeria, Egypt, Iraq, Lebanon, and West Bank and Gaza.

Firms in MENA take costly actions to influence the outcomes of policy implementation by government officials. The degree to which firms take actions to influence policy implementation varies across firms within countries. Table 2.3 shows the time firms' senior management spent, on average, with government officials. It reveals that firms

TABLE 2.3

The Extent to Which Firms Take Action to Influence Policy Implementation across Types of Firms in MENA

Country	Percentage of management time spent dealing with officials (average)									
	Jordan, 2006	Morocco, 2007	Lebanon, 2006	Egypt, Arab Rep., 2008	Tunisia, 2013	Algeria, 2007	Yemen, Rep., 2010	Syrian Arab Republic, 2009	Iraq, 2011	West Bank and Gaza, 2006
Total	8.4	13.2	10.5	11.0	24.8	25.1	17.4	13.2	6.2	7.1
Firms located in capital city	12.7	7.7	13.4	8.4	36.0	21.2	21.5	13.2	5.0	6.4
Firms not located in capital city	4.3	15.6	12.1	11.7	17.7	27.5	16.0	13.2	6.5	7.9
Small (5 to 19 employees)	7.0	10.6	11.6	8.5	27.2	22.9	14.7	14.6	4.2	6.6
Medium (20 to 99 employees)	10.6	14.0	13.3	13.1	24.8	27.7	19.8	14.1	10.2	7.7
Large (100 or more employees)	6.8	13.3	13.3	10.9	22.1	27.9	24.3	9.7	8.3	8.5
Food sector	10.1	11.9	13.3	11.6	21.0	26.9	19.1	15.0	6.8	7.8
Textiles and garments	7.1	9.0	12.8	12.7	22.1	24.7	14.2	8.8	1.6	6.2
Chemicals	7.9	12.2	11.1	11.0	20.5	23.8	37.5	11.8	4.4	8.4
Other manufacturing	9.9	14.6	17.5	10.2	25.9	28.4	15.1	12.0	4.1	6.6
Services	5.5	16.2	12.0	na	29.1	21.2	22.4	16.8	7.7	7.4
Construction and Transport	12.2	21.3	na	na	na	26.3	20.4	16.5	10.3	8.3

Source: Calculations using World Bank Enterprise Surveys in 2006–13.

are more likely to spend time with government officials where regulatory implementation is uncertain. For example, in the Republic of Yemen senior managers spent on average 35 percent of their time influencing policy; the effort was especially high among firms in the chemicals sector. Moreover, large firms tend to spend more time influencing policy. In Tunisia, firms in the services sector, which includes tourism and hotels, are more likely to spend time dealing with government officials. In Morocco and Jordan, senior management in the construction and transport sectors spent more time dealing with government officials.

Firms are more likely to take costly actions when faced with higher policy implementation uncertainty. The variations across firms' access to regulatory services may stem either from a subset of firms that have privileged access, such as large politically connected firms, or from differences in the performance of officials implementing policy. Regression analysis shows, however, that there is a systematic correlation between policy implementation uncertainty and firms' actions to influence the implementation suggesting that differences in the enforcement by government officials is not random but discriminatory. In particular, we group firms by their location, sector, and size. The coefficient of variation is computed for the perceived consistency of policy implementation across firms in each group. We refer to this explanatory variable as policy implementation uncertainty. The average management time firms spend interacting with, for example, lobbying with government officials, is also computed for each group (dependent variable); it is used as a proxy for quantifying firms' actions to influence the outcome of policy implementation. The results shown in table 2.4 indicate that more management time is spent dealing with officials when firm groups face greater policy implementation uncertainty.

TABLE 2.4

Higher Policy Implementation Uncertainty Induces Senior Managers to Spend More Time with Government Officials

Dependent variable:	Average management time (in %) spent dealing with officials
Coefficient of variation of firm reporting implementation as consistent and predictable	0.234**
	(2.13)
R^2	0.331
Number of location-sector-size firm groups	55

Source: World Bank (2012).
Note: Each entry reflects the results of a regression including sector dummies and heteroscedasticity robust standard errors; t-values are presented in parenthesis. The correlation coefficient between management time and reported bribes is 0.305 (some countries are excluded).
Significance level: * = 10% and ** = 5%.

Policy implementation uncertainty is associated with lower competition, innovation and firm growth in Jordan and Egypt. The WBES for Egypt and Jordan demonstrate that variations in implementing legislation among firms, rather than the legislation itself, distinguishes these countries from fast-growing emerging economies in other regions. Moreover, we contend that discriminatory policy implementation reduces economic dynamism—competition and innovation—as well as firm growth. Table 2.5 reports empirical findings for Jordan and Egypt. It suggests that policy implementation uncertainty reduces perceived pressure from domestic competition.[15] In contrast, it is not correlated with pressure from

TABLE 2.5

Policy Implementation Uncertainty Reduces Innovation and Firm Growth in Jordan and the Arab Republic of Egypt

Jordan

Dependent variables:	Pressure from domestic competition to reduce cost		Pressure from foreign competition to reduce cost	Employment growth, 2003–06		Probability to innovate	
	(1)	(2)	(3)	(4)	(5)	(6)	(7)
Coefficient of variation of firms reporting implementation as consistent and predictable	−1.01* (−1.76)		0.822 (0.75)	−.647** (−2.24)		−.807 (−.97)	
Difference 75–25 percentile firms reporting implementation as consistent and predictable		−.155** (−2.04)			−.072** (−1.95)		−.206* (−1.85)
R-squared	0.120	0.122	0.336	0.199	0.197	0.238	0.241
Number of firms	467	467	419	436	436	487	487

Egypt, Arab Rep.

Dependent variables:	Pressure from domestic competition to reduce cost		Pressure from foreign competition to reduce cost	Employment growth, 2006–07		Probability to innovate	
	(1)	(2)	(3)	(4)	(5)	(6)	(7)
Coefficient of variation of firms reporting implementation as consistent and predictable	0.025 (0.36)		0.060 (1.00)	−.111** (−2.57)		−.787** (−2.96)	
Difference 75–25 percentile firms reporting implementation as consistent and predictable		0.013 (0.53)		.	−.002 (−0.09)		−.090 (−1.04)
R-squared	0.031	0.031	0.043	0.420	0.418	0.109	0.106
Number of firms	902	902	899	878	878	905	905

Source: World Bank (2012) and World Bank (2013).
Note: Results are from World Bank 2012 for Jordan; calculations for the Arab Republic of Egypt. The results for Jordan are based on ES data for 2006, for Egypt on ES data for manufacturing firms in 2007. All regressions include sector dummies (apart from specification (1), heteroscedasticity robust standard errors that are clustered at the group level; t-values are presented in parenthesis. The average and standard deviation are computed over grouped firms in each location-sector-size group. Innovation is a binary variable equal to 1 if the firm introduced a new product or new process, or licensed a foreign technology in the last 3 years and 0 otherwise (roughly half of the firms in sample innovated).
Significance level: * = 10%, ** = 5%.

foreign competition (specification 3). Taken together, this suggests an indirect test against spurious correlation, since variations, or uncertainty, in policy implementation are expected to reduce domestic competition, but should not affect competition from imports. Furthermore, empirical findings for Jordan and Egypt reveal that the greater the disagreement with the statement that government implementation is "consistent and predictable" within a location-sector-size firm group, the lower is employment growth and the probability to innovate for firms in these groups.

The results suggest that de facto discriminatory implementation of policies, rather than laws themselves, deter competition, innovation, and employment growth, by granting privileges to selected firms. In other words, we expect to find that firms with certain characteristics, or that undertake certain actions, benefit from streamlined regulatory services and procedures. This can lead to the lack of a level playing field, and undermine the competitiveness of firms in the region. The data suggest that:

a. firms' characteristics (size, age, or ownership) and actions (bribes and lobbying) systematically influence policy implementation, and

b. the resulting uncertainty reduces competition, innovation, and employment creation.

Notes

1. The impact of FDI is measured on employment instead of productivity spillovers as in Javorcik (2004), since no reliable output data for establishments was available. Focus was given to the long-term employment growth effects of the presence of foreign firms in 2006 and subsequent employment growth until 2011. Thus, we assume that over a five-year period learning effects (technology spillovers) of domestic suppliers materialize into job growth. Moreover, in contrast to Javorcik (2004), our data allow measuring spillovers to manufacturing and services firms.
2. See Marotta et al. (2014) for related work on Tunisia.
3. It is important to note that the net welfare effect might still be positive even in the case of complete crowding-out if foreign firms pay higher wages.
4. More details and additional analyses are described in the companion paper by Gasiorek et al. (2014). See also Appendix F for more details on data sources, methodology, and a summary table with the main empirical results.
5. Table F.2 in appendix F summarizes the results for regressions of the aggregate net job creation rate on business environment variables classified into (a) regulatory environment, (b) competition, and (c) access to finance. The first column shows the coefficients for these variables without any interaction, while the subsequent columns represent the policy-interacted coefficients for different 'types' of firms. Access to finance and competition

variables are observed at the firm level (combining the census and WBES data at the firm level), while the regulatory variables are aggregated to the sector level.

6. The classification of industries in high, medium, and low energy-intensities is based on the UNIDO (2010), "Compilation of Energy Statistics for Economic Analysis," Development Policy and Strategic Research Branch Working Paper 01/2010. High energy-intensive industries account for 22 percent of all mining and manufacturing four-digit industries, medium energy-intensive industries for 37 percent, and low energy-intensive for 42 percent.

7. The total number of employees working in the industrial sector in the Arab Republic of Egypt is based on the Egypt Labor Market Panel Survey, and in Turkey on the yearly labor force survey from *Turkstat*.

8. The numbers here differ from the Egypt Labor Market Panel Survey number of industrial employment in 2012 in the previous paragraph as the census was conducted in a different year (2006) and does not cover all informal or part-time workers.

9. This section follows the methodology in Hallward-Driemeier et al. (2010).

10. The *Doing Business* indicators measure the time and costs of official legal procedures for a representative domestic firm based in the capital or the largest business center of the country. The measured policy dimensions are the cost of starting a business, dealing with construction permits, registering property, getting credit, protecting investors, paying taxes, trading across borders, enforcing contracts, closing a business, and getting electricity.

11. MENA countries underperform systematically in two dimensions: access to bank finance and enforcing contracts. "Access to finance" primarily measures laws regarding credit information, collateral, and bankruptcy. "Enforcing contracts" measures the number of official procedures, time, and costs to enforce a sale of goods dispute from the moment of filing until actual payment. Hence, it indicates a problem of implementation rather than legislation.

12. The countries are Algeria, Egypt, Iraq, Jordan, Lebanon, Libya, Morocco, the Syrian Arab Republic, Tunisia, the Republic of Yemen, and West Bank and Gaza.

13. Comparing average waiting times across countries should be viewed with caution for some regulatory services. Receiving or renewing an operating license may be associated with mandatory complementary registrations or inspections (safety or health inspections) in many countries, which would bias the mean upwards. However, comparing the dispersion of waiting times across countries does not suffer from this bias, since the coefficient of variation corrects for such level differences across each country.

14. The coefficient of variation, which is defined as the ratio of the standard deviation to the mean, is a normalized measure of dispersion of a probability distribution. The coefficient of variation should be used only for measures which take nonnegative values. It is independent of the unit in which the measure has been taken (in contrast to the standard deviation which can only be understood in the context of the mean of the data). Thus, one should use the coefficient of variation instead of the standard deviation for comparison between data with widely different means.

15. The variable approximating "policy implementation uncertainty" is constructed as follows. Firms are grouped by their location, sector, and size, for

30 groups of firms (each containing at least five firms). For each group, the coefficient of variation of the perceived consistency of policy implementation across firms is computed. The spread between the 75th and 25th percentiles of the perceived policy implementation consistency is computed as an alternative measure of policy implementation uncertainty. In addition, control variables measuring the initial size, location, age, exporting status, and the initial level of employment of firms are included in the regressions. The results for the control variables are consistent with findings in the literature on firm growth (not shown in the table). The probability of innovating is estimated with a probit regression, whereby the dependent variable is a binary variable equal to one if a firm either introduced a new product or a new process, or licensed a new technology within the last three years, and equal to zero otherwise. About 50 and 42 percent of firms in the sample in Jordan and Egypt, respectively, were innovators.

References

Aghion, P., C. Harris, P. Howitt, and J. Vickers. 2001. "Competition, Imitation and Growth with Step-by-Step Innovation." *The Review of Economic Studies* 68 (3): 467–92.

Arnold, Jens, B. Javorcik, M. Lipscomb, and A. Mattoo. 2012. "Services Reform and Manufacturing Performance—Evidence From India." Policy Research Working Paper 5948, World Bank, Washington, DC.

Augier, Patricia, Dovis Marion, and Gasiorek, Michael. 2012. "The Business Environment and Moroccan Firm Productivity." *Economics of Transition Volume* 20(2): 369–99.

Bartelsman, Eric, J. Haltiwanger, and S. Scarpetta. 2004. "Microeconomic Evidence on Creative Destruction in Industrial and Developing Countries." Working Paper, World Bank, Washington, DC.

Blankespoor, B., R. van der Weide, and B. Rijkers. 2014. "How Valuable is Market Access? Evidence from the West Bank." Mimeo, World Bank, Washington, DC.

Borchert, Ingo, Batshur Gootiiz, and Aaditya Mattoo. 2012. "Guide to the Services Trade Restrictions Database," World Bank Policy Research Working Paper WPS6108, Washington, DC.

Caves, D. W., Christensen, L. R., and Diwert, W. E. 1982. "The Economic Theory of Index Numbers and the Measurement of Input, Output, and Productivity." *Econometrica* 50: 1393–414.

Davis, Steven J., John C. Haltiwanger, and Scott Schuh. 1996. *Job Creation and Destruction*. MIT Press.

Gasiorek, Michael, Novella Bottini, and Charles Lai Tong. 2014. "Employment Dynamics in Morocco: The Role of the Business Environment and Asymmetrical Policy Treatment." Mimeo, World Bank, Washington, DC.

Hallward-Driemeier, M., G. Khun-Jush, and L. Pritchett. 2010. "Deals versus Rules: Policy Implementation Uncertainty and Why Firms Hate It." Working Paper 16001, NBER, Cambridge, MA.

Henderson, Vernon, Adam Storeygard, and David N. Weil. 2012. "Measuring Economic Growth from Outer Space." *American Economic Review* 102(2): 994–1028.

Hsieh, Chang-Tai, and Benjamin Olken. 2014. *"The Missing 'Missing Middle'."* Working Paper 19966, NBER, Cambridge, MA.

Hussain, Sahar, and Marc Schiffbauer. 2014. "Struggling for Growth: Labor Demand and Job Creation in Egypt." Mimeo, World Bank, Washington, DC.

Javorcik, Beata. 2004. "Does Foreign Direct Investment Increase the Productivity of Domestic Firms? In Search of Spillovers through Backward Linkages." *American Economic Review* 94 (3): 605–27.

Javorcik, Beata, and Mariana Spatareanu. 2011. "Does It Matter Where You Come From? Vertical Spillovers from Foreign Direct Investment and the Origin of Investors." *Journal of Development Economics* 96 (1): 126–38.

Jones, C. 2011: "Intermediate Goods and Weak Links in the Theory of Economic Development." *American Economic Journal: Macroeconomics* 3 (2): 1–28.

Keller, W. 2004. "International Technology Diffusion." *Journal of Economic Literature* 42 (3): 752–82.

Kremer, Michael. 1993. "The O-Ring Theory of Economic Development." *The Quarterly Journal of Economics* 108 (3): 551–75.

Lamla, Michael, and Marc Schiffbauer. 2014. "Employment Spillovers from FDI in Jordan." Mimeo, World Bank, Washington, DC.

Marotta, Daniela, Christian Ugarte, and Leila Baghdadi. 2014. "Weak Links in Tunisia." Mimeo, World Bank Washington, DC.

Olley, G., and A. Pakes. 1996. "The Dynamics of Productivity in the Telecommunications Equipment Industry." *Econometrica* 64: 1263–79.

Rodrik, Dani. 2004. "Industrial Policy for the Twenty-First Century." Discussion Paper 4767, Centre For Economic Policy Research, London.

———. 2008. "Normalizing Industrial Policy." Commission on Growth and Development, Working Paper 3, World Bank, Washington, DC.

Sahnoun, Hania. 2014. "Discriminatory policy implementation in the Middle East and North Africa." Mimeo, World Bank, Washington, DC.

Sutton, John. 2005. "The Auto-Component Supply Chain in China and India: A Benchmark Study." *In Annual Bank Conference on Development Economics 2005: Lessons of Experience*, edited by Francois Bourguignon and Boris Pleskovic. Washington DC: World Bank.

World Bank. 2009. *From Privilege to Competition: Unlocking the Private-Led Growth in the Middle East and North Africa*. MENA Development Report. Washington, DC: World Bank.

———. 2011. "Financial Access and Stability: A Road Map for the Middle East and North Africa." Working Paper, World Bank, Washington, DC.

———. 2012. "Jordan Development Policy Review." Mimeo, World Bank, Washington, DC.

———. 2013. "Jobs for Shared Prosperity: Time for Action in the Middle East and North Africa." Mimeo, World Bank, Washington, DC.

———. 2014b. "Why Doesn't MENA Export More? A Firm-Level Perspective." Mimeo, World Bank, Washington, DC.

Avoiding the Pitfalls of Industrial Policy: Program Design in MENA and East Asia

Efforts to stimulate private sector growth and jobs in MENA have often taken the form of active industrial policies with, however, limited evidence of success and many instances where policies have been captured by only a few firms. This chapter reviews these policies over the past decades and compares them with the experiences of East Asian countries. Several critical differences in policy design and implementation that underpin the success of industrial policies in East Asian countries compared with MENA countries are highlighted. These differences point to a list of key ingredients for an effective industrial policy: (a) there is consensus on a common strategic vision and objectives at the country level, and a focus on new economic activities where market failures are more likely to have a binding influence on industrial development; (b) policies are connected to performance and evaluation systems in which both the effectiveness of policies and officials can be assessed; (c) policies promote and safeguard competition and equality of opportunity for all entrepreneurs in the domestic market and provide incentives for firms to compete in international markets.

Many countries in MENA have taken the route of an active industrial policy in an effort to address the deficiencies in their business environment and stimulate private sector growth, job creation, and structural transformation. The previous chapters have shown that a host of policies across MENA countries undermine the underlying firm-level fundamentals of job creation by limiting competition and tilting the playing field. While confronting these constraints directly would have been more effective, many countries in MENA have adopted industrial policies in an effort to encourage private sector growth, job creation, and structural transformation. In MENA, as in many other countries around the world, industrial policy has often included subsidies and tax breaks, which must be large to compensate for the deficiencies in the business environment and spur investment, growth, and job creation. Both MENA countries and many East Asian countries have used this alternative strategy extensively. In the following, we discuss the extent to which these indus-trial policies have been successful and the factors that explain the differ-ent experiences of the two regions.

The MENA region has many decades of experience with industrial policy, but there is limited evidence of success. Few observers argue that the experience has been successful: despite aggressive actions to drive industrial development, structural transformation, and job creation, results have been scarce and low. What should the region's policy makers con-clude from this experience? Should they, in the future, rely more on mar-ket forces, and less on government direction? Or should they improve on the quality of government interventions? The second option appears par-ticularly attractive to policy makers and analysts who observe the remark-able success of East Asian economies, where the government role has been large and ongoing (Box 3.1).[1]

The analytical and data challenges in assessing whether a particular constellation of industrial policies triggered growth that otherwise would not have occurred are considerable. Did a sector emerge and prosper because of industrial policy? Despite it? More important, did industrial

---

BOX 3.1

Market Failure and Industrial Policy

Government intervention has a role to play in structural transformation when market forces are disrupted. A long-standing argu-ment for industrial policy is coordination failure: firms may not invest when the profit-ability of their own potential investments depends on whether other firms make com-plementary investments.[a] This argument is more difficult to sustain when there is an active world market in the complementary products, attenuating the need for within-country coordination of investments. Harrison and Rodriguez-Clare (2010) sum-marize more recent versions of this argu-ment. Learning externalities or knowledge spillovers yield large productivity benefits for all firms, but no single firm takes them

into account when deciding whether to enter a sector. For example, firms may not know how costly it is to produce in a new sector, or how profitable an export market is. Their investments in discovering these costs yield benefits for all firms that they individually do not take into account (Hausmann and Rodrik 2003). Thus, market forces are dis-rupted by information asymmetries related to the economic returns to investment; coordination difficulties among entrepre-neurs in complementary industries; and the absence of markets.

Three concerns about industrial policy preoccupy observers and analysts. First, can market failure be reliably identified? A major difficulty in identifying market failures

(continued on next page)

BOX 3.1 *Continued*

---

is that they may be difficult to disentangle from government policy failures. Arguably, East Asian industrial policies have not targeted market failures directly, but appear to have particularly succeeded at offsetting, for selected industries, *government*-related obstacles to growth, such as those rooted in governance challenges, red tape, and political risk.[b] Second, can industrial policy work given the significant technical and informational demands in crafting and implementing industrial policy? Rodrik (2008) suggests an active public-private dialogue to overcome information asymmetries, citing the positive experiences with deliberation councils or private-public venture funds in East Asia. However, these dialogues are likely to succeed only to the extent that the obstacles to collective action among

firms are resolved.[c] *Third, do governments really want to fix it?* Governments may place a higher priority on alternative uses of funds or pursue other goals that are potentially incompatible with growth; these include, but are not limited to, incentives to extend open-ended benefits to supporters.

While research is convincing that industrial policy aimed at attenuating the effects of market failure is necessarily selective, a crucial point is that it must be selective at the level of industries and sectors, not at the level of firms.[d] Market failures do not, again by definition, afflict some firms in a sector, but not others. Moreover, recent research by Aghion et al. (2012) indicates that industrial policy can promote productivity growth when it favors competition—and that industrial policy in China has done precisely this.

Note:
a. See also Murphy, Vishny, and Schleifer (1989).
b. Where political risk is high—and in many East Asian countries it was very high—governments cannot easily attract private investment. To increase investment, they can either rely on state-owned enterprises—for which political risk is irrelevant—or offer large subsidies to private entrepreneurs to raise their risk-adjusted rates of return. As the subsequent discussion makes clear, during a period in which private investors confronted substantial political risk, the Republic of Korea embraced both strategies.
c. When the problem is the identification of new markets, however, neither side of the dialogue is likely to be especially well-informed; it is precisely because they do not know about potential opportunities that the need for industrial policy might exist. Lin and Monga (2010) point out that a few private entrepreneurs might have already entered new profitable industries. They conclude that these local success stories are themselves informative. Public-private dialogues could bring such examples to light.
d. The essentially selective characteristic of industrial policy prompts critics to describe it as "picking winners." However, market failures are typically related to particular sectors or types of economic activity. Hence, industrial policies intended to correct them are necessarily selective.

---

policy initiatives correct market failures, or did they simply offset, for some firms, policy distortions in other areas, such as cumbersome regulations, public infrastructure, financial markets, or the rule of law? Given this problem of missing data, this section follows the alternative strategy to directly compare elements of industrial policy design in MENA and East Asian countries, and in particular the Republic of Korea. It revisits in some detail the Arab Republic of Egypt and Morocco's industrial policy framework as well as some aspects of industrial policy in Jordan, the Syrian Arab Republic, and Tunisia ("Industrial Policy in MENA Has

Had Limited Success and Many Instances of Policy Capture") and compares it to the experience of East Asia ("What Did Successful Countries Do? The Case of the Republic of Korea" and "Lessons from East Asia Are More Difficult to Implement than Is Commonly Understood").

Industrial Policy in MENA Has Had Limited Success and Many Instances of Policy Capture

Industrial Policy in Egypt

After independence, the state invested in heavy industry and used its regulatory powers to direct private sector investment into favored sectors. Among MENA countries, we know the most about the industrial policies of Egypt, the largest economy in the region. It has pursued policies meant to encourage particular economic sectors since its independence in 1952. From 1956 to 1970 the state invested in heavy industry, authorized favorable tax treatment for some private investments, and heavily regulated private sector industrial activity. Confronted with the failure of state-led industrialization, but reluctant to abandon state-owned enterprises, from 1970 to 1981 Egypt focused even more intently on using its regulatory powers to direct private sector investment into favored sectors and to discourage it in others (Loewe 2013).

Between 1981 and 1990, the most important adjustment in state-led development was a dramatic expansion in the business interests of the army. Price regulations, customs, and financial sector policies continued to favor state-owned enterprises from 1981 to 1991. However, the devaluation of the Egyptian pound, incremental deregulation of domestic markets, and some tax breaks for manufacturing brought benefits to the private sector as well. Private investment rose from approximately 16 percent of total investment over the period 1960–82, to 41 percent over the period 1983–90 (Loayza and Honorati 2007). During this latter time, the business interests of the army expanded dramatically into tourism, construction, white goods, vehicles, fertilizer, mineral water, olives, and bread, with much of it financed by the sale of government land in Cairo and on the seaside (Loewe 2013).

The fiscal crisis forced a change in industrial policies in the 1990s. Egypt shifted somewhat to more favorable conditions for private investment, though not to the point that the government embraced a more economic approach to industrial policy (identifying market failures and carefully constructing policies to correct them). While maintaining important privileges for favored sectors and enterprises, more favorable conditions for all private investors included tax holidays and steps to liberalize the financial sector, deregulate commodity prices, and reduce barriers to trade and international capital movements (Loewe 2013). Private investment reached 51 percent of total investment during 2001–06, although due in part to declining public sector investment (Loayza and Honorati 2007).

Despite numerous efforts, structural transformation did not fully materialize in Egypt. Galal and El-Megharbel (2005) indicate that industrial policies through 1999 did not achieve the goals of structural transformation. They consider two markers of structural transformation: whether product variety increased and total factor productivity improved. From 1980 to 1999, product concentration actually *increased* (variety fell), total factor productivity scarcely improved, and those industrial sectors that received the greatest assistance exhibited the lowest rates of productivity improvement.[2] They argue that this is not surprising: policy over this period did not particularly target new activities; did not condition assistance to firms on concrete goals, such as export success; left open the possibility that support to firms could continue indefinitely; and supported sectors rather than activities.

The period from 2004 to 2011 is typically seen as representing a sharp turn towards a private sector-driven structural transformation, export growth, and job creation. In 2004–05, the government privatized 87 state-owned enterprises and reduced income taxes, before moving on to simplify customs procedures and business start-up regulations, while continuing to liberalize the financial sector. Policies seemed to focus on new markets (subsidies to exports), and new production technologies (subsidies for modernization), and they were more substantial. However, vast areas of the economy remained closed to foreigners, including aviation and engineering services, and heavy industry (energy production, steel and aluminum production, construction, insurance, and fertilizer).

Moreover, in this period, more individual business people benefitted from first-tier personal connections with the government. Prior to 2000, approximately 8 percent of ruling party deputies were business people; from 2004 to 2011, these numbers increased to 17 percent of ruling party deputies and five ministers. The business people represented a miniscule fraction of firms in Egypt and were not politically accountable to them. Hence, they had stronger incentives to use their political positions to improve the investment climate for their own enterprises instead of the private sector in general. Because these business people typically represented large enterprises, their closer ties with the government could have triggered observable improvements in Egyptian growth over the period.

A centerpiece of the 2004–11 period was the Egypt Industrial Development Strategy (EIDS), drafted by the Ministry for Trade and Industry (MFTI). The Strategy tracked closely the ideal prescriptions for successful industrial policy (Loewe 2013). It was designed to address: coordination failures in human capital by training workers and entrepreneurs (the Industrial Training Council); quality assurance (through the National Quality Council); financial markets (the Industrial Modernization Center); innovation and technology transfer (Technology and Innovation Centers); imperfect information about market opportunities (Export Council and Export Development Bank); and coordination problems in infrastructure and plant location (Industrial Development Agency). Loewe (2013) judges the EIDS to be an improvement over past industrial policies; he argues that FDI and exports surged as a result from 2004 to 2008.

However, the EIDS was surrounded by both opacity with respect to the targeting of benefits to "insider" firms (Roll 2013), and weakness in measuring actual impact and costs and benefits of EIDS subsidies. For example, the composition of total FDI inflows into Egypt (and other MENA countries) is mostly concentrated in real estate and mining, which together account for 75 percent of total FDI. The high share of FDI flows into real estate, primarily from GCC countries, relativizes the importance for economic development. This is because capital accumulation in this sector typically has very limited scope for technology spillovers, expanding production capacities, or generating employment effects beyond construction periods.[3] In addition, on other dimensions of private sector growth and structural transformation, the effects of EIDS were more ambiguous. Symptoms of market failure—limited research and development, insufficient coordination of complementary economic activities—seemed to barely change as a consequence of EIDS. In 2004, for example, total R&D spending was an almost imperceptible 0.27 percent of GDP; by 2008, it had actually declined to 0.23 percent. While the activities under EIDS were consistent with efforts to solve coordination failures, the program was not set up either to identify market failures or to evaluate whether it corrected them.[4]

The absence of clarity in the targeting of these subsidies and lack of rigorous tracking of their efficacy raised questions of privileges to specific firms. What explains the mixed results for EIDS? The most plausible reasons for greater exports were simply large government subsidies. Under EIDS the government made substantial financial transfers to beneficiary firms, particularly export subsidies (up to 15 percent of the value of goods) and modernization (up to 95 percent of the costs). These subsidies were likely sufficient to offset significant public policy distortions in finance, human capital, and administrative interference. On the other hand, the subsidies were also large enough to yield significant rents for beneficiaries. Given the absence of rigorous tracking of their efficacy, this raised questions of privileges to specific firms in the distribution of EIDS benefits.

For example, when tariff rates were reduced in Egypt at the end of the 1990s, Egypt apparently responded by increasing the use of nontariff technical import barriers.[5] A new World Bank database allows measuring NTMs in various countries. Figure 3.1 illustrates the decline in average weighted tariffs from about 16.5 percent in 1995 to 8.7 percent in 2009—but also shows a steady and offsetting increase in NTMs. Of the 53 different NTMs in place in Egypt in 2009, almost half (24) were introduced or amended around 2000, and 21 percent between 2005 and 2009. Of these, most were issued by the Ministry of Industry and Trade, which was headed at the time by a prominent businessman. As a result, Egypt had one of the highest NTM frequencies in the world in 2010 (Malouche, Reyes, and Fouad 2013; see also figure 4.5).

Even if discrete policy initiatives were well designed and effectively implemented—a disputed assumption—the broader policy framework in Egypt did not constitute a successful industrial policy. While political connections evidently did not lead to broad benefits for all Egyptian industry, they delivered substantial benefits to the connected firms

FIGURE 3.1

The Evolution of Average (Weighted) Tariffs and NTMs on Imports, 1995–2010

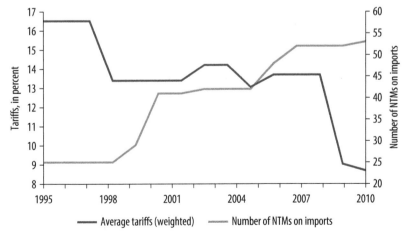

Source: Data are from WITS.
Note: Rate reflects most-favored nation tariffs. The NTMs data provides either the year when an NTM has been introduced or the latest year in which it is has been substantially revised.

themselves. Diwan and Chekir (2012) identify 22 politically connected firms among the 116 largest Egyptian firms traded on the Egypt Stock Exchange. Following the Arab Spring revolution, they estimate the value of connected firms dropped 23 percentage points more than nonconnected firms—that is, 23 percent of the expected future returns to investments in these firms were contingent on political connections.

Industrial Policy in Morocco

Dramatic movements in the exchange rate, however, have consistently dwarfed the impact of other industrial policy initiatives targeting export. Moroccan industrial policy has long vacillated between providing selectively targeted benefits and benefits to all exporters. In the 1980s, Morocco sought to increase manufacturing with tariffs and licenses. However, over the same period the currency experienced a large, 40 percent real depreciation. This likely played the largest role in the significant rise in exports and manufacturing that occurred over the period (Achy 2013). The government liberalized in the 1990s, reducing tariffs, margin controls, and other licensing requirements; it halted direct credits for exporters and increased the role of the market in the allocation of credit. Neither manufacturing nor the economy in general prospered during this time—but this was likely the result of the 22 percent appreciation of the exchange rate over the period.

In the 2000s the government began to use several selective investment promotion schemes to encourage job creation, export growth, and structural transformation. Several investment promotion and tax exemption programs were used in the early 2000s to stimulate investment and structural transformation. The largest was the Hassan II Fund for Economic and Social Development, which provided investment subsidies amounting to about US$560 million (4.5 billion dirham), mostly to textile manufacturers and automotive suppliers. Starting in the mid-2000s many existing instruments were redefined to fit within a more comprehensive industrial policy program called Plan Emergence. It focused on the modernization of the industrial sector and offshoring. Eight sectors were initially selected: agro-food industry, seafood industry, textiles, automotive, aeronautics, electronics, and offshoring services particularly in French and Spanish languages. Investment incentives were granted to foreign as well as domestic firms. Again, as was the case throughout the region, market failures were not defined, nor were the efficiency effects of the subsidies ever evaluated.

Moroccan industrial policy was not accompanied by significant administrative reforms. A group of prominent and politically loyal business firms also enjoyed the capacity to act collectively, through the business

TABLE 3.1

The Cost of Industrial Policy in Morocco, 2010
millions of Moroccan Dirham

Industrial policy measure	Estimated cost, 2010
Value-added tax exemptions/rebates for capital goods	102
Tax exemptions for exporters	2,502
Tax exemptions for new enterprises in Tangiers, other targeted locations	697
Tax exemptions for locating in free export zones	55
Customs exemptions for capital goods imports by large investors	283
Auto industry customs exemptions	365
Hassan II Fund for Economic and Social Development	900
Total	4,904

Source: Adapted from Achy 2013, table 6.
Note: US$ 1 = 8 Moroccan Dirhams.

organization the *Confédération Général des Entreprises du Maroc* (CGEM). They saw their interests hurt by the removal of tariff protections, but when they used the CGEM to resist these reforms, the government responded by expanding the ranks of the CGEM to include more small and medium-sized firms. The government also began an anti-corruption campaign that targeted some in the business community (Achy 2013). Concurrently, and as in Egypt, the government also brought business representatives into the legislature. In addition, the reorganized CGEM began to call publicly and insistently for a level playing field in economic policy, and to act autonomously of the government. The degree to which this ability to act autonomously also protected member firms from opportunistic changes in government policy is, however, unclear.

One reason for the modest effect of these programs is that they were small. None of these policy initiatives seemed to have a perceptible effect on structural transformation. Achy (2013) catalogs all of the subsidies and their cost. In 2010, they amounted to approximately US$612 million, less than 0.7 percent of GDP (see table 3.1). Even if exceedingly well-targeted to market failures and credibly implemented with respect to time-bound goals, the industrial policy program in Morocco was small relative to the spending associated with industrial policy in East Asia.

Industrial Policy in Syria, Jordan and Tunisia

In Syria, the 10th five-year development plan (2006–10) emphasized the more rapid growth of manufacturing exports. Accordingly, similar to the EIDS effort in Egypt, investment and export promotion agencies were created, as were "industrial cities," meant to support the clustering of manufacturing firms. In cooperation with UNIDO, the government launched the Industrial Modernization and Upgrading Program, which focused its support on the textile and clothing sectors. Nevertheless, the program did not respond to any explicit analysis of market failures, nor was there an evaluation of the efficiency gains from allocating subsidies to these sectors rather than to other sectors, or to allocating no subsidies at all. Chahoud (2011) found little evidence that these initiatives were broadly implemented during the period.

Similar to Syria, Jordan created a variety of programs to support industry, with responsibilities dispersed across several ministries. The Ministry of Trade and Industry created a strategy to support small and medium-sized enterprises, the Jordan Investment Board, which was charged with improving the business environment and, especially, allocating tax incentives to investors; the Development and Free Zones Commission was created to develop four regional development zones, meant to target specific industries with substantial tax and other benefits. Even the Central Bank adopted a policy of reducing reserve requirements for private banks by an amount equal to their SME loans.

Among all these programs in Jordan, perhaps the most significant has been the least systematic: tax incentives granted to selected firms and industries by the Council of Ministers. These are issued without transparent conditions or evaluation procedures, and outside of a bureaucratic apparatus that could monitor the contribution of beneficiary firms towards growth or employment.

BOX 3.2

Are GCC Countries an Exception?

The GCC provides some cases of what appear to be successful industrial policy interventions. One class of successes relates to the energy sector development. The GCC countries entered the 1970s almost entirely concentrated in crude oil production operated by international companies, and with basic needs for access to services and infrastructure still unmet. In that decade, Saudi Arabia embarked upon a strategy to develop its own technical capacity in oil production along with facilities for oil refining and petrochemicals. Among the most ambitious of these interventions was the creation of two industrial cities, in Jubail (on the Gulf Coast) and Yanbu (on the Red Sea). These cities are governed by a Royal Commission (set up in 1975), which operates outside the administrative ministry structure and has complete autonomy over spatial planning, regulation, and investment in the cities.

(continued on next page)

BOX 3.2 *Continued*

The intention of the two cities was to transform the energy sector by promoting a cluster of subindustries related to petroleum products and petrochemicals, including associated logistics. All major production operations in the industrial cities are owned by Saudi Arabian Aramco, Saudi Arabian Basic Industries (Sabic, a government-created petrochemicals company), or joint ventures of one of these two companies with international partners.

As a result of these efforts, Saudi Arabia now has a broad-based hydrocarbons sector, in which its massive oil endowment is complemented by a downstream value chain. Of course, this industrial capacity reflects a policy decision to provide industry with oil and gas inputs at below export price. The key to avoiding dissipation of this cost advantage lies in the effective commercialization of these companies through professional management, insulation from political pressures, and exposure to international best practices by forcing foreign investors into joint ventures (Hertog 2008).

Whereas the Saudi Arabian example can be linked to its energy endowment, Dubai presents a more complex case where a services industry specialization did not have an obvious starting point. Instead a few critical decisions made by the leadership—dredging Dubai Creek to facilitate bigger ships; establishing a free zone around the new port at Jebel Ali to encourage transit and assembly activity; building up the airport and the airline; and encouraging foreign investment in finance and real estate (not least through liberal visa policies)—combined to set in motion a sustained boom and an acquired comparative advantage in logistics.

While virtually every element of this strategy was implemented by state-owned companies, emirates were in constant competition with other emirates. As in Saudi Arabia, these companies were professionalized and run on a commercial basis. The context of Dubai provided further discipline. The emirate was in constant competition with other emirates and some decisions came as competitive responses to them. For example, Jebel Ali port was triggered by Sharjah's initial moves to attract container traffic and Abu Dhabi has mimicked elements of the Dubai logistics strategy.

Finance provides an additional lever. As a subnational entity without its own large oil resources, Dubai companies had to fund themselves through operations or debt—the latter forcing some analysis of viability and profitability from banks or securities markets. While banks were themselves closely linked to the government, they were run along sufficiently commercial principles to induce some genuine economic pressures on the SOEs. The irony was that the growth strategy, initially presented as diversification, was in fact linking the various facets of the growth closely together, as the Dubai debt crisis of 2008 showed. Nonetheless, the logistics network saw little adverse impact even at the peak of the crisis, indicating its resilience.

At least part of the apparent success of GCC countries' industrial policies is explained by the sheer size of the programs made possible by oil revenues. This contrasts starkly with the initiatives in other MENA countries.

In contrast with the Korean experience subsequently described, Jordanian benefits were uncoordinated, relatively small, and not conditioned on performance. In addition, there was no effort to identify market failures. Instead, government policy sought, as is often the case, simply to create industrial activity in sectors or regions where there was little. It did not distinguish whether there was little activity because of market failure or because of a simple lack of comparative advantage.

Industrial policy in Tunisia took the form of special regulatory regimes for exporters, including generous tax and tariff rules. A central feature of Tunisian industrial policy was the formal offshore regulatory framework. For nonexporters, the firms in the onshore economy, the regulatory and tax environment did little to promote competition and innovation. On the contrary, they established significant barriers to entry of foreign or domestic firms, especially in service sectors where most of the politically connected firms close to the Ben Ali family operated. The protection of rents in service sectors likely also reduced the quality of backbone services provided to the rest of the economy (creating *weak links*), potentially also constraining productivity in the offshore economy despite the generous tax and tariff exemptions.

What Did Successful Countries Do? The Case of the Republic of Korea

Successful firms emerged despite the fact that the political challenges of promoting private sector job creation and structural transformation in Korea in the 1960s echoed those of the MENA region in the 2000s.[6] The 1960s in Korea were a period of significant political unrest. Student demonstrations and military coups drove regime change, the president faced few institutional controls on his authority, and top officials earned significant rents (Kang 2002). Even as late as 1982, the first year for which governance indicators are available, Korea looked little different than Egypt in 2010, according to the *International Country Risk Guide* indicators of Political Risk Services. In sharp contrast to MENA and such programs as EIDS in Egypt, however, the firms supported by Korean industrial policy rose to become world-class producers. One of the outstanding success stories of Korean industrial policy was the formerly state-owned Pohang Steel Company (POSCO). What explains these different outcomes, despite similar governance challenges and political risks?

Ironically, in one important respect, Korean policies appear very much like those undertaken in MENA: selected industries received support with little attention to the identification of market failures or cost-benefit analysis. However, Korean policies were substantially more generous, tightly linked to the achievement of private sector growth and structural transformation goals, and supported by significant organizational changes in both the public and private sectors.

The magnitude of government intervention to drive private sector growth and structural transformation in Korea is well known. Private investors shy away from large commitments of capital in environments where leaders can predate on their investments with impunity. The policies that Korea pursued in the 1960s and 1970s had precisely the effect of offsetting the reluctance of private investors to commit capital. First, President Park bypassed private investment altogether and placed heavy reliance on state-owned enterprises; government investment is naturally free from the hazards of government predation. The government established more than 20 major state enterprises in capital-intensive sectors (electricity, airlines, shipbuilding, steel, and so on). Second, private firms in priority sectors received massive direct and indirect subsidies, ranging from direct cash payments and tax exemptions to favorable import and foreign exchange regimes. These subsidies compensated investors in priority sectors for the political risks they incurred in committing substantial amounts of capital to the private sector growth and structural transformation agenda. The government's massive infrastructure investments also effectively raised the private return to investment. From 1960 to 1970, Korea dedicated one-third of gross domestic investment to infrastructure and dramatically increased electricity generation and installed telephones. Why did these policies succeed in Korea? Three responses to this question are most plausible.

First, by implementing policies to stimulate activities where none previously existed, industrial policy in Korea was effectively, if not intentionally, more likely to address market failure. Subsidies aimed at—and were conditioned on—creating economic activities in areas where there was none, most famously in the heavy and chemical industries. In addition, the state aggressively funded information acquisition—again, at least potentially addressing a market failure. For example, the state funded 97 percent of research and development expenditures in Korea in the early 1960s (Evans p. 147). In contrast, Galal and El-Megharbel (2005) show that industrial policy in the MENA region, including Egypt's EIDS initiative in the mid-2000s, did not effectively target new markets or products—the ones most exposed to market failures.

Second, the Republic of Korea credibly linked subsidies to export performance; even those that benefited insiders and cronies. In contrast with MENA, the implementation of industrial policy was conditional on firm success in pursuing private sector growth and structural transformation. Not only were subsidies contingent on firms entering new activities, but they had to succeed in those activities in order to continue to receive subsidies. That is, even if subsidies might also have been disproportionally channeled to politically connected firms in East Asian countries, these firms still had to meet the performance targets aligned with economic growth.

Time-bound goals are central in order to provide entrepreneurs with incentives to innovate and invest. However, if political incentives to pursue growth are weak, friends of the regime are unlikely to regard deadlines as credible. They will anticipate that governments will prefer to extend deadlines in exchange for rents, weakening their incentives to innovate. More generally, the efficacy of industrial policy hinges on entrepreneurs' confidence that successful firms will not confront an abrupt and opportunistic change in the rules of the game (higher taxes, more intense regulation, and predatory behavior by officials).[7] The greater this threat, the less credible are government promises and the larger must be the industrial policy subsidies that governments use to accelerate growth.

In contrast, the policy benefits offered to firms in MENA were not conditioned on concrete goals, such as export success. Instead, the policy regime left open the possibility that support to firms could continue indefinitely.

Third, the government made public and private sector organizational reforms to ensure the successful implementation, and the credibility, of industrial policy. On the one hand, it is technically difficult to design subsidies, their timing and their expiration; on the other hand, the private sector response to subsidies is greater to the extent that private firms trust in the credibility of future policies. President Park mandated wholesale changes in government and in the industrial structure of the economy to improve the government's implementation capacity, and to make it costly for him to act opportunistically. In the narrow pursuit of better industrial policy, he established a super-ministry, the Economic Planning Board, to consolidate functions—previously scattered across various ministries—related to the formulation and implementation of industrial policies. More broadly, though, he substantially moderated the tendency, manifest over the years 1948–60, to treat the public administration as a spoils system, where civil service positions were used to reward political allies and supporters. Instead, the public administration reform imposed to practically all positions the requirement that appointments be made on the basis of open, competitive examinations; increased the difficulty of those examinations[8]; linked promotions strictly to job performance; and provided civil servants with job security. The administrative reforms immediately improved the capacity of the civil service to implement industrial policy: expertise was higher and promotion systems were linked more transparently to success in the public sector mission, which was private sector growth, jobs, and structural transformation.

Administrative reforms also improved the credibility of the presidential commitment to industrial policy. They increased the ability of the bureaucracy to resist opportunistic policy reversals by the president. On the one hand, the elite Economic Planning Board, with widely recognized levels of expertise, gave the civil service an informational advantage with respect to the president. On the other hand, consistent with Gehlbach and Keefer (2011), the administrative reforms improved the ability of officials and firms to act collectively in the event that President Park reneged on his commitments. In contrast, before the civil service reforms, there was little horizontal cohesion among civil servants, who received their jobs through connections with higher level patrons. Gehlbach and Keefer (2011) argue that these institutional changes are sufficient to generate credible commitments. They also document similar changes undertaken by Deng Xiaoping in China, when he changed state and party organizations to support increased investment and faster economic growth. For example, promotions in the Chinese public sector (for example, from county executive to provincial executive) are contingent on achieving economic growth in their jurisdiction.

These administrative reforms contrast sharply with the MENA experience. The Social Fund for Development was once one of the most efficient and transparent agencies in Egypt (Loewe 2013). However, its preeminence faded in the face of political pressure to use the fund as a source of patronage jobs. This weakened the capacity of the government to implement industrial policy, but it also undermined the credibility of its policies, since bureaucracies organized around patronage are less effective checks on opportunistic behavior by leaders.

Fourth, the emerging industrial organization of the country also supported collective action by the private sector. The Korean government famously encouraged very large industrial enterprises, the Chaebols. Large conglomerates, each representing substantial shares of total industrial employment in the country, and each the potential source of rents and campaign contributions to politicians, could more easily defend their interests before the state. For example, the nine Chaebols that received the plurality of bank loans in 1964 all had family members in high positions of the ruling party or the bureaucracy (Kang, 189). Kang (190–192) argues that the arrangements between the Chaebols and the government allowed each to hold the other hostage—and, therefore, to make credible commitments. The top 20 Chaebols accounted for nearly 15 percent of nonagricultural GDP in 1975, but they were also heavily indebted, with debt-equity ratios approaching on the order of 350 percent. They needed the government, and so had every incentive to fulfill their commitments to pursue export growth, and to provide private financing to government.

However, the government needed them and could not let large swaths of the economy go out of business.

Despite similarities between MENA and Korea in the linkages between large businesses and high positions in the ruling party, the political commitment to economic growth was more deeply rooted in Korea, taming the extent of rent-seeking. The prominence of individual families in the economic life of low and middle-income countries is a common occurrence, and also pervasive in the MENA region. Korea appears to stand out, though, in two important ways. The "mutual hostage taking" characterized by Kang was more extensive and pervasive than in MENA. More important, the political commitment to economic growth was more deeply rooted, taming the extent of rent-seeking that typically accompanies oligarchic industrial structures.

In this regard, all observers agree that the leadership in the Republic of Korea had a single-minded commitment to economic growth. From the Republic of Korea and China to Malaysia and Singapore, the governments of East Asia structured their bureaucracies and ruling parties around the goal of economic growth. The political imperative of generating growth motivated leaders to embrace organizational reforms that substantially reduced their discretion over the decisions of the bureaucracy. Indeed, this commitment is the reason that the institutional reforms (civil service reform, Chaebols, infrastructure, and so forth) did not collapse into patronage, rent-seeking, and stagnation, as in other parts of the world. For example, when the political process allows bureaucrats to focus more on collecting rents from industrial policy than on using it to transform the economy, private-public dialogue is likely to yield correspondingly less useful information and leads potentially to counterproductive policies. What explains this commitment? This question is not unique to Korea. It also arises in the case of other East Asian "miracles."[9] The question persists because there is no systematic explanation of the unusually focused dedication of Park Chung Hee, Deng Xiao Pen, and Lee Kwan Yu to the goal of economic growth. Most explanations plausibly refer to the devastation of war, the need to support a large military, the tapering of aid, and concerns about public support (despite the nondemocratic nature of these regimes).

Lessons from East Asia Are More Difficult to Implement than Is Commonly Understood

East Asia implemented its industrial policies much differently than MENA and in ways that leaders in many countries often resist. The modalities these countries used to implement industrial policy imposed considerable limits on the discretion of leaders. These also included organizational reforms that restricted their discretion and strengthened the credibility of their commitments to the reforms. In addition, the pursuit of growth as a strategy of gaining political support necessarily substituted for other strategies. However, this focus on growth came at a cost. Comparing only the within-sector benefits of industrial policy (abstracting from important potential spillover benefits on other sectors), the resources used for private sector growth and structural transformation were, in many cases, diverted from uses that might have delivered greater welfare to citizens, including Koreans' own consumption. For example, East Asian leaders could have preferred large consumer subsidies to build legitimacy. However, private sector growth and structural transformation, Korean style, is expensive and incompatible with the subsidies common in the MENA region.

Other attributes of industrial policy in East Asia are, however, worthy of replication. Industrial policies

- offset governance and political risks;

- were complemented by infrastructure construction and ample support for human capital acquisition;

- focused on activities that were entirely absent in the economy;

- were accompanied by far-reaching organizational reforms in the public sector;

- were implemented in an environment of a single-minded focus on growth;

- tightly linked subsidies to the success in more competitive export markets; and

- were applied at the sector, rather than the firm level.

The firm-directed industrial policies common in the MENA region distorted competition and growth. Industrial policy in MENA had a tendency to privilege individual (connected) firms instead of benefitting all firms (and new entrants) in targeted sectors.[10] These firm-specific policies concentrated benefits on privileged firms, not sectors. These policy privileges provide these firms with potentially large exogenous cost advantages over their competitors in the same sector. Thus, the Schumpeterian growth framework predicts that they lead to less *neck-and-neck* competition and hence growth; that is, they drive nonconnected firms out of the market and suppress the incentives to innovate (to escape competition) for all firms in the sector. In contrast, Aghion et al. (2012)

indicate that industrial policy can promote productivity growth when it favors competition by reducing costs for all firms and entrants in a sector. The authors argue that industrial policy in China has done precisely this. Moreover, they show that sectors in China that benefited from more uniform intra-sector subsidies exhibited greater productivity growth.

The even-handed, effective application of the policy requires that government decision makers be relatively immune to the influence of vested interests, at least in fast-growing modern sectors. In the absence of a single-minded focus on growth, the political cost of catering to vested interests is low, political incentives are correspondingly higher to privilege some firms over others, and to pursue industrial policy even when it has no demonstrated positive effect on development.

The single-minded focus on growth, however, might be the most difficult to replicate as it implicitly requires a new social contract between government and citizens. Much is made of the social compact in MENA, one that trades government employment and consumer subsidies for limitations on expressions of citizen voice. These same limitations were pervasive in East Asia, but the social compact took a different form, emphasizing jobs and productivity growth. Moreover, the organizational changes in the public sector have been consistently some of the hardest for MENA governments to accommodate, and yet played an essential role in the success of industrial policies in East Asia.

Policy makers can choose an alternative and potentially cheaper strategy to accelerate private sector job creation and structural transformation, by reducing the impact of policy failures before seeking to address market failures; or by using expensive subsidies to offset the costs of both. Government policy failures can rival or exceed market failures as obstacles to job creation and structural transformation. In many countries, however, industrial policies such as those followed in East Asia are too expensive or too difficult to implement credibly. Moreover, government-induced market failures in MENA have arguably been at least as significant a barrier to growth as information asymmetries and coordination difficulties in private markets.

Notes

1. This section is based on Keefer (2014).
2. TFP grew in the Arab Republic of Egypt at a 3.3 percent annual rate from 1983 to 1990, before dropping to 1.6 percent from 1991 to 2000 and to 1.1 percent from 2001 to 2006. TFP growth in the private sector soared to 5.6 percent in the 1980s, falling to 1.9 percent from 1991 to 2006 (Loayza and Honorati 2007).

3. In contrast, figure 2.1 shows that FDI inflows into China, Brazil, Indonesia, and India were concentrated in manufacturing or high technology services which typically have high potential for spillovers in technologies, production capacities, and employment.

4. In discrete cases, however, government efforts to solve coordination failures may have succeeded. Loewe (2013) points in particular to the marble sector and fashion industry.

5. The World Bank database on NTMs provides either the year when a particular NTM has been introduced or the latest year in which it is has been substantially revised. Unfortunately, the database does not distinguish between the two.

6. In 1980, Korea's real purchasing parity power-adjusted income per capita ($5,543) was the same as Egypt's in 2010 ($5,760).

7. These problems of credible commitment are pervasive. In monetary policy, for example, governments have an incentive to deviate from low inflation policies to reduce government debt burdens. They increase the credibility of their low inflation commitments by increasing the independence of central banks.

8. Only about 4 percent of those filling the higher entry-level positions had taken the civil service exam (Evans, 52). Under Park, the civil service became more strictly meritocratic, such that approximately 20 percent of those taking high entry level positions had passed the civil service exam. The exam also became more difficult. One sign of its difficulty: between 1963 and 1985, 157,000 persons took the civil service exam and 2,600 passed it.

9. Outside of East Asia, Rodrik and Subramanian (2005) argue that Indian growth was driven by a change in attitude of Indian leaders: they began to see growth as a viable strategy for political survival.

10. Some have argued that industrial policies should be "horizontal," applying to all sectors. This has the appeal of at least superficially preserving a "level playing field." However, for two reasons horizontal policies may be incompatible with this goal. First, identical policies have heterogeneous effects across sectors (cheap capital or energy favor capital- or energy-intensive industries). Second, horizontal policies have a limited economic rationale to the extent that market failure drives industrial policy, since market failures are heterogeneous across sectors. Sectoral policies could, however, be broadly targeted. For example, countries could promote an export sector, comprised of many different lines of economic activity, by undervaluing their exchange rates.

References

Achy, Lahcen. 2013. "Structural Transformation and Industrial Policy in Morocco." Economic Research Forum Working Paper 796, Economic Research Forum, Cairo.

Aghion, P. M., Dewatripont, L. Du, A. Harrison, and P. Legros. 2012. "Industrial Policy and Competition." Mimeo (April 24).

Chahoud, Tatjana. 2011. "Syria's Industrial Policy." Working paper, Deutsches Institut fuer Entwicklungspolitik (DIE), Bonn.

Diwan, I., and H. Chekir. 2012. "State-Business Relations in Mubarak's Egypt." Mimeo, World Bank, Washington, DC.

Galal, Ahmed, and Nihal El-Megharbel. 2005. "Do Governments Pick Winners of Losers? An Assessment of Industrial Policy in Egypt." Working Paper 108, The Egyptian Center for Economic Studies, Cairo.

Gehlbach, Scott, and Philip Keefer. 2011. "Investment without Democracy: Ruling-Party Institutionalization and Credible Commitment in Autocracies." *Journal of Comparative Economics* 39 (2): 123–278

Harrison, Anne, and Andres Rodriguez-Clare. 2010. "Trade, Foreign Investment, and Industrial Policy for Developing Countries." In *Handbook of Development Economics* 5: 4039–214.

Hausmann, Ricardo, and Dani Rodrik. 2006. "Economic Development as Self-Discovery." *Journal of Development Economics* 72.

Hertog, Steffen. 2008. "Petromin: The Slow Death of Statist Oil Development in Saudi Arabia." *Business History* 50 (5): 645–67.

Kang, David C. 2002. "Bad Loans to Good Friends: Money Politics and the Developmental State in South Korea." *International Organization* 56 (1): 177–207.

Keefer, Philip. 2014. "Industrial Policy and MENA—Lessons from Research and East Asia." Mimeo, World Bank, Washington, DC.

Loayza, Norman, and Maddalena Honorati. 2007. "Investment and Growth in Egypt." Mimeo, World Bank, Washington, DC.

Loewe, Markus. 2013. "Industrial Policy in Egypt 2004–2011." DIE Discussion Paper 13/2013, Deutsches Institut fuer Entwicklungspolitik, Bonn.

Malouche, Mariem, José-Daniel Reyes, and Amir Fouad. 2013. "New Database of Nontariff Measures Makes Trade Policy More Transparent." Mimeo, World Bank, Washington, DC.

Murphy, Kevin, Andrei Schleifer, and Robert W. Vishny. 1989. "Industrialization and the Big Push." *Journal of Political Economy* 97 (5): 1003–1026.

Rodrik, Dani. 2008. "Normalizing Industrial Policy." Commission on Growth and Development, Working Paper 3, World Bank, Washington, DC.

Rodrik, Dani, and Arvind Subramanian. 2005. "From Hindu Growth to Productivity Surge: The Mystery of the Indian Growth Transition." *IMF Staff Papers* 52 (2): 193–236.

Roll, Stephan. 2013. "Egypt's Business Elite after Mubarak: A Powerful Player between Generals and Brotherhood." SWP Research Paper 8 (September), Stiftung Wissenschaft und Politik, Berlin.

CHAPTER 4

Privileges Instead of Jobs: Political Connections and Private Sector Growth in MENA

This chapter shows that policies in MENA have often been captured by a few politically connected firms. This has led to a policy environment that created privileges rather than a level playing field, undermining competition, the ability of all entrepreneurs to pursue opportunities on an equal footing, and job creation. The analysis builds on new data and information on first-tier politically connected firms in the Arab Republic of Egypt and Tunisia that became available after the Arab Spring—and from more qualitative evidence from other countries in the region—that allow us for the first time to provide direct quantitative evidence on how firm privileges affect competition, the level playing field, and job growth in the region. Taken together, the findings shed light on the entire microeconomic transmission mechanism, from privileges to limited competition and unleveled playing fields, to weak firm dynamics and slow aggregate job growth.

This chapter provides evidence that many policies in MENA favor privileges over innovation and jobs. In the Schumpeterian growth framework, influential political connections provide firms with an outside option to escape competition by tilting regulations towards their favor instead of innovating. Aghion et al. (2001) predict that growth declines if a few colluding market leaders have sizeable cost advantages, which are unbridgeable by competitors operating in the same sector. Chapters 2 and 3 document examples of policies in MENA that favor specific types of firms over others. If these privileges are large enough, the model predicts that sectors end up with a few colluding, politically connected market leaders; a potentially large number of unproductive micro firms; and most important, lower productivity and job growth. The more widespread these firm-specific privileges across sectors, the lower are aggregate growth and job creation.

The literature on Arab capitalism contains rich analyses of how autocrats granted exclusive privileges to business elites allowing them to dominate the business sector in exchange for support for the regime. Qualitative research has documented barriers to entry that excluded opponents and provided privileges to a small coterie of friendly capitalists (Henry and Springborg 2010; Heydemann 2004; King 2009; Owen 2004). In the Arab Republic of Egypt, observers argue that cronyism thrived in the "businessmen" cabinet headed by Ahmad Nazif from 2004 to 2011 (Kienle 2001; Sfakianakis 2004). In Tunisia, the Ben Ali and Trabelsi families monopolized business opportunities and even expropriated the real estate and business holdings of wealthy elites. Similar stories about favoritism and insiders abound in the Syrian Arab Republic, Libya, the Republic of Yemen, and Algeria, where political cronies seem to control large chunks of the private sector (Alley 2010; Haddad 2012; Tlemcani 1999). However, previous work came short of providing quantitative evidence associating the privileges to specific policies or showing their impact on economic performance.

We use novel data from Egypt and Tunisia to test whether political connections lead to large privileges, and hence lower competition and growth. Chapter 2 analyzed several policies in MENA that benefit specific types of firms, potentially distorting neck-and-neck competition; these include energy subsidies to industry, licenses, access to land, and biased regulatory enforcement. Two novel data sets on politically connected firms in Mubarak's Egypt and Ben Ali's Tunisia allow quantifying for the first time whether these policies disproportionally benefitted connected firms. They also allow us to quantify for the first time if the presence of politically connected firms changes sectors' market structures and aggregate job growth in line with the predictions of Aghion et al. (2001). Moreover, this chapter provides evidence from other MENA countries and discusses to which extent privileges are a regional phenomenon.

In "Privileges to Politically Connected Firms Undermine Competition and Job Creation: Evidence from Egypt and Tunisia" section, we use novel data sets on first-tier politically connected firms in Egypt and Tunisia to quantify their economic impact in both countries.[1] "The Available Qualitative Evidence Points to Similar Mechanisms of Policy Privileges in Other MENA Countries" section presents more qualitative evidence on policy privileges in other MENA countries. In "The Extent to which Political Connections Hampered Competition Differed in MENA and East Asia" section, we highlight potential factors that explain why private sector and jobs outcomes were different in MENA than East Asia, in spite of the presence of politically connected firms in both regions.

Privileges to Politically Connected Firms Undermine Competition and Job Creation: Evidence from the Arab Republic of Egypt and Tunisia

The governments in Egypt and Tunisia erected barriers to entry and competition even as they engaged in economic liberalization. In Egypt, President Hosni Mubarak's son, Gamal, working closely with a group of economic experts and ambitious businessmen, shifted the country's policies in the early 2000s towards accelerated privatization and financial sector and trade reforms. Insider firms were able to capture the opportunities that emerged with the modernization of the economy[2]; these included massive real estate and construction projects, tourism at coastal areas, the oil and gas sectors, the banking sector, telephony, and local distribution of international consumer brands. Government decisions were key in all of these areas—for example, connected families invested in specific manufacturing or mining sectors such as cement or oil and gas where each new factory required government approval; they obtained privileged access to state procurement contracts or exclusive licenses to distribute international brands in Egypt, shielding them from domestic competition; they entered the real estate, tourism, and transport sectors by acquiring large sections of prime land from the government, reportedly, involving closed and nontransparent deals.[3] In fact, connected businessmen were well placed to influence these decisions: they were not only personally well connected with the political leadership, but they themselves also occupied important post in government, the ruling party, parliament, and various influential boards and committees.

In Tunisia, the Investment Law was amended several times in the 2000s to provide incentives for private sector investments in the offshore economy but, at the same time, also to protect connected firms from competition in the onshore economy. The amendments included generous tax breaks for firms operating in the offshore economy. In addition, it stipulates the freedom to invest for both foreign and domestic entities. However, it also contains provisions that restrict this freedom, including authorization requirements and FDI restrictions in the onshore economy, which allow the government to control the entry of selected firms in some lucrative service activities. The Ben Ali family's business interests in these services sectors were not a secret. In part, however, because Tunisia registered stable positive growth rates hovering around 4–5 percent per year, Ben Ali also had a somewhat favorable external image. The World Economic Forum repeatedly ranked Tunisia as the most competitive economy in Africa, and the IMF and the World Bank heralded Tunisia as a role model for other developing countries. Yet, at the same time there were few formal sector jobs and perceptions of corruption was high.

This section demonstrates that policies in both countries have often been captured by a few privileged firms, thereby limiting competition, distorting the playing field, and curtailing job creation. First, we discuss our measures of political connectedness and highlight the characteristics specific to connected firms. Second, we document that politically connected firms profited disproportionately from policy privileges in Egypt and Tunisia, distorting the playing field in both countries. The evidence implies that business regulations in Egypt and Tunisia were abused as a rent creation vehicle for friends and family of the two former presidents. Third, we show in more detail for Egypt that the presence of connected firms reduced the dynamism and growth opportunities for the rest of the economy; i.e., firm entry is lower in sectors where connected firms are already present and aggregate employment growth declines once connected firms enter new, previously unconnected sectors. The results suggest that distortive policies, such as authorization requirements, energy subsidies to industry, trade protection, and burdensome regulation benefit a small group of "profitable" firms, but reduce the total number of jobs created in Egypt and Tunisia. Notably, most of these business regulations are still in place.

Identifying the Politically Connected Firms and Their Economic Significance

Who Are They?

To examine the economic effects of insider privilege, we need both a data set of politically connected firms and information about firm performance. In Tunisia, we use government data on 214 Ben Ali firms confiscated by the Tunisian authorities in the aftermath of the Jasmine revolution. The confiscation involved 114 individuals, including Ben Ali himself, his relatives, and his in-laws, and involved the period from 1987 until the outbreak of the revolution. The seized assets included some 550 properties, 48 boats and yachts, 40 stock portfolios, 367 bank accounts, and approximately 400 enterprises, not all of which operate in Tunisia. The confiscation commission estimates that the combined total value of the confiscated assets of the Ben Ali clan is approximately US$13 billion, about one quarter of Tunisian GDP in 2011. We obtained a list of 252 confiscated firms from the Tunisian authorities, of which we were able to identify 214 firms with available data in the Tunisian annual firm census (Tunisian Business Register).[4] The census contains information on the size, age, location, and legal form of all private nonagricultural registered firms in Tunisia, including one-person firms without paid employees.

The census data are further merged with administrative data from the tax authorities, containing balance sheet information, and information on business regulations from the Tunisian Investment Law from 1993 to 2010.

To identify politically connected individuals in Egypt, we followed Fisman (2001) and interviewed managers of banks and private equity funds, lawyers, and nongovernmental organizations (anti-corruption organizations) after the fall of Mubarak in 2011 to create a list of politically connected businessmen. We confirmed the representativeness of this list in two ways. First, we matched this list with the names of businessmen whose assets were frozen immediately after the regime change. Second, we pruned the list to include only those businessmen who had political posts in the ruling party or in the government, or whose immediate family members did. We also had sufficient information to identify long-term friends of the Mubarak family; these were also identified as connected businessmen.[5] We matched this list with firm data from the OECD Orbis database, which includes information on the board members, managing directors, and major shareholders for 854 firms that are currently or were formerly traded on a stock exchange.[6] We were able to unambiguously match the names of the 32 businessmen identified in step one with board members, managers, and major shareholders of 104 firms.

Several of the connected firms in Egypt are holding companies and investment funds. Using the Internet, we identified the names of all subsidiaries—up to two tiers—of these 104 firms, and matched these subsidiaries with firms in the Orbis database. This process identified 469 firms that are unambiguously controlled, directly or indirectly, by a connected businessman. Of these firms, 47 have at least one politically connected businessman as a general manager (CEO) and in 334, at least one connected businessman or firm was unambiguously identified to have an ownership stake. In addition, in 172 firms a private equity fund owned by at least one politically connected businessman an ownership stake.[7] Moreover, politically connected firms are widely spread across the 320 nonfarm, nongovernment four-digit ISIC Rev.4 sectors: about half (49 percent) of the sectors include connected firms (186 out of 372). Within manufacturing, where 41 percent of the connected firms operate, they are present in 58 percent of the four-digit industries (73 out of 126).

We combine the information on politically connected firms in Egypt with four sources of data. First, the Orbis database has firm characteristics—including firm names—and balance sheet variables for a panel of over 20,000 establishments between 2003 and 2012, which allows us to compare the performance of connected and unconnected firms.[8] While production data on small enterprises are frequently missing in Orbis, the data on medium and large establishments, the right comparison group for politically connected firms, are comprehensive. Second, establishment census data from the department of statistics in Egypt (Central Agency for Public Mobilization and Statistics) do not contain firm names, but they do allow us to estimate how the dynamics across detailed four-digit sectors change depending on the presence of connected firms. The census includes employment and firm characteristics of over two million nonfarm economic establishments in 1996 and 2006. Third, World Bank Enterprise Survey (WBES) data allows us to assess correlations between the presence of connected firms and perceived policies.[9] Fourth, to investigate whether connected firms benefitted from state-supported barriers to entry or energy subsidies, we use information on nontariff barriers to trade (NTMs) from the World Bank (WITS), and UN data on the energy intensities of manufacturing industries.

We only observe a subset of politically connected firms in Egypt and Tunisia: those private sector firms with first-tier political connections to the Mubarak or Ben Ali family. However, there are other connected firms. Reportedly, the most important group of firms is controlled directly or indirectly by the Egyptian army, which operates businesses in tourism, construction, white goods, vehicles, fertilizer, mineral water, olives, and bread. Most of these businesses initially were financed by the sale of government land in Cairo and on the seaside (Loewe 2013). Similarly, the sample of 214 connected firms in Tunisia is most likely skewed towards the largest and economically most relevant firms since these are easier to identify.

Where Are They?

A direct comparison of the distribution of politically connected firms across countries would suggest that this phenomenon was more widespread in Egypt. While the number of connected firms should be regarded as a lower bound in both countries, we observe fewer connected firms in Tunisia (214) relative to Egypt (469). Moreover, connected firms were substantially larger and economically more significant in Egypt: connected firms employ on average 941 workers in Egypt 66 relative to workers in Tunisia; they accounted for about 7 percent of total private sector employment in Egypt relative to about 1 percent in Tunisia.[10] These disparities might originate from the different nature of the data. The nature of political connections is also different, since the confiscation commission in Tunisia focused exclusively on firms owned by members of the Ben Ali family. In contrast, the Egypt data also include first-tier Mubarak associates—connected businessmen with influential political posts, whose assets were also confiscated in 2011. It is unclear to which extent first-tier political connections beyond the extended Ben Ali family played a role in the Tunisian economy.

The presence of politically connected firms appears to be more wide-spread across various economic activities in Egypt, especially among manufacturing industries. Despite the differences in the nature of the data, the distribution of connected firms across sectors exhibits some similarities (table 4.1). In both countries, connected firms are concentrated in real estate, business services, tourism, wholesale and retail trade, mining, telecommunications, and transport services. In Egypt, however, their activities reach far beyond these sectors. Politically connected firms operate in 49 percent of all nonfarm, nongovernment four-digit sectors (186 out of 372). In contrast, Ben Ali firms operate in only 14 percent of all five-digit sectors in Tunisia (45 out of 321). In particular, the concentration of politically connected firms in various Egyptian manufacturing industries is striking: 42 percent of politically connected firms operate in manufacturing in Egypt relative to 13 percent of connected firms in Tunisia (table 4.1). Manufacturing industries are typically considered harder to protect from (international) competition. In fact, the subsequent analysis shows that, in Tunisia, policies protecting connected firms from competition focused on service sectors in the onshore economy while such restrictions were absent for manufacturing firms in the offshore economy. For example, Ben Ali firms dominated the telecommunications

TABLE 4.1

Number of Politically Connected Firms, by Economic Sectors

Sector	Egypt, Arab Rep.	Tunisia
Mining	12	8
Manufacturing	193	31
Food and beverages	33	9
Textiles and apparel	22	2
Chemicals	28	3
Base metals	19	2
Machinery and equipment	27	2
Other manufacturing	64	13
Utilities	18	0
Construction	36	9
Services	388	166
Wholesale trade	91	38
Retail trade	25	3
Transport	13	16
Hotels and restaurants	43	7
Finance	53	8
Real estate and construction	138	59
Other services	25	35
Total	647	214

Source: World Bank calculation.
Note: The last row represents the total number of politically connected firms operating in each four-digit sector. In Egypt, it amounts to 647 because several of the 469 connected firms operate in more than one four-digit sector. In Tunisia, we observe only one (i.e., the main) sector for each firm in the data.

and air transport sectors, and were also important players in other transport sectors and real estate, all sectors in which entry is highly regulated. In contrast, policies favoring connected businessmen in Egypt (e.g., trade protection or energy subsidies to industry) also profited selected manufacturing firms.

The stronger presence of first-tier politically connected firms across sectors in Egypt over the past decade might indicate that the regime aimed to tighten control of the economy (i.e., the recipients of extracted rents and their potential use for political financing). By 2010, the activity of politically connected firms in Egypt was not constrained to more mature traditional sectors but they also operated in some younger modern sectors (e.g., *manufacture of* pharmaceuticals or *plastics*). Moreover, table G.2 in Appendix G shows that connected firms entered various new sectors between 1997 and 2006 which had been *open* (i.e., not connected) before (e.g., *manufacturing of batteries* or *computer programming services*) while they did not enter others (e.g., *manufacturing of optical instruments* or *specialized design services*). Thus, there is also substantial variation of the presence of politically connected firms even across four-digit industries within the same two-digit sector. These attributes of the distribution of connected firms across sectors in Egypt aid in the empirical identification of the impact of political connections on four-digit sector outcomes in the subsequent analysis.

Politically Connected Firms Are Highly Profitable

The few politically connected firms in both countries accounted for the lion's shares of profits. Profits are measured as operating profits declared to the tax authorities.[11] Among medium and large establishments in Egypt, politically connected firms accounted for only 11 percent of total employment, but 60 percent of total net profits.[12] The average net profits were 13 times higher for the 49 connected establishments included in the available data, indicating that at least some of the politically connected firms make excessively high profits (table 4.2). Among all firms in Tunisia, the 214 confiscated Ben Ali firms appropriated 21 percent of all net private sector profits in 2010.[13] In contrast, they accounted for only about 1 percent of all wage jobs. Ben Ali firms also report significantly higher profits when looking at within-sector comparisons (table 4.2, last column).

The potential advantages of connected firms that lead to their higher profits are specific to the individual firm, or to the product it sells. Table 4.2 reports the descriptive statistics among politically connected and other firms in Egypt and Tunisia. Politically connected firms are significantly larger than other firms, both in terms of employment and output. The fourth column reports the difference in performance between connected and other firms that operate in the same two-digit sectors. It shows that the performance differences are not specific to the broader

TABLE 4.2

Within-Sector Differences, Politically Connected and Other Firms

	No. of PC establishments	No. of other establishments	PC vs. other establishments	PC vs. other establishments, within two-digit sector	PC vs. other establishments, within four-five-digit sector
Egypt, Arab Rep.					
Ln(Employment)	436	19,375	1.40**	1.02**	0.97**
Ln(Revenues)	67	611	1.61**	1.59**	1.50**
Ln(Profits)	49	239	1.43**	1.37*	1.29
Ln(Profits/Rev)	47	236	1.88**	2.17**	1.02
Tunisia					
Ln(Employment)	114	81,180	1.61**	1.49**	1.05**
Ln(Revenues)	81	250,340	5.17**	4.27**	2.38**
Ln(Profits)	94	93,098	−1.41**	0.10	1.10**
Ln(Profits/Empl)	64	41,760	−0.08	0.88**	0.01

Source: World Bank calculation.

Note: Data are from the Orbis database (Egypt) and the firm census (Tunisia). In contrast to the firm census in Tunisia, the Orbis data for Egypt primarily include medium and large establishments, which are the correct comparison groups when comparing politically connected and unconnected establishments. The statistics in Egypt show the results for the broadest measure of political connections, which also include firms that received significant investments from politically connected private equity funds. Columns 3–5 report the coefficient and *t*-statistic on the politically connected dummy variable, from an OLS regression of the performance variable (e.g., Ln(employment)) on the dummy variable which is equal to 1 for politically connected firms and 0 otherwise. In the fourth (fifth) column, we also include two(four/five)-digit sector dummies so that the connection dummy coefficient measures the difference between connected and unconnected firms operating within the same two(four)-digit sector. * and ** indicate that the coefficients are significant at the 5 percent and 10 percent level, respectively. Note that to account for negative profits, we use a transformation of the log profits measure that also accounts for negative profits, notably $\log\left(Profits + \sqrt{Profits^2 + 1}\right)$. Similarly, ln(Profits/L) is constructed as $\log\left(Profits + \sqrt{Profits^2 + 1}\right) - lnL$.

sectors in which firms operate. In other words, if connected firms receive preferential benefits or treatment, these must not be sector specific, but rather specific to the connected firm or the individual product it sells. The last column shows that after controlling for detailed four-digit sectors (product classes), politically connected firms in Egypt cease to have significantly higher profit margins relative to other firms, suggesting that portions of their higher profits originate from characteristics specific to the product classes they are selling.

The significantly larger net profits in Egypt were systematically related to the survival of the regime. Figure 4.1 plots the evolution of the differences in (log) net profits between politically connected and other large firms from 2003 to 2011. After the fall of the Mubarak regime on February 11, 2011, the positive profits differential of politically connected firms suddenly disappeared.[14] The finding suggests that the larger profits of politically connected firms originated from firm-specific factors directly related to the existing political regime, such as firm-specific privileges in the form of subsidies or trade protection, rather than the greater entrepreneurial skills of the managers, which are independent from regime shifts. The fact that the profit differential between connected and unconnected firms disappears shortly after the fall of Mubarak also corroborates the quality of our empirical measurement of politically connectedness in Egypt.[15]

FIGURE 4.1

The Evolution of Net Profit Differentials between Connected and Other Firms, 2003–11

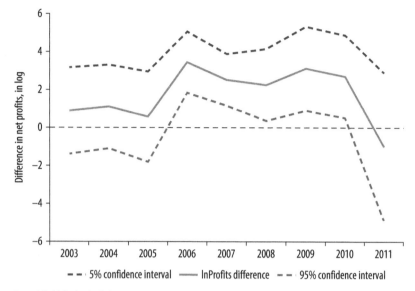

Source: World Bank calculation.
Note: Data are from Orbis establishment database and establishment census.

Connected Businessmen Capture Policies to Secure a Range of Privileges

Trials of leading businessmen since the Arab Spring have shed light on the potential mechanisms through which privileges were granted to connected firms; they revealed several common practices to favor politically connected firms in Egypt and Tunisia, including land appropriation at below-market prices; the manipulation of government regulations to stifle competition; and privileged access to subsidized energy and state procurement contracts.[16] Our newly constructed data allows for the first time to uncover empirically the main policy privileges granted to connected firms and show how they tilt the level playing field and affect competition. Lastly we show that these privileges led to large profits of connected firms but came at a high cost for private sector growth and job creation.

Politically Connected Firms Are Insulated from Competition through Various Entry Barriers

The Investment Law in Tunisia requires prior authorization from the government in order to operate legally for a number of activities; including fishing, tourism (travel agencies), air transport, maritime transport and road transport, telecommunications, education, the film industry, real estate, marketing, and health-related industries. If not administered equitably, these authorization requirements can be abused to create market power and stifle competition, both from prospective entrants and incumbents. Anecdotal evidence suggests this happened in the case of the closing of the Bouebdelli School, a highly respected private school from which many of Tunisia's elite have graduated. This school was perceived to be in direct competition with an international school founded by the Ben Ali family. In spite of widespread public protests, the Minister of Education ordered the school closed for failure to comply with registration regulations.[17]

The Investment Law also stipulates a number of activities for which foreign firms are required to obtain permission from the Investment Commission (CSI), when their foreign equity exceeds 50 percent of capital. These include transport, communications, tourism, education, cultural production, entertainment, construction, real estate, computer services, and a select number of other services. Obtaining such permission is notoriously difficult. Since 2005, the CSI has been processing between two and three applications per year with roughly half of all applications being successful. The list of sectors subjected to restrictions on foreign investment overlaps considerably with those that are subjected to government authorization. We note that many other sectors are also subject to government intervention, but not through the Investment Code.

Restrictions on foreign entry likely limit foreign competition and can also be used to direct foreign funds to certain domestic firms. The failed entry of McDonald's into the Tunisian food market is often used to illustrate the Ben Ali family's hold on specific sectors. The exclusion of McDonald's from the Tunisian market followed from their unwillingness to grant the sole license to a franchisee with family connections. The government of Tunisia in turn refused to grant authorization to invest.[18]

Connected firms are more likely to operate in sectors which are protected from competition through entry barriers. Figure 4.2 illustrates that 39 percent of the sectors with at least one Ben Ali firm require previous authorization by the government, relative to 24 percent of nonconnected sectors.[19] Similarly, 43 percent of connected sectors are protected from foreign entry relative to only 14 percent of nonconnected sectors. Moreover, 64 percent of Ben Ali firms are in sectors subject to authorization requirements and 64 percent are in sectors subject to restrictions on FDI. For nonconnected firms the comparable numbers are 45 percent and 36 percent, respectively.[20]

Egypt imposed more nontariff barriers to import than most other countries in the world. Tariff rates were reduced in Egypt at the end of the 1990s; at the same time, however, the government increased the use of

FIGURE 4.2

Authorization Requirements and FDI Restrictions Protect Politically Connected Firms in Tunisia

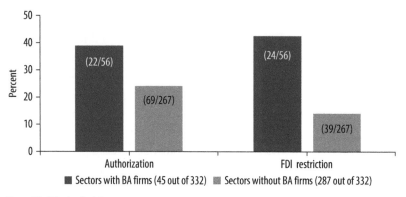

Source: World Bank calculation.

Note: Differences between Ben Ali and other firms are measured at the five-digit sector level (no. of restricted sectors/total no. of sectors). The difference in authorization requirements Fisher's *t* test probability = 0.04) and FDI restrictions Fisher's *t* test probability = 0.00 between connected and nonconnected sectors is significant at the 5 percent level.

nontariff technical import barriers (see figure 3.1). As a result, Egypt had one of the highest nontariff measures (NTM) frequencies in the world in 2010 (Malouche, Reyes, and Fouad 2013). Most NTMs in Egypt are "Class B" NTMs, legal technical barriers to import, including license or registration requirements for importers; regulations on production and distribution processes; traceability; and product quality requirements. They are imposed on 65 percent (96 out of 147) of the four-digit manufacturing industries. All of these restrictions make it harder for foreign companies to sell their goods and services in Egypt and thus can be abused to create market power and protect domestic firms from foreign competition.

Politically connected firms in Egypt are more likely to sell products protected from foreign competition. Table 4.5 shows that NTMs disproportionally benefitted politically connected firms[21]; i.e., manufacturing and mining industries in which politically connected firms are present are more likely to be protected from import competition by NTMs than sectors without politically connected firms. Politically connected firms are also more likely to be protected by NTMs at the individual establishment level; 82 percent of all politically connected manufacturing and mining establishment sell products that are protected by technical nontariff import barriers. In contrast, only 56 percent of all manufacturing or mining establishments in Egypt in 2006 operated in these sectors.

The gap in trade protection between politically connected and other firms increases substantially with the number NTMs imposed on a single product class. Table 4.5 shows that 82 percent of connected firms, but only 27 percent of all firms, sell products that are protected by at least two technical import barriers. Seventy-one percent of connected firms, but only 4 percent of all firms, sell products that are protected by at least three technical import barriers. These benefits accrued to connected firms despite the fact that, at the same time, Egypt was acclaimed for its efforts to reverse decades of state control of the economy.

Politically Connected Firms Enjoy Privileged Access to Subsidized Inputs and Assets

Both regimes appear to have moved away from the most visible modes of support for connected firms in the 2000s. The most direct way to subsidize firms connected to or owned by members of the political regimes are probably direct fiscal transfers through tax breaks or directed lending by state banks. However, these are also the most visible channels for outside observers. Both regimes aimed to attain an image of a reformer, business-friendly government in the late 1990s and 2000s partly because of reform pressure accompanying IMF programs. Obvious tax evasion or direct fiscal transfers to politically connected firms might have made it more difficult for the regimes to maintain that image potentially making them more vulnerable.

We do not find evidence that fiscal advantages disproportionally benefitted politically connected firms in Tunisia. The Tunisian Investment Law also stipulates that firms engaging in particular activities are eligible for special fiscal incentives. While these fiscal transfers seem to be more frequent for activities conducted by Ben Ali firms, we cannot reject the null hypothesis that they are equally prevalent in sectors in which connected firms were active as in sectors in which they were not. Thus, in contrast to authorization requirements and FDI restrictions, the special

TABLE 4.3

Politically Connected Firms and All Firms Protected by Nontariff Trade Barriers in the Arab Republic of Egypt

Number of class B NTMs per industry	Firms			Sectors		
	PC firms (%)	All firms (%)	Pearson χ^2 test (p)	PC sectors (%)	Non-PC sectors (%)	Pearson χ^2 test (p)
At least 1	82	56	0.00	76	55	0.01
At least 2	82	27	0.00	76	52	0.00
At least 3	71	4	0.00	59	38	0.01
At least 4	26	3	0.00	22	7	0.01
At least 5	18	3	0.00	15	5	0.05
At least 6	15	2	0.00	14	5	0.08
At least 7	13	0	0.00	9	3	0.09
At least 8	10	0	0.00	5	1	0.37

Source: World Bank calculation; WITS Comtrade.
Note: Because of small samples, we use the Fisher test to test for the significance in differences between PC and non-PC sectors for all comparisons with more than five NTMs per industry. The statistics show the results for the broadest measure of political connections, which also include firms that received significant investments from politically connected private equity funds.

fiscal incentives appear not to be the preferred way of supporting politically connected firms in Tunisia.

After the financial crises in the late 1990s in Egypt, advantages of connected firms shifted away from directed lending by state banks to other policy areas. The most commonly documented advantage enjoyed by connected firms is access to capital. This was also the case in Egypt before the financial crisis at the end of the 1990s, when connected firms enjoyed privileged access to credit from state-owned banks. After the banking crisis in the late 1990s, however, policy reforms circumscribed the activities of state banks and opened the financial sector for (foreign) private banks. As indicated earlier, we still find that connected firms in Egypt absorb most bank loans. However, interviews with foreign banks operating in Egypt suggest that private banks compete to lend to these firms as they are the most profitable in the country. Thus, the concentration of bank loans among connected firms in Egypt appears to be an equilibrium outcome of a system of privileges guaranteeing higher profits for connected firms rather than a direct policy privilege. Instead, the available evidence suggests that privileges shifted to other more subtle mechanisms such as energy subsidies to industry, land deals, trade protection through NTMs, or discretion in rule enforcement.

Politically connected firms in Egypt benefit disproportionally from energy subsidies. Chapter 2 documented that large establishments are more likely to benefit from the generous energy subsidies to industry in Egypt. Figure 4.3 shows that among large firms, the few politically connected ones are much more likely to operate in energy-intensive industries. That is, 45 percent of all connected establishments operate in energy-intensive industries, compared with only 8 percent of all establishments. In contrast, there is no statistical difference between the number of connected firms and all establishments operating in low or moderate energy-intensive industries. Likewise, at least one connected firm operates in 81 percent of all high energy-intensive industries. In contrast, connected firms are present in only 43 percent of low energy-intensive industries, and entirely absent in 57 percent.

Firms operating in sectors with more connected firms are more likely to have access to government land. In the manufacturing sector, access to land includes access to industrial zones, which guarantee several benefits relative to competitors outside of these zones, including tax exemptions from corporate taxes or customs duties, better infrastructure, and more streamlined regulations.[22] In the following, we test whether firms in sectors with a higher intensity of political connections in Egypt are more likely to obtain land from the government and/or be located in an industrial zone. To do this we employ the WBES data between 2004 and 2008, which contains information for all of these variables for about 3,000 firms

FIGURE 4.3

Share of Politically Connected Firms in High and Low Energy-Intensive Sectors in the Arab Republic of Egypt

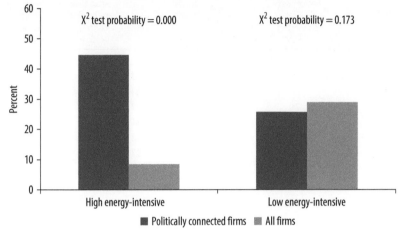

Source: World Bank calculation.
Note: The difference between politically connected and all other firms is significant at the 1 percent level in high energy-intensive industries but not significant in low energy-intensive industries. The percentage of firms in medium energy-intensive sectors has been excluded. The statistics show the results for the broadest measure of political connections which also include firms that received significant investments from politically connected private equity funds.

in Egypt. Firm responses to the WBES are anonymous, so we cannot distinguish connected and unconnected firms directly. However, as with NTMs and energy subsidies, we can identify the detailed four-digit industries in which politically connected firms are active by supplementing the WBES data with the information on the number of politically connected firms per four-digit sector.[23] Descriptive statistics show that firms in politically connected sectors (i.e., with at least one connected firm) are 11–14 percent more likely to have acquired land from the government and 7–11 percent more likely to be located in an industrial city (table 4.4). In the following, we test more systematically if politically connected firms benefitted disproportionally from government relations using regression analysis.[24] We emphasize that all results reflect the most conservative empirical tests, since we only compare differences in the impact of the intensity of political connections among firms located in the same two-digit manufacturing sector (e.g., textiles), but in different four-digit subsectors (which vary in the number of politically connected firms). We find that with each additional politically connected firm in a four-digit manufacturing sector, the probability of obtaining land from the government increases by 1.8 percentage points. Thus, assuming linearity, sectors with five connected firm owners are 9 percentage points more likely to have obtained land from the government than sectors without connected firm owners, which is a significant effect.

TABLE 4.4

Government Relations and Competition in Sectors with Politically Connected Firms versus Nonconnected Sectors in the Arab Republic of Egypt

	Sectors with politically connected CEOs	All other sectors	Sectors with politically connected owners	All other sectors	Sectors with any politically connected firm	All other sectors
Government relations						
Share of firms acquired land from government (%)	48	37	44	33	44	30
Share of firms in industrial city (%)	47	36	42	33	41	34
Share of firms with bank loan (%)	21	17	19	17	19	13
Waiting days for construction permit	595	642	608	681	610	696
Coefficient of variation (construction permit)	0.56	0.45	0.54	0.33	0.53	0.30
Number of tax inspections per year	4.6	5.7	5.1	5.7	5.3	5.2
Coefficient of variation (tax inspections)	1.34	1.32	1.35	1.25	1.34	1.27
Number of inspections by municipal authorities	1.6	1.9	1.7	2.0	1.6	2.5
Coefficient of variation (municipal inspections)	2.23	2.19	2.31	1.92	2.23	2.03
Share of firms' total sales to government	21	16	19	14	19	12
Competition						
Share of firms <10 domestic competitors (%)	36	29	32	30	32	29

Source: World Bank calculation.

Note: Data are from WBES 2004–08 and number of politically connected firms in Egypt. Politically connected four-digit sectors have at least one politically connected firm while all other sectors include zero connected firms depending on the type of political connection. The types of political connections are ranked according to their restrictiveness. The incentive of the connected individual to leverage connections on behalf of the firm is strongest if he is the CEO (almost all connected CEOs also own at least part of their companies). It is less strong for politically connected owners and weakest for any type of connected firms for which we also include firms which received significant investments from connected private equity funds.

Trials of leading businessmen after the fall of Mubarak in Egypt corroborate our empirical finding that connected firms profited from cheap access to prime land. There is plenty of anecdotal evidence that politically connected firms in Egypt have superior access to land and credit. Reportedly, the government not only sold the land but also guaranteed to connect the land with the necessary electricity, telecommunication, and transport infrastructure; this practice immediately increased the value of land, which the businessmen used as collateral to get bank loans far exceeding the initial purchase value of the land. The past practice of selling prime land below market value in closed deals also became apparent in the emergence of numerous court disputes filed against major real estate developers after the regime change in 2011. These trials aimed to force these real estate firms to revalue past land deals with the state and pay the difference. Several of these disputes have been settled outside courts in recent months (Ahram Online, various issues).

Large firms are more likely to be located in an industrial zone if they operate in politically connected industries (containing a higher number of connected firms). Figure 4.4, panel a, illustrates how the probability that a large firm with at least 100 employees is located in an industrial zone increases with the number of firms managed by a politically

FIGURE 4.4

Large Firms in Politically Connected Industries Are More Likely to Be Located in an Industrial Zone

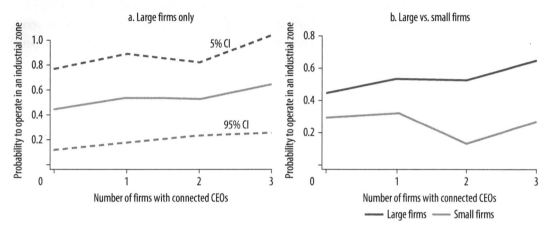

Source: World Bank calculation.

Note: Data are from WBES 2004–08 and number of politically connected firms in Egypt. Large firms have at least 100 employees. The graph illustrates how the probability that a large firm with at least 100 employees operates in an industrial zone increases 'the number of firms with a politically connected CEO across four-digit industries. The number of firms with politically connected CEO across four-digit industries in the sample ranges from 0 to 3. It is based on a probit regression of a dummy variable if the firm is located in an industrial zone and the number of firms with a politically connected CEO within a four-digit sector. The regression controls for firm level size, age, export shares, and two-digit sector dummies. We also include interaction terms between firm size categories (small versus large) and the number of connected firm per four-digit sector.

connected CEO across four-digit industries. Note that this result is likely to be driven by the connected firms in these sectors, since large firms are generally much more likely to be politically connected.[25] It shows that approximately 41 percent of all large firms in four-digit sectors without connected firms operate in industrial zones. This share increases to about 58 (respectively 62 percent) in sectors with one firm (respectively three firms) managed by a politically connected CEO.

Among politically connected industries, large firms are more likely to be located in an industrial zone than small firms. Figure 4.4b illustrates how the probabilities that large and small firms operate in an industrial zone increases with the number of firms led by a politically connected CEO across four-digit industries. Given that the majority of connected firms in our sample are large, the results strongly indicate that it is the connected firms within four-digit sectors that are located in industrial zones.

Reportedly, the identification of activities benefitting from tax exemptions in special economic zones was also driven by vested interests; for example, the list of sectors eligible for tax exemptions was expanded to include media companies after the construction of a new media complex (including the media company's offices, hotels, theatres, and so forth) of a politically connected businessman. The complex was declared a special economic zone shortly after, allowing him to benefit from tax exemptions (Ahram Online, various issues).

Politically Connected Firms Benefit from Discretionary Policy Implementation

Connected firms disproportionately benefit from the enforcement of rules. Politically connected firms also used their connections to minimize their regulatory burden and the threat of predatory behavior by government officials, relative to the burden and threats faced by their competitors. To analyze this situation, we again employ the WBES data, which contains firms' assessments of the implementation of various government policies and regulations. Following Hallward-Driemeier et al. (2010), we also examine within-industry variations of firm reports regarding the regulatory environment. Descriptive statistics show that firms in politically connected sectors (i.e., with at least one connected firm) report much lower waiting times for construction permits. For example, for the most conservative measure of political connections, table 4.4 shows that firms in connected sectors wait on average 47 days less.[26] In the following, we test more systematically if politically connected firms benefitted disproportionally from discretion in rule enforcement using regression analysis.[27] The data show that, for the most conservative measure of political connections, an additional firm with a politically connected CEO reduces the average waiting time in a four-digit sector by 51 days. Furthermore, large firms in industries that are less/not connected have to wait substantially longer (between 11 and 48 days, depending on the type of connection) than large firms in sectors with more politically connected firms. Given that politically connected firms are much more likely to be large relative to the average firm in the WBES, the finding suggests that connected firms have access to fast-track enforcements relative to other large firms in the same two-digit (but different four-digit) manufacturing sector. The data indicate that sectors with more politically connected firms exhibit a significantly higher coefficient of variation in the waiting days for construction permits, consistent with the argument that connected firms are able to access fast-track regulatory services while unconnected firms in the same four-digit industry are not.

Discretionary enforcement of rules can also be used to keep out or weaken potential competitors. For example a businessman, that pursued new investment abroad, recalls his encounter with a prominent local entrepreneur (World Bank 2009):

> *"As I was going through the investment process in that country and had already transferred the initial capital, I was contacted by a local entrepreneur whom I knew was close to the country's leadership. He offered to take part in my venture with a 25 percent share, bringing in a free land plot . . . and assurances that the investment would proceed smoothly with 'no administrative hassle'. I knew what that meant, of course, and the risk it*

involved for my control of the enterprise. Fortunately, I knew of ongoing investment in my own country. I made him understand that we would both gain in our respective countries to have our investments proceed smoothly, but also by staying away from each other's businesses as I could also make things difficult for him in my country, thanks to my own connections."

Firms that are not politically connected appear to be more frequently targeted by government inspections. Reportedly, using political connections to increase the number of inspections by government officials for a direct competitor is a mechanism to prevent a potential competitor from growing. The WBES for Egypt contain information on the number of tax and other inspections. Table 4.4 shows that, on average, firms in sectors with at least one politically connected CEO are inspected by tax officials 4.6 times a year. In contrast, the frequency of tax inspections increases by 24 percent (to 5.7 times a year) for firms in sectors without a connected CEO. Similarly, the frequency of inspections by the municipality is about 20 percent higher in sectors without politically connected firms. What is more, the dispersion (coefficient of variation) of reported inspections across firms is significantly higher in the connected sector (table 4.4). Thus, some firms received very few inspections while others are inspected frequently when connected firms are present in the sector. While we do not directly observe if connected firms report very few inspections, it is likely that the nonconnected firms are the ones targeted by government officials more frequently. The finding is also consistent with the notion that nonconnected small firms or firms in the informal sector stay small (under the radar of large connected competitors) in order to avoid being targeted by anti-competitive actions or government scrutiny.

BOX 4.1

Did Ben Ali Firms Dictate Amendments to the Investment Law in the 2000s?

The establishment of new entry barriers was more likely in sectors hosting Ben Ali firms. The list of activities which are subject to authorization requirements and FDI restrictions changed since 1993; they were supplemented by 22 subsequent presidential decrees, resulting in 73 amendments at the NAT 96 level, which is the five-digit sector level. Table B4.1.1 summarizes changes made to the Tunisian investment code between 1994 and 2010 through 22 decrees issued by Ben Ali himself. These decrees introduced new authorization requirements pertaining to 45 sectors and new FDI restrictions in

(continued on next page)

BOX 4.1 *Continued*

TABLE B4.1.1

Correlation between New Barriers to Entry and the Presence of Ben Ali Firms

New regulations and presence of Ben Ali firms							
Ben Ali presence		New Authorization requirements			New FDI restrictions		
	N	n	%	Fisher's F-test	n	%	Fisher's F-test
At least one firm	451	7	1.55	Table Pr 0.0195	9	2.00	Table Pr 0.0195
None	5058	38	0.75	0.046	19	0.38	0.000
All	5509	45		$p = 0.0961$	28		$p = 0.000$

New regulations and entry of Ben Ali firms							
Ben Ali entry in the same or the subsequent year		New Authorization requirements			New FDI restrictions		
	N	n	%	Fisher's F-test	n	%	Fisher's F-test
At least one entry	168	4	2.35	Table Pr 0.0195	3	1.76	Table Pr 0.0195
None	5031	41	0.82	0.043	25	0.50	0.049
All	5199	45		$p = 0.0582$	28		$p = 0.0619$

Source: World Bank calculation.
Note: The test for equality is Fisher's exact t test. It tests the null hypothesis that the introduction of new regulations referred to in the column heading pertaining to narrowly defined five-digit sectors is independent of the presence (top row) and start-up (bottom row) of connected firms within such sectors. The entry indicator is a sector-level binary indicator taking the value 1 if a Ben Ali firm entered in the same or following year.

28 sectors. Table B4.1.1 (upper panel) shows that connected firms were present in seven (nine) of the 45 (28) sector-years in which new authorization requirements (FDI restrictions) were imposed. The null hypotheses that the likelihood of new FDI restrictions (authorization requirements) does not depend on the presence of connected firms is rejected at the 1 percent (10 percent) significance level. While the number of observations is again small, the data also reject the null hypothesis of independence between the startup of new Ben Ali firms and the introduction of new authorization requirements and FDI restrictions at the 10 percent significance level (table B4.1.1, lower panel).

A few anecdotal clues support the view that the investment code has been actively manipulated by the Ben Ali family. For example, *Décret n° 96-1234*, issued in 1996, amended the investment code by introducing authorization requirements for firms engaging in the handling and transfer of goods in ports and the towing and rescue of ships. The decree also introduced restrictions on FDI for firms involved in the transport of red meat. In the same year, a shipping and logistics company focused on the transport of refrigerated products was established by a member of the Ben Ali family. Moreover, immediately after the entry of a politically connected firm into the cement sector, *Décret n° 2007–2311* was introduced stipulating that government authorization was required for firms producing cement.

Privileges to Politically Connected Firms Undermine Private Sector Development and Job Creation

The theory developed in Aghion et al. (2001) points to an indirect empirical strategy for assessing whether the advantages of political connections constitute a drag on growth. First, if political connections are a drag on growth, it must be the case that the policy privileges of the politically connected firms drive a wedge between the prices of inputs and outputs that they face compared with the prices encountered by unconnected firms. If this is the case, the policy privileges that connected firms receive should account for their better performance relative to unconnected firms. The subsequent evidence shows that this is the case.

Policy Privileges Explain the Superior Profits of Connected Firms

Connected firms in Egypt are more profitable because they benefit more from trade protection and energy subsidies. The joint distribution of NTMs, energy subsidies, and politically connected firms across four-digit industries accounts for the entire profitability differential between connected and other firms. That is, politically connected firms are significantly more profitable than unconnected firms if their products are protected from import competition, but are not so otherwise. We find similar results once we account for the joint distribution between political connections and energy subsidies in high energy-intensive industries.[28]

These results indicate that nontariff barriers and energy subsidies are targeted to connected firms. These barriers and subsidies appear to exclude unconnected firms operating in the same sectors. For example, some barriers to entry limit the ability of unconnected domestic firms to benefit from the privileges granted to connected firms. In the case of energy subsidies, firms are required to obtain a government license to build a factory in energy-intensive sectors such as steel and cement. This license was issued by the Ministry of Industry and Trade, or the Ministry of Investment, and had to be renewed annually. The licensing procedure favored politically connected firms, which were both more likely to get the license and less likely to be exposed to predatory behavior (the non-renewal of a license after they had undertaken large sunk investments). In the very profitable energy-intensive and trade-protected cement and steel sectors, by 2010 only a few connected firms had obtained the license guaranteeing access to energy subsidies. In the case of NTMs, some of these measures also required explicit licenses to import specific intermediates from foreign manufacturers (as in the automobile industry). Table 4.6 shows that connected firms are significantly more likely to benefit from authorization requirements for importing. Moreover, enforcement of NTMs requires government action, which has been shown to be uneven across firms operating in the same sector when connected firms are present.[29]

Connected firms in Tunisia are more profitable because legal barriers to entry guaranteed their market power. Ben Ali firms only have higher market shares and value added per worker if they are protected by authorization requirements and FDI restrictions.[30] In sectors covered by the Investment Code but not subject to these regulatory requirements, the differences are statistically negligible once the larger size of connected firms is taken into account. On average, the market shares of Ben Ali firms exceed that of nonconnected firms in sectors with authorization requirements and FDI restrictions by 4 percentage points and 6.4 percentage points, respectively. These are sizeable differences considering that the average market share of nonconnected firms in sectors subject to authorization requirements is only 0.27 percent. Notably, Ben Ali firms are also significantly larger in sectors with entry restrictions. Ben Ali firms employ 137 percent and 285 percent more salaried employees than nonconnected firms when authorization requirements or FDI restrictions are present, respectively. Moreover, we find that the growth differences in these variables between Ben Ali and other firms also fluctuate systematically with the prevalence of regulations.

Business regulations helped generating higher profits for Ben Ali firms. Ben Ali firms are especially more profitable than their peers in sectors subject to authorization requirements and FDI restrictions. In sectors not subject to these restrictions, however, Ben Ali firms make significantly lower profits than their competitors. These results suggest regulatory capture by connected firms.

Given our findings that political connections in Egypt and Tunisia translate into large policy privileges, we also expect to find that the presence of connected firms affects competition and firm dynamics as predicted in Aghion et al. (2001). Sectors including politically connected firms should see less firm entry and weaker competition among firms. Likewise, sectors dominated by these firms should have a more skewed firm distribution, characterized by a large connected market leader and a potentially large number of small or informal micro firms using vintage technologies to serve local market niches. In the following, we use our newly constructed data set for Egypt to present empirical evidence consistent with these predictions.

Politically Connected Firms Are Insulated from Competition

Large firms in connected sectors—those with more connected firms—report fewer domestic competitors. The analysis is based on approximately 3,000 firms from the WBES data for Egypt which report their number of domestic competitors. Descriptive statistics show that firms in politically connected sectors (i.e., with at least one connected firm) are more likely to report fewer than 10 competitors in the domestic market (table 4.4). In the following, we test more systematically if firms in politically connected sectors report less competition using regression analysis.[31] The information is observed at the firm-level, allowing us to test for complementarities between the effect of political connections at the four-digit sector level and specific characteristics of firms in these sectors, such as their size. This is important because large firms in the WBES data are much more likely to be connected. Thus, the data make possible measuring the intensity of domestic competition faced by large firms in connected sectors relative to other large firms in less/nonconnected sectors. In other words, the competition results are much more likely to be driven by the politically connected firms (even though we cannot identify them directly in the WBES) when we focus on the subgroup of large firms across all sectors. The findings confirm that large firms report fewer domestic competitors when they operate in more connected manufacturing sectors. Moreover, within more connected sectors, large firms are more likely than small firms to report fewer domestic competitors. Taken together, large firms in connected sectors report facing fewer domestic competitors. In sum, the findings suggest that connected manufacturing firms are more likely to be protected from domestic competition than other large firms.

Privileges to Politically Connected Firms Suppress the Firm Dynamics Associated with Job Creation

Low rates of entry in sectors dominated by connected firms—despite higher rents in these sectors—are further evidence that connected firms benefit from barriers to entry. We expect to find that the presence of politically connected firms discourages the entry of unconnected firms, as the latter cannot compete with the connected firms' privileges. Thus, unconnected firms would have to specialize in unproductive local market niches in these sectors. While the counterfactual of firm entry in the absence of connected firms in the same sectors is not observable, our empirical strategy is to compare firm dynamics across detailed four-digit sectors, which differ in their intensity of political connections in a given year and over time. The cross-sector comparison can be biased because of an endogenous selection effect of connected firms into sectors with specific characteristics, such as growth opportunities associated with their maturity. The findings in the previous sections help us assess the potential direction of such bias. First, the sizeable rents from energy subsidies, trade protection, and the use of prime land should attract substantial entry into these sectors, implying that the observed correlation between political connections and firm entry is biased downward. Second, the analysis has shown that the presence of connected firms is relatively broad-based across economic activities; including manufacturing and modern service sectors (machinery and ICT services) with arguably higher sector-specific growth opportunities (table 4.1 and table G.2 in appendix G). Thus, we argue that there is sufficient variation in the distribution of connected firms across sectors with high- and low-growth potential in Egypt in the 2000s to detect whether firm dynamics vary across sectors depending on the presence of connected firms. In addition, we control for sector-specific characteristics that are correlated with sectors' growth opportunities in all estimation specifications (for example, average size and age of establishments in a sector and sector dummies). Thus, we only use four-digit sectors with comparable characteristics to empirically identify the impact of political connections on establishment entry.[32]

Firm entry is lower in connected sectors. Table 4.5 summarizes the descriptive statistics of selected variables from the establishment census across four-digit sectors with at least one politically connected firm and all other sectors with zero connected firms. Entry rates into sectors with at least one politically connected firm were 0.8 percentage points lower in 2006 (based on the most restrictive measure of sectors with politically connected CEOs); this corresponds to 11 percent lower entry rates in connected sectors. The difference is even larger for employment weighted entry rates which are 28 percent lower in connected sectors. Moreover, connected sectors had a higher share of old establishments in 2006 pointing to either lower firm entry or exit in previous years. As discussed in chapter 3 there is evidence that the extent of privileges to politically connected firms increased between 1996 and 2006.[33] Thus, if privileges to politically connected firms discourage firm entry (of unconnected firms), we expect declining firm entry rates in connected sectors between 1996 and 2006. Table 4.5 shows that this was indeed the case. Entry rates into unconnected sectors increased significantly between 1996 and 2006 but hardly changed in sectors with at least one connected firms over the same period. Likewise, the share of young firms increased more rapidly in connected sectors without connected firms. The results are robust when controlling for sector-specific characteristics (e.g., average size and age of establishments in a sector as well as one- or two-digit sector dummies). For example, an increase in the number of firms with a connected CEO in a four-digit sector from zero to one increases the share of old establishments in that sector by 1.7 percentage points after controlling for average firm size and two-digit sector dummies. Thus, either entry or exit between 1996 and 2006 has been significantly lower in politically connected four-digit subsectors relative to not/less connected four-digit subsectors belonging to the same two-digit sector.

The findings suggest that the presence of politically connected firms crowds out the type of firms that have the highest potential for job creation. The presence of connected firms appears to discourage new (unconnected) entrepreneurs to enter as they cannot compete with the connected firms' privileges. Chapter 1 suggests that this decline in the share of young firms reduces job growth.

The presence of political connected firms tends to push the majority of unconnected firms towards unproductive small-scale, potentially informal activities. Table 4.5 shows that the coefficient of variation (standard deviation divided by the mean) and skewness in the establishment size distribution are almost twice as high and 50 percent higher in sectors with at least one politically connected firm, respectively. Both measures also increased substantially in politically connected sectors between 1996 and 2006 but hardly changed or even declined in unconnected sectors. Note that a higher coefficient of variation implies fewer medium-size establishments since either the share of micro or of large establishments increased (or both); given that the distribution of employment across establishments is right-skewed, i.e., characterized by many micro and few large establishments, a higher skewness in the establishment size distribution implies that the employment share of micro establishment increased or the employment share of large establishment declines. Taken together, the simultaneous increase in the coefficient of variation and the skewness

TABLE 4.5

Firm Dynamics in Sectors with Politically Connected Firms versus Nonconnected Sectors in the Arab Republic of Egypt

	Sectors with politically connected CEOs	All other sectors	Sectors with politically connected owners	All other sectors	Sectors with any politically connected firm	All other sectors
Level effects, 2006						
Entry rate (%)	6.5	7.3	7.0	7.4	6.9	7.6
Entry rate, employment weighted (%)	3.6	4.6	4.4	4.5	4.2	4.8
Share old establishments (age 11–30 years) (%)	26.1	24.0	24.5	24.1	25.3	23.2
Coefficient of variation (empl)	2.6	1.5	2.0	1.4	2.0	1.3
Skewness (empl)	8.9	5.8	7.3	5.4	7.4	5.0
Dynamic effects, 1996–2006						
Growth entry rate (decade)	0.1	1.2	0.2	2.3	0.2	2.9
Growth entry rate empl-weighted (decade)	0.4	3.6	2.0	4.1	2.0	5.0
Change share young establishments (age ≤10)	5.7	9.1	7.5	9.2	7.4	13.5
Change coefficient of variation (empl)	2.7	0.5	1.8	−0.3	1.7	−0.4
Change skewness (empl)	7.5	3.3	6.2	0.9	6.1	0.5

Source: World Bank calculation.

Note: Data are based on the Egyptian establishment census in 1996 and 2006 and number of politically connected firms. Politically connected four-digit sectors have at least one politically connected firm while all other sectors include zero connected firms depending on the type of political connection. The incentive of the connected individual to leverage connections on behalf of the firm is strongest if he is the CEO (almost all connected CEOs also own at least part of their companies). It is less strong for politically connected owners and weakest for any type of connected firms for which we also include firms which received significant investments from connected private equity funds.

in a four-digit sector thus indicate that the employment share of micro establishments increased in connected sectors while the employment shares of medium and large establishments declined; this is consistent with the predictions of Aghion et al. (2001). Since most micro enterprises in Egypt are informal, the presence of political connections appears to push the majority of unconnected firms towards informal activities.[34]

These findings suggest that unconnected firms are not able to compete with politically connected firms in the same sector because they do not receive the same policy privileges. Instead, unconnected firms in these sectors are forced to cater to local market niches involving typically small-scale, potentially informal activities. If these activities are also less productive the result signals a higher misallocation of labor across firms in political connections sectors. In that case, the dynamic impact of privileges to politically connected firms on the firm size distribution comes with a loss in aggregate productivity, because of a less efficient allocation of resources.

Although comparable evidence is not available for Tunisia because of data limitations, the Schumpeterian growth framework suggests that major policy privileges, such as those granted in the form of entry barriers, also distort competition and firm dynamics in Tunisia. Figures 1.19 and 1.12 documented that firm turnover in Tunisia is low and job creation is skewed towards small-scale, unproductive activities especially in the service sectors. Both stylized facts are consistent with the predictions of the adopted Schumpeterian growth framework; i.e., they are symptoms of a lack of private sector competition. That is, Aghion et al. (2001) predict that the large cost advantages of Ben Ali firms resulting from the biased legislation limit neck-and-neck competition among firms, reducing their incentives to adopt new (foreign) technologies. All together, the findings in this section suggest that at least in part the distortions to firm dynamics and competition in Tunisia documented in chapter 1 originate from legislative barriers to entry that benefitted a few connected firms.

Entry Barriers in Backbone Services Has Likely Limited Growth in Downstream Manufacturing Industries

Barriers to entry and competition are expected to have reduced the quality of services provided by the few firms authorized to operate in these sectors in Tunisia. The entry barriers translate into sizeable cost advantages for the few connected firms authorized to operate in these sectors. They lead to a monopolistic market structure that helps the few connected firms shielded from competition to achieve abnormally high profits. Aghion et al. (2001) show that the resulting market structure discourages the incentives of market leaders to improve the quality of their services; hence, it is expected to reduce the aggregate service sector performance.

While services are an important part of the economy, the results do not directly explain why the generous tax breaks provided to manufacturing firms in the offshore economy in Tunisia did not generate more growth and jobs. While the Schumpetarian growth framework explains the distorted dynamics and firm performances in protected service sectors, it falls short of explaining the modest productivity and job growth of manufacturing firms in the offshore economy. Manufacturing firms in the offshore economy benefitted from generous tax incentives. For example, the investment code stipulates that offshore firms—those that export at least 70 percent of their output (Articles 10 and 16 of the code)—do not have to pay profit and turnover taxes. Moreover, they usually did not have to compete directly with Ben Ali firms. The tax incentives have helped Tunisia attract foreign investors in spite of the onshore sector being highly protected and largely closed to foreign competition, as subsequently discussed.

The protection of Ben Ali firms from competition in Tunisia's onshore economy is likely to have reduced the quality of backbone services provided to downstream manufacturing firms, limiting their growth.[35] The theory of weak links (Jones 2011; Kremer 1993) highlights that the performance of manufacturing firms cannot be analyzed in isolation from the performance of nontradable service sectors. Weak performances in backbone service sectors lead to lower quality services provided to firms in downstream using industries. Hence, despite the generous tax regime, productivity and job growth in the downstream manufacturing industries that use these lower quality services can be limited. In fact, the results in chapter 2 show that FDI in services led to significant jobs spillovers in downstream using sectors in Jordan. Given the sizeable entry barriers in backbone service sectors in Tunisia because of the presence of Ben Ali firms—which primarily operated in service sectors—we would anticipate the potential impact of *weak links* in Tunisia to be significant. The recent work of Marotta, Ugarte, and Baghdadi (2014) supports this hypothesis showing that *weak links* led to lower levels of productivity per worker in Tunisia.

The Presence of Connected Firms Reduces Aggregate Job Creation

The findings thus far provide ample indirect evidence that privileges lead to firm dynamics associated with lower aggregate job growth. All of these findings—the higher profitability of connected firms due to granted policy privileges and the adverse impact of their presence on competition, entry, and employment in medium and large firms—are consistent with the empirical hypotheses derived from the Schumpeterian growth model of Aghion et al. (2001). They suggest that aggregate employment growth would have been higher if the intensity of political privileges declined. This would necessitate a decline in the intensive margin, measured by the number of firms with a strong political influence within sectors, and the extensive margin, measured by the expansion of politically connected firms into new, initially unconnected sectors.

We cannot observe directly if employment growth in connected sectors would have been higher in the absence of political connections. Employment growth in politically connected sectors between 1996 and 2006 was comparable to other sectors. Thus, if connected firms indeed have positive employment growth, the effect is offset by the negative employment growth of unconnected firms in these sectors. Still, drawing conclusion from directly comparing employment growth among connected and unconnected sectors has limitations since we do not observe simultaneous changes in various other determinants of employment growth in our data. Instead, we would like to measure to what extent employment growth in connected sectors would have been higher in the absence of politically connected firms. This relevant counterfactual is of course not directly observable.

The nature of our data, however, provides a quasi-experimental setting which allows determining the aggregate employment impact of the entry of politically connected firms into new, previously unconnected sectors. We do observe the year in which politically connected firms entered into new sectors. Therefore, we can observe when connected firms enter into sectors which were previously unconnected. There are 41 such sectors: 18 service sectors, 16 manufacturing, 8 utilities, and 4 mining sectors. These include several sectors with high growth potential in Egypt, such as *manufacture of primary cells and batteries, television and radio receivers, wholesale of solid, liquid and gaseous fuels, inland water transport, legal activities, and advertising.*

We test whether aggregate employment growth over a 10-year period between 1996 and 2006 declined after the entry of politically connected firms into new, previously unconnected (*open*) sectors. Holding all else constant, entry always increases employment in the sector regardless of whether the entrant is connected or not. Thus, we expect that the entry of connected firms leads to sector employment growth, unless the adverse impact of connected firms on the growth opportunities of their unconnected peers leads to their exit or shrinkage. In contrast, we do not expect to observe the latter adverse effect (or at least expect it to be less pronounced) when connected firms enter into sectors which were already dominated by privileged connected firms in previous years. Therefore, negative aggregate employment growth after the entry of connected firms into previously unconnected sectors implies that the decline in employment in unconnected firms—which cannot compete—outweighs

BOX 4.2

Political Connections and Patronage in the Republic of Yemen

Large government spending on maintenance of oil infrastructure has benefitted a small group of Yemeni companies and individuals.[a] Revenues from oil exports substantially contributed to economic growth and imported goods subsidies in the years before 2011. However, the government spent US$ billions over the past three decades on maintenance of oil infrastructure because of the cost-inflation actions of a small, well-connected business elite. These elites are local intermediaries that connect foreign oil companies with local governments; they have either close ties to former President Saleh and his subordinates, or to powerful tribal sheikhs. Owners of dominant oil-related service providers in engineering and construction, transport and logistics, facilitation, and security sectors are relatives of, or closely connected to, the former president, military generals, and ministers. The most lucrative aspects of the energy sector are oil exports and fuel imports, which in turn are controlled by powerful persons including the former president, sheikhs, and military commanders. Their behavior leads to inflated production costs, lost revenues, diesel smuggling, and likely diminish the multiplier effect of investment in the sector.

A handful of firms connected to the military or the former president control the production of water-consuming *Qat* and the lucrative food import market. Insecure food and water supplies are chronic issues in the Republic of Yemen. Two problems worsen the situation. First, the production of a

water-consuming narcotic leaf, *Qat*. Second, the dominance in the food import market of a small number of private and public players with ties to the regime of former President Saleh. Reforming the water sector has proved to be extremely difficult as the direct beneficiaries of *Qat* production are the Saleh family and other landowners with significant stakes in the political regime. Moreover, the Republic of Yemen has to import nearly all of its wheat and rice, the two most important staples of national diet. Major importers are a military-run firm (Yeco), and three private entities of which former President Saleh is a shareholder. These few connected firms reportedly influence the regulations in the sector to their own favor.

The lucrative telecommunications sector in the Republic of Yemen has been beset with government monopoly, privileges to politically connected firms, and opacity since market liberalization began in the 1990s. The state-run public telecommunication corporation (PTC) has been the sole provider of broadband Internet in the country. While the telecom market appears to be competitive when looking at the market shares of three major private and public operators, most entrants in the sector were linked with the former president's family and his close connections. The first two private mobile licenses were granted to business groups supported by, or financially and personally connected to, former President Saleh. The third and last private mobile license was awarded to a company whose ultimate owner remains opaque and is widely

(continued on next page)

BOX 4.2   *Continued*

seen as an attempt by the Saleh family to take a stake in the lucrative telecom market. Furthermore, former President Saleh and his relatives are widely rumored to own shares in the sole public mobile operator, Yemen Mobile. It has increased its share of subscribers as a result of substantial government assistance. Some of these supports include applying lower tariffs; privileged access to private infrastructure networks built by other operators; compelling entire ministries to use Yemen Mobile's services; and direct intervention from the former president by refusing import and export licenses crucial to the day-to-day business of other operators. Given the importance of the lucrative sector, it remains to be seen whether the state will allow fairer competition among current and future players in the market.

The structure of Yemen's financial sector in 2012 privileges a small group of politically connected firms. Yemen's formal banking system was small, underdeveloped, poorly regulated, and limited to a small group of elite actors, all of whom had a close relationship with former President Saleh. The banking system is accessible only to the tiny middle class and wealthy elites. This restrains the growth potential of nonconnected firms. While the private sector accounts for the largest share of formal banking, its few major financial institutions were founded by elites with strong connections to Saleh's family. The central bank's upper management is well-respected by international institutions, but the bank itself is reputedly used to launder the profits of illicit activities. Moreover, it is hamstrung by poor government fiscal position and limited foreign currency reserves. The informal banking system, on the other hand, is reportedly as large as its formal counterpart; it serves as the source of microfinance, for example, for firms in food production and water merchants.

Note:
a. The following analysis is based on a series of papers analyzing political patronage in different economic sectors in the Republic of Yemen produced by the Chatham House (2013).

any positive job creation by the connected firm(s).[36] We test this hypothesis in a difference-in-difference estimation (also controlling for other industry-specific characteristics correlated with job growth).[37]

We find that aggregate employment growth declines by about 1.4 percentage points annually when connected firms enter new, previously unconnected sectors. The economic impact is large. The magnitude of the corresponding coefficient suggests that aggregate employment in these sectors shrinks by 25 percent over the 10-year period from 1996 to 2006. Note that the connected firms did not necessarily enter directly in 1997, so the employment growth might have been positive in earlier years, but then declined substantially because of the sudden presence of the connected firm with access to policy privileges, itself guaranteed a large cost advantage over the existing competitors or potential new, unconnected entrants.

These findings provide quantitative evidence that the growth impact of connected firms' entry is more than offset by their adverse impact on the growth opportunities of the majority of unconnected firms that stop growing or exit. As a consequence, political connections reduce aggregate employment growth in this sector. This conclusion is consistent with the indirect evidence that political privileges lead to firm dynamics associated with lower aggregate job growth presented earlier. It is also consistent with the prediction of the model of Aghion et al. (2001), who show that less neck-and-neck competition because of large exogenous cost advantages of market leaders reduce aggregate long-term growth. In the case of Egypt and Tunisia, such large exogenous cost advantages are granted by policy privileges such as licenses requirements, trade protection, energy subsidies, access to prime land, or biased regulatory enforcement. Even though these policy privileges might help the few benefitting firms grow and create jobs, we show that the aggregate employment impact is negative because of the adverse effects of such policies on competition, and thus on the growth opportunities for the large majority of firms, which are unconnected.

Available Qualitative Evidence Points to Similar Mechanisms of Policy Privileges in Other MENA Countries

The results so far show that politically connected firms in Egypt and Tunisia received large privileges that distorted competition and thus firm dynamics associated with job creation. What is more, the evidence in Tunisia suggests that firms connected to Ben Ali used their political influence to affect the regulatory environment to their favor. In addition, there is direct evidence in Egypt that the presence of firms connected to Mubarak led to similar capture and also to lower aggregate job creation.

This section argues that policy privileges and their adverse impact on regulations, competition, firm dynamics, and ultimately job creation are also frequent in other countries of the MENA region. We do not have comparable detailed data listing politically connected firms for other MENA countries. However, there is ample qualitative evidence from other countries in the region which we review. The section points out that the system of closed deals between the state and businesses in Egypt and Tunisia are not outliers, but rather representative of the way business is conducted in MENA.

The frequent use of nontariff measures in Egypt documented in "Privileges to Politically Connected Firms Undermine Competition and Job Creation: Evidence from the Arab Republic of Egypt and Tunisia"

FIGURE 4.5

Nontariff Barriers Are Frequently Imposed in MENA

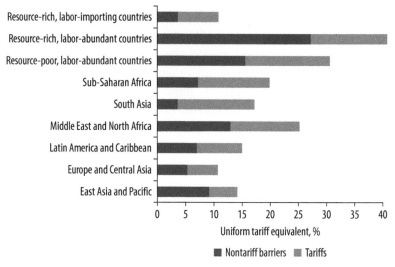

Source: from Malik (2013).
Note: Figure shows the average tariff equivalent value of tariffs and nontariff measures by region of the world and categories of MENA countries by level of endowment.

section is representative for oil-importing MENA countries. Malik (2013) indicates that nontariff measures are more frequently used in MENA countries than in other regions and argues that they are likely exploited to protect connected firms from import competition (figure 4.5).

MENA Lags Behind Other Regions in Governance and Corruption Indicators, Especially in Corruption in Defense and Military Involvement in Business

The relative prevalence of the role of privileges in MENA can also be characterized through a number of qualitative governance indices, especially in regards to the military sector. For example, the Transparency International (TI) Government Defense Anti-Corruption Index analyzes corruption risk in defense establishments worldwide. This index assesses and compares levels of corruption risk and vulnerability across countries. TI assessed 82 countries in 2012 and classified each country in a category[38] from A to F, with A being the lowest corruption risk and F the highest. The countries included in this index accounted for 94 percent of global military expenditure in 2011. TI's evidence suggests that poor rankings are associated with patronage networks. The report found that networks based on close family ties between the military and businesses and restrictions on public debate and civil society freedom are features of most MENA countries. All of the MENA countries assessed have high to critical risk of corruption (categories D, E, or F). Out of these 18 MENA countries, twelve were placed in category E and F, corresponding to very high or critical corruption risk (33 percent of all countries); these include Egypt, Algeria, Libya, Syria, and the Republic of Yemen, along with non-MENA countries like Angola. Three were ranked D+: Kuwait, Lebanon, and UAE, along with countries like India, Israel, and Thailand (18 percent of all countries surveyed); and two were placed in category D-: Jordan and West Bank and Gaza, along with countries like China, Pakistan, the Russian Federation, and Turkey (18 percent of all countries surveyed). Figure 4.6 lists the remaining MENA countries according to their ranking.

Patronage networks between the military and business are common features in most MENA countries. Looking at the financial risk subindex

FIGURE 4.6

Transparency International: Defence Anti-Corruption Index

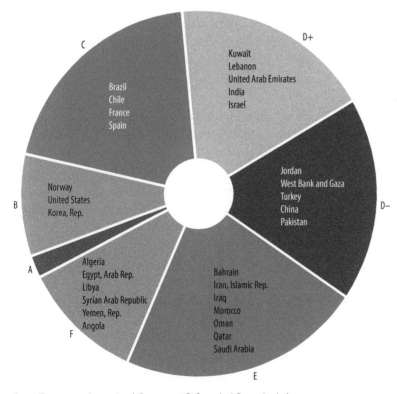

Source: Transparency International: Government Defence Anti-Corruption Index.

of TI's Government Defence Anti-Corruption Risk Index allows us to refine our qualitative assessment of MENA countries. Countries in the report were categorized into five risk areas: political, financial, personnel, operations, and procurement. Financial corruption risks are linked to the abuse of large, potentially secretive defense budgets and asset disposal and links to businesses. Countries were asked 5 questions (2 for asset disposal and 3 regarding links to businesses); scores were associated according to the responses.[39] TI reports that military institutions' commercial interests (military ownership of businesses) creates substantial conflicts of interest and thus an increased risk of corruption. The results for MENA are summarized in table 4.6. Military-owned businesses are common in 11 MENA countries (out of 18). For example, in Jordan, TI reports that in recent years the line between business and the military has become blurred with the government's efforts to focus more on profit-generating activities. Anecdotal evidence indicates that this closer relationship between business and military actors has not been accompanied by adequate controls. There is no evidence of military institutions owning commercial businesses at a significant scale in Morocco, Tunisia, and West Bank and Gaza (equivalent to only 1 percent of the defense budget or less). Still, there are reports of military personnel engaging in unauthorized private enterprise in Morocco. In Tunisia, while the armed forces did not appear to own businesses or engage in illicit economic activities, security forces exploited their political power to own commercial businesses and attain licenses and other privileges during the previous regime. Military-owned businesses exist and are lacking scrutiny in the Islamic Republic of Iran and Iraq.

There is a severe lack of institutional controls to contain corruption in defense in a number of MENA countries. There is no evidence of institutional activity and transparency to prevent corruption in the disposal of assets for defense. Military-owned businesses[40] are prevalent in each country, and are characterized by a complete lack of transparency and absence of any form of oversight. For example, the military in Egypt has considerable economic interests and assets, estimated at between 10 and 40 percent of the country's economy, according to TI. The profits of these firms are deemed "national secrets."[41] In Algeria, an anti-corruption law attempts to prohibit participation of the military in corrupt private enterprises, but this type of illicit activity is still common practice because of the lack of implementation of this law. In Syria, there is no evidence that military-owned businesses are subject to any scrutiny or auditing processes. The entire budget of the military is "off-budget." Defense and security institutions have ownership of several commercial businesses, which are not independently scrutinized.

TABLE 4.6

Financial Corruption Risk Subindex: Asset Disposal and Links to Business, MENA Countries

Country name	Asset disposal		Links to business		
	Asset disposal controls	Asset disposal scrutiny	Mil. owned businesses exist	Mil. owned business scrutiny	Unauthorised private enterprise
Band D+					
Kuwait	4	4	4	..	2
Lebanon	0	0	2	2	2
United Arab Emirates	2	0	3	2	4
Band D–					
Jordan	1	2	1	1	2
West Bank and Gaza	1	2	1	1	1
Band E					
Bahrain	1	1	4	..	3
Iran, Islamic Rep.	0	1	1	1	0
Iraq	0	0	0	0	1
Morocco	1	0	4	..	1
Oman	0	1	4	..	4
Qatar	1	0	2	0	0
Saudi Arabia	2	0	2	1	0
Tunisia	1	0	..	4	2
Band F					
Algeria	0	0	0	0	2
Egypt, Arab Rep.	0	0	0	0	2
Libya	0	0	..	0	0
Syrian Arab Republic	0	0	0	0	0
Yemen	0	0	0	0	0

Q22: How effective are controls over the disposal of assets, and is information on these disposals, and the proceeds of their sale, transparent?

Q23: Is independent and transparent scrutiny of asset disposals conducted by defence establishments, and are the reports of such scrutiny publicly available?

Q30: Do national defense and security institutions have beneficial ownership of commercial businesses? If so, how transparent are details of the operations and finances of such businesses?

Q31: Are military-owned businesses subject to transparent independent scrutiny at a recognised international standard?

Q32: Is there evidence of unauthorised private enterprise by military or other defence ministry employees? If so, what is the government's reaction to such enterprise? Hint: Such enterprises may operate under the pretence of being part of official military activity.

Source: Transparency International: Government Defence Anti-Corruption Risk Index.

Note: 4 = High transparency; strong, institutionalized activity to address corruption risks, 3 = Generally high transparency; activity to address corruption risks, but with shortcomings. 2 = Moderate transparency; activity to address corruption risks with significant shortcomings. 1 = Generally low transparency; weak activity to address corruption risks. 0 = Low transparency; very weak or no activity to address corruption risks.

Qualitative evidence exemplifies how military businesses can use their connections to stifle competition. A former entrepreneur from a large country in the region founded a larger investing in the dairy and meat sector company in his country. After he entered the market he learned that his company would potentially compete regionally with an incumbent business run by a military general. He describes his experience as follows:

> We (my father, brother, and I) decided to invest in cattle production in our country. We pooled our money together and invested about 300,000 euros to develop our cattle production since there is a supply shortage. Our live cargo arrived at port in containers and was not released to us as we were told that we were missing crucial documents for customs clearance. This was evidently a new procedure we had not heard of before. We learned that a Military General had cornered the market in that part of the country and had decided he would not sustain any competition. The amount of red tape and delay to get the approval took more than three weeks with the cattle sitting in their containers. When the paperwork finally arrived and we were cleared to take our live cargo out of the port, the cattle headcount had dropped to 15 cattle from 100 and that was the end of our business venture.

BOX 4.3

The Islamic Republic of Iran: Privatizations without the Private Sector

Between 2006 and 2010, Iran engaged in a large and wide-ranging privatization program with a goal of privatizing 80 percent of the public sector. The program had the blessings of Ali Khomeini, Iran's leader and supreme jurist, who formulated the 80 percent privatization goal.[a] By late 2009, the government had divested over 800 trillion rials (about US$80 billion) in more than 370 state-owned enterprises (SOEs), including petrochemical plants, fuel refineries, airlines, banks, insurance companies, telecommunication companies, and so forth. However, in 2010 an Iranian parliamentary commission on privatization found that among all the SOE assets divested since 2006, only about 13 percent of the shares went to the private sector. The remainder of the shares was transferred to what constitutes the pseudo or parastatal state, including military firms, pension funds, state-linked investment and holding companies, endowed foundations, and recipients of the "Justice Shares" program. Harris (2013) shows how different political economy factors have shaped the pseudo-privatization process in Iran and the distribution of privatized assets to various constituencies between 2006 and 2010.

"Justice Shares" and the social politics of privatization. Following his election in 2005, President Mahmoud Ahmadinejad announced that the SOE privatization program, legitimated by Iran's supreme leader through an executive order, would move forward but with the benefits distributed to the people via a program called "Justice Shares." The program was designed such that the bottom six income deciles of the population were eligible to buy "justice shares" of the privatized SOEs; the bottom two income

(continued on next page)

BOX 4.3 *Continued*

deciles were able to buy shares at half their face value, and the third to sixth deciles were permitted to buy "justice shares" at full price (payable over 10 years). However the program was expanded to various groups while it was implemented; these included low-income villagers and nomads, public sector retirees, beneficiaries of the Imam Khomeini Relief Committee and other welfare organizations, and families with martyr status. These groups represented already existing categories of beneficiaries within the Iranian welfare system. The Iranian Parliament Research Center found that among 264 privatized SOEs initially valued at US$54 billion, over 68 percent of shares went to "justice shares." Harris (2013) further argues that Ahmadinejad's push for privatization constituted a strategic component of the president's public relations campaign against its critics.

Pension funds and pseudo-privatization: Harris (2013) suggests that pension financing in Iran created a sizable interest group for pseudo-privatization, namely the Iranian middle class and formal labor force. Fiscal pressures because of an overly generous system pushed the Social Security Organization (SSO) to become more active in the acquisition of SOEs, both in the stock market and in negotiations over government debt. In 2001, for example, the government transferred assets worth US$400 million to the SSO to cover mandated obligations to pensioners. In 2011, the SSO claimed that the fund was owed nearly US$24 billion by the government, pointing to a high likelihood of future demands for pseudo-privatization from the SSO and other pension funds.

Privileged access to SOE privatization for the military. The military establishment (retired and acting) benefitted largely from privileged access to privatized SOEs from 2006 to 2009. Harris (2013) documents how large divestment scandals involving privileged access to privatization for the military made front pages amid post-election street demonstrations in 2009. For example, 51 percent of the Telecommunications Company of Iran was sold to a conglomerate linked to the Islamic Revolutionary Guards Corps Cooperative Foundation, a large investment company and service contractor. The auction was limited to only two bidders, with the second linked to the *Basij* (voluntary militia) investment cooperative. Hence, two military parastatals were competing for a major share in the lucrative domestic telecom market. The International Exposition Center was also transferred to the Armed Forces Social Security Organization.[b]

Notes:
a. This section is based on Harris (2013).
b. Harris (2013) also documents how the engineering arm of the Islamic Revolutionary Guards Corps, Hatam al-Anbiya, (which emerged during the Iran-Iraq war and was subsequently involved in postwar reconstruction) has over the past decade (along with its subcontractors) replaced foreign firms in the development of oil and gas fields, pipeline projects and highway and tunnel construction.

Public perceptions of corruption in business are strongly correlated with perceptions of government corruption in MENA. The favors exchanged between business and political elites include official bribes, illegal funding of political campaigns, and the manipulation of the financial markets for the benefit of both firm and government insiders.

These favors have sometimes also been documented in the media, influencing public opinions. figure 4.7 reveals the consequences: public perceptions of corruption in business are strongly correlated with perceptions of government corruption. As a result, popular perceptions about business elites became negative in the region in the years before the recent uprisings. For example, a Pew survey reveals that in 2010 corruption was the top concern of Egyptians, with 46 percent listing it as their main concern, even ahead of a lack of democracy or poor economic conditions.

Also, changes in the corruption ratings of MENA countries in the overall Transparency International corruption index confirm popular perceptions. In 2005, Egypt ranked 70, Tunisia ranked 43, Libya ranked 117, and the Republic of Yemen ranked 103, out of 158 rankings on TI's Corruption Perceptions Index (CPI). Perceived corruption increased markedly in the following three years. In 2008, Egypt dropped to 115, Tunisia to 62, Libya to 126 and the Republic of Yemen to 141, out of 180 rankings on the CPI.

Governance indicators suggest that MENA lags behind other regions. The World Bank Governance Indicators measure government effectiveness, regulatory quality, the rule of law, and control of corruption. Figure 4.8 reports the relative performance of MENA countries. MENA countries are typically ranked in the bottom 40 percent worldwide in all four dimensions.

FIGURE 4.7

Perceptions of Corruption in Government and Business, Middle East and North Africa, 2011

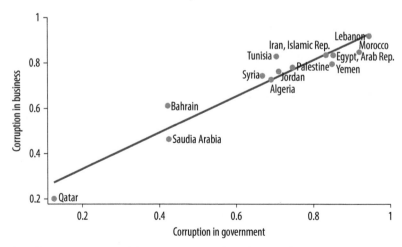

Source: Transparency International Corruption Perception Index; in Diwan (2012).

FIGURE 4.8

Worldwide Governance Indicators

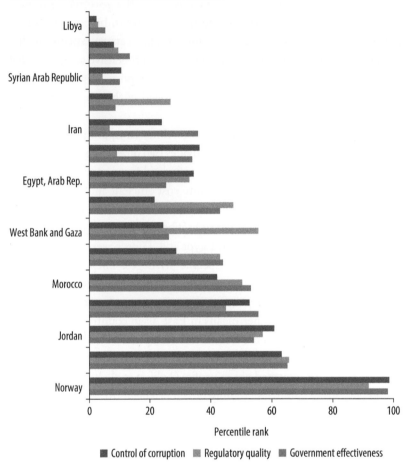

Source: World Bank's Worldwide Governance Indicators 2012.
Note: Normalized to 1–100.

What Explains the Different Outcomes in MENA and East Asia?

The Extent to Which Political Connections Hampered Competition Differed in MENA and East Asia

The analysis suggests that privileges limit job creation in MENA. The report provides novel empirical evidence on how business regulations in MENA countries are distorted to protect the interests of a few politically connected firms. The results further suggest that these political privileges tend to reduce competition and job creation.

However, the occurrence of politically connected firms is not specific to MENA economies. There is also evidence that politically connected firms were common among East Asian countries at the time when their economies started to grow at double-digit rates (see the discussion on the Republic of Korea in chapter 3). What is more, the governance framework of East Asian countries at the time appears to be comparable to governance levels among MENA countries. How can we explain the different experiences of these two regions? A comprehensive answer to this important question is beyond the scope of this report. Nevertheless, the theoretical and empirical framework employed in this chapter point to potential explanations.

The extent to which political connections hampered competition differed in both regions. Chapter 3 provides two different arguments that politically connected firms in East Asia indeed faced more competitive pressures, forcing them to become more cost efficient and grow.

First, there is evidence that political connections were not sufficient for East Asian firms to escape competition. The previous analysis has shown that politically connected firms in Egypt and Tunisia were able to transform their connections into firm-specific privileges. They found ways to exclude their competitors from access to these privileges and made higher profits. Chapter 3, however, suggests that government support in the form of subsidies, credit, and other means in East Asian countries was granted at the industry rather than the firm level. Thus, politically connected firms still encountered higher domestic competition and higher firm entry into their sectors once they made high profits (Aghion et al. 2012).

Second, Asian countries credibly linked privileges to performance targets; even those that benefitted insiders and cronies. Chapter 3 documents that in Korea a few large businesses families controlled large parts of the economy. These families were often also politically connected through family members in high positions in the ruling party or the bureaucracy (Kang, p. 189). "Privileges to Politically Connected Firms Undermine Competition and Job Creation: Evidence from the Arab Republic of Egypt and Tunisia" section reveals similar structures in Mubarak's Egypt.[42] Nevertheless, chapter 3 provides evidence that in East Asia politically connected firms still had to meet performance (export) targets to continue to benefit from industrial policies.

Taiwan, China, provides an example of the enforcement of performance targets in East Asia. It conditioned its sector subsidies on performance criteria, such as export growth, and performance was regularly reviewed. One target sector, the video industry, fell slightly below its target growth and the government withdrew support. As a result, three large firms went bankrupt and in contrast to other East Asian countries, the industry never developed in Taiwan, China. However, the example sent a clear signal to firms in all other sectors that benefitted from industrial policy support.

East Asia's export orientation exposed firms to competition in highly contested global markets. Even if politically connected firms faced only a few domestic competitors, which was the case initially in Korea, they had to meet credible performance targets to continue to benefit from government support. To a certain extent, this policy offset the initial lack of domestic competition. In other words, East Asian governments imported competition through their focus on exports. The destination of exports may also have mattered. East Asian firms targeted highly contested export markets in the US and EU. In contrast, manufacturing exporters in the Middle East often target local market niches in other Middle Eastern or African markets, which are typically less contested. For example, pharmaceutical companies in Jordan are the only foreign firms that are allowed to sell medicines in Algeria.

In other words, sector-specific policies in East Asia tended to offset governance challenges whereas in MENA sector-specific policies may have reinforced those challenges. Thus, while the overall governance framework was comparable in both regions, there is evidence that East Asian countries designed industrial policy to mitigate policy distortions in the few targeted sectors, while firm-directed industrial policies worsened policy distortions in MENA. Moreover, chapter 3 argues that the costs of catering to vested interests for government officials were higher in East Asia because bureaucrats were committed to, and benefitted directly from economic growth.

In a Schumpeterian world, the impact of privileges to politically connected firms on growth also depends on countries' barriers to innovation. The process of foreign technology adoption is costly and risky. Therefore, firms are likely to use cheaper options to escape competition if they exist. Political connections provide such an option. More specifically, in the Schumpeterian growth framework, firms are more likely to use their connections if the expected costs of seeking policy protection are lower than the costs of innovating. The argument essentially indicates that the costs to lobby for policy protection were higher in East Asian countries because of their industrial policy design and complementary reforms of the public sector. At the same time, however, firms are also more likely to rely on their political connections to escape competition if they face higher barriers to innovate. Thus, for any given level of governance, growth in a country is more likely to suffer from privileges if firms' costs to innovate are higher. The adopted Schumpeterian growth framework predicts that, among two regions (such as MENA and East Asia) with the same level of governance, the adverse impact of privileges on growth is stronger in the region where firms' face higher costs to innovate. Given a higher regulatory burden for firms to innovate and MENA countries' weaker integration into global markets (through trade or FDI), we should expect higher costs for MENA firms.

Notes

1. The methodologies and additional country-specific analysis are described in detail in the corresponding companion papers of this report including Diwan, Keefer, and Schiffbauer (2014); Rijkers, Freund, and Nucifora (2014).
2. See chapter 3 for a detailed review of Egypt industrial policy program at the time.
3. The Egyptian military implicitly or explicitly agreed on all government land sales, as they had a de facto veto right to any land deal. The Egyptian Minister of Defense can intervene to block a land deal—especially in coastal areas—if the land is considered strategically important by the military.
4. The group of Ben Ali firms is highly. While three connected firms feature in the list of the 10 largest firms in Tunisia, 100 connected firms did not report using any paid laborers at any point in time. Some such firms may have served as shell companies for money laundering or to benefit from tax breaks.
5. Out of the 32 PC businessmen, 18 had high political posts after 2002 (either in the ruling party or in the government) and controlled 307 of the 469 firms we ultimately identified as connected. Among the other 14 businessmen, the most important ones are long-term friends of Hosni Mubarak from his military period or cofounders of a large investment bank partly owned by a Cyprus registered company said to be owned by the Mubarak family.
6. Many large firms were listed at stock exchanges in Egypt, since gains from selling shares of listed companies are exempted from taxation. Reportedly, several politically connected firms exploited this legal tax loophole to avoid paying taxes for takeovers; that is, instead of selling firms directly, which is taxable, the transaction was conducted as an untaxed market transaction by first listing the company for sale at the stock exchange (Ahram Online, various issues).
7. Note that these types of political connections can be ranked according to their restrictiveness. The incentive of the connected individual to leverage connections on behalf of the firm is strongest if he is the CEO of the company (almost all politically connected CEOs also own at least part of their companies). It is less strong for politically connected owners and weakest for any type of connected firms for which we also include firms which received significant investments from politically connected private equity firms. Of course, it also matters how "close" the political connection is to the businessman. However, we do not have information to distinguish between different types of connections, as all connected businessman are considered to have first-tier political influence over regulations and their implementation.
8. Employment is observed for about 20,000 establishments, while operating revenues and profits are only available for about 700 and 400 large establishments, respectively.
9. We pool all available surveys for Egypt between 2004 and 2008 in order to maximize the representativeness of the perceived policy data at the sector level. Overall, there are more than 4,200 firms which are aggregated into 90 (ISIC Rev. 3.1) four-digit sectors. We exclude sectors for which we observe less than 4 firms, which produces on average 38 firms per four-digit sector.
10. See Rijkers, Freund, and Nucifora (2014) and Diwan, Keefer, and Schiffbauer (2014) for details. The total share of employment in Egypt is calculated as

the approximate total number of employees in connected firms in 2010 (550,000) relative to the total number of about 7.5 million private sector employees.

11. As in any country, we expect that several firms underreport their output, employment, and profits. It is difficult to assess if connected firms are more or less likely to underreport.

12. The Orbis data for Egypt primarily includes medium and large establishments which are the correct comparison groups when comparing politically connected and unconnected establishments. Large firms are well-distributed among connected and unconnected establishments with available data.

13. The high share of net profits is in part the result of many firms reporting losses. When only firms reporting positive profits are considered, Ben Ali firms account for about 7 percent of all profits.

14. Longer time series data for profits are not available in Orbis. We note that the precision of estimated profit differential in 2003 and 2004 is low because of the few available observations.

15. We note that most of the regulatory privileges favoring connected firms (e.g., energy subsidies to industry or trade protection) are still in place until today. Thus, the decline in the profit differential for connected firms immediately after Mubarak's fall might reflect that other policy privileges (temporarily) disappeared (e.g., implementation bias) or that the new regime at least initially made it generally more difficult for these businessmen to operate in Egypt.

16. In the following, we document only selected channels of policy privileges for which we have available data in Egypt and Tunisia. For example, we neither have sufficiently detailed data on licenses requirements and FDI restrictions for specific sectors in Egypt nor on input subsidies in Tunisia.

17. Wikileaks cables 09TUNIS372_a and 07TUNIS1489-a: see https://wikileaks.org/plusd/cables/09TUNIS372_a.html, https://wikileaks.org/plusd/cables/07TUNIS1489_a.html, accessed February 23, 2013.

18. Wikileaks cable 08TUNIS679_a, https://wikileaks.org/plusd/cables/08TUNIS679_a.html, accessed February 23, 2013.

19. One issue we encountered was matching the activities listed in the Investment Code to specific five-digit sectors, which do not perfectly overlap. In some cases, the Investment Code provides a more detailed description of activities, whereas in others, the code is more general than the Tunisian NAT 96 classification that we use. With the help of officials at the Tunisian Institut National de la Statistique we created a correspondence between activities and sectors, but in some cases multiple activities were mapped to the same sector and vice versa. As a consequence, it is possible for some sectors to be subjected to several regulations of the same kind.

20. Note that the number of observations on these variables is limited to 64 because we confine attention to enterprises operating in sectors in which the investment code is binding; this reduces the nonconnected firm sample to 70,259. This amounts to about 55 percent of the full sample for both connected and nonconnected firms. The regressions are also confined to this group of firms.

21. In order to test this hypothesis, we first match data on NTMs (at the six-digit product level harmonized system classification) from the World Bank data set with the Orbis data (which is at the four-digit industry level). The NTM

measures are available for tradable goods, corresponding broadly to the manufacturing and mining industries. We therefore limit the analysis of NTMs to these 147 sectors. Our data includes 200 politically connected firms operating in at least one of these sectors.

22. Industrial zones in Egypt include qualified industrial zones (QIZs) which guarantee firms duty and quota free exports to the U.S. Abdel-Latif and Nugent (2010) review the impact of QIZs in Egypt and find that large firms disproportionally benefit from the QIZ agreement: in the 17 industrial zones hosting QIZ factories, 88 percent of exports are concentrated in firms with more than 500 workers. Textiles and garments account for 89 percent of QIZ exports, followed by plastics and chemicals.

23. The WBES data include firm-level data for 95 four-digit (ISIC Rev. 3.1) sectors, including 84 manufacturing and 11 services sectors. All of the 11 four-digit services sectors include multiple connected firms (in hotels and restaurants, retail and wholesale trade), so we restrict the analysis to the four-digit manufacturing sectors including 3,040 firms.

24. We use the following regression model: $Pol_{is} = \beta_c\ connected_s + \beta_s\ Size_{is} + \beta_{cs}\ connected_s * Size_{is} + \beta_X X_{is} + \beta_{St} S + \varepsilon_{is}$. The dependent policy variable Pol_{is} is a dummy variable for firm i in the four-digit sector s. It is 1 if the firm bought land from the government or it is located in an industrial zone, respectively, and zero otherwise; *connected* measures the number of politically connected firms by type in the four-digit sector s. *Size* is the dummy variable *Small*, which is equal to 1 if the firm has less than 100 employees and zero otherwise. X_{is} is a matrix of firm level control variables: age, export share, S is a matrix of two-digit sector dummies. If we include the dummy variable "*Small*" for the "Size" variable, β_c measures if large firms' access to land is different in sectors with more connected firms while measures if large firms' access differs from small firms' access in sectors with more politically connected firms relative to sectors without (or fewer) political connections. See Diwan, Keefer, and Schiffbauer (2014) for more details.

25. Overall, 85 percent of manufacturing firms with available employment data have at least 100 employees. In contrast, among all manufacturing firm in the WBES, only 33 percent have at least 100 employees (on average, we observe about 12 large firms in a four-digit manufacturing sector in the WBES data). Thus, large firms in the WBES data are much more likely to be politically connected. We also tested for differences in firm age between connected and unconnected sectors. However, the age distribution of politically connected firms and all firms in the WBES data are very similar; the median age among the former is 18, and among all WBES firms it is 19.

26. Table 4.4 also shows that the share of output directly sold to the government is 5–7 percent higher for firms in politically connected sectors indicating that connected firms have preferential access to government procurement contracts.

27. The following results are based on a regression model analog to the ones testing for access to government land but using waiting time for construction permits as the dependent variable. See Diwan, Keefer, and Schiffbauer (2014) for more details.

28. The results are based on regression analysis, including interaction terms between the number of NTM restrictions (at the industry level) or a dummy

for high energy intensive industries and a dummy variable indication if a firm is politically connected or not. This framework allows testing the hypothesis that connected firms outperform their competitors when trade protection or energy subsidies are prevalent. The sample is confined to 2003–11 because of lack of profits and output data in earlier years. See Diwan, Keefer, and Schiffbauer (2014) for more details.

29. In some sectors we observe several politically connected firms, which could in principle lead to competition among them. Instead, however, we observe a web of intertwined ownership structures and co-investments among politically connected firms. For example, the 6 (10) most intertwined businessmen together control stakes directly or indirectly in 240 (322) firms. In addition, 85 firms (18 percent) managed or owned by a connected businessman received significant investments from private equity funds controlled by *other* politically connected investors. Thus, collusion among politically connected firms is much more likely.

30. The results are based on regression analysis, including interaction terms between authorization requirements and FDI restrictions (at the sector level) and a dummy variable indication if a firm is politically connected or not. This framework allows testing the hypothesis that Ben Ali firms outperform their competitors when regulatory restrictions are prevalent. The sample is confined to activities covered by the investment code. Only firms which report hiring paid workers at some point during the year are included; we exclude the self-employed and those without employees. The sample is confined to 2000–10 because of lack of profits and output data in earlier years. See Rijkers, Freund, and Nucifora (2014) for more details.

31. The following results are based on a regression model analog to the ones testing for access to government land but using the following dependent variable instead: a dummy variable which is equal to one if a firm reports less than 10 competitors in domestic markets and zero otherwise. See Diwan, Keefer, and Schiffbauer (2014) for more details. Comparable data is not available for Tunisia.

32. The analysis is based on the establishment census, which includes more than 2,000,000 establishments across all nonagriculture, nongovernment economic sectors in 1996 and 2006. The entry rates and parameters of the distribution of employment across establishments (coefficient of variation, skewness, and share of micro establishments) are computed at the four-digit sector level and then matched with our information on the number of politically connected firms per sector. Employment weighted entry rates are weighted by the number of employees in entering firms relative to the total number of employees in the four-digit sector. The descriptive statistics are summarized in table 4.6. Moreover, we estimate the effects of the number of connected firms (*connected*) in the four-digit sector s on (changes in the) measures of firm dynamics, e.g., entry, (Z) for sector s, controlling for the average log of the number of employees and the average establishment age (X) as well as sector dummies at the one- or two-digit level b: $Z_{s,2006} = \beta_c\ connected_{s,2006} + \beta_X lnX_{s,2006} + S_B + \varepsilon_{s,2006}$.

33. First, this period witnessed more widespread political connections across sectors. Second, state-business relations intensified as several well-connected businessmen took high political posts, allowing them to directly steer economic policies (Demmelhuber and Roll 2007; Roll 2013).

34. The results are robust when controlling for sector-specific characteristics (e.g., average size and age of establishments in a sector as well as one- or two-digit sector dummies) in a regression framework.
35. Arnold, et al. (2012) document that service trade liberalizations—the removing restrictions on FDI in India's service sectors over the previous decade—led to large productivity gains in downstream using manufacturing industries.
36. The estimation procedure and results are outlined in detail in Appendix E.
37. The estimation is based on establishment census data from 1996 and 2006, including more than 2,000,000 establishments in all nonagriculture, non-government economic sectors. We control for specific sector characteristics such as establishment size and age, and for broad sector dummies in all estimation specifications.
38. These bands are based on scores from an assessment consisting of 77 questions—for each question, the government was scored from 0 to 4. TI considered a range of institutions in each country: the defense and security ministries, and armed forces in each country, including any other government institutions with the potential to influence levels of corruption risk in the sector.
39. 4 = high transparency; strong, institutionalized activity to address corruption risks. 3 = generally high transparency; activity to address corruption risks, but with shortcomings. 2 = moderate transparency; activity to address corruption risks with significant shortcomings. 1 = generally low transparency; weak activity to address corruption risks. 0 = low transparency; very weak or no activity to address corruption risks.
40. Civilian businesses and defense companies owned, in whole or part, by the government defense establishment or the armed forces. This does not include private businesses lawfully owned by individuals in the defense establishment.
41. This also explains why we were unable to obtain information on politically connected military firms in sections "Privileges to Politically Connected Firms Undermine Competition and Job Creation: Evidence from the Arab Republic of Egypt and Tunisia" and "The Available Qualitative Evidence Points to Similar Mechanisms of Policy Privileges in Other MENA Countries."
42. One might argue that the political influence of connected businessmen was still stronger in Egypt, since some of these businessmen were ministers and did not have to rely on the influence of family members to direct economic policies.

References

Aghion, P. M., Dewatripont, L. Du, A. Harrison, and P. Legros. 2012. "Industrial Policy and Competition." Mimeo (April 24).

Aghion, P., C. Harris, P. Howitt, and J. Vickers. 2001. "Competition, Imitation and Growth with Step-by-Step Innovation." *The Review of Economic Studies* 68 (3): 467–92.

Alley, April Longley. 2010. "The Rules of the Game: Unpacking Patronage Politics in Yemen". *Middle East Journal* 64 (3): 385–409.

Arnold, Jens, B. Javorcik, M. Lipscomb, and A. Mattoo 2012. "Services Reform and Manufacturing Performance—Evidence From India." Policy Research Working Paper 5948, World Bank, Washington, DC.

Demmelhuber, T., and S. Roll. 2007. "Maintenance of Domination in Egypt: The Role of Reforms and Economic Oligarchs." Stiftung Wissenschaft und Politik (SWP), Deutsches Institut für Internationale Politik und Sicherheit.

Diwan, Ishac. 2012. "A Rational Framework for the understanding of the Arab Revolutions." CID Working Paper 237, Center for International Development, Harvard University, Cambridge, MA.

Diwan, I., and H. Chekir. 2012. "State-Business Relations in Mubarak's Egypt." Mimeo.

Diwan, Ishac, Philip Keefer, and Marc Schiffbauer. 2014. "On top of the Pyramids: Cronyism and Private Sector Growth in Egypt." Working Paper, World Bank, Washington, DC.

Faccio, M. 2007. "Politically Connected Firms." *American Economic Review* 96: 369–86.

Fisman, R. 2001. "Estimating the Value of Political Connections." *American Economic Review* 91: 1095–02.

Haddad, Bassam. 2012. *Business Networks in Syria: The Political Economy of Authoritarian Resilience*. Stanford, CA: Stanford University Press.

Hallward-Driemeier, M., G. Khun-Jush, and L. Pritchett. 2010. "Deals versus Rules: Policy Implementation Uncertainty and Why Firms Hate It." Working Paper 16001, NBER, Cambridge, MA.

Harris, Kevan. 2013. "The Rise of the Subcontractor State: Politics of Pseudo-privatization in the Islamic Republic of Iran." *International Journal of Middle East Studies* 45: 45–70.

Henry, Clement Moore, and Robert Springborg. 2010. *Globalization and the Politics of Development in the Middle East*. Cambridge University Press.

Heydemann, Steven. 2004. *Networks of Privilege in the Middle East: The Politics of Economic Reform Revisited*. New York: Palgrave Macmillan.

Jones, C. 2011. "Intermediate Goods and Weak Links in the Theory of Economic Development." *American Economic Journal: Macroeconomics* 3 (2): 1–28.

Kienle, Eberhard. 2004. "Reconciling Privilege and Reform: Fiscal Policy in Egypt, 1991–2000." In *Networks of Privilege in the Middle East: The Politics of Economic Reform Revised*, edited by Steven Heydemann, 281–96. New York, NY: Palgrave Macmillan.

King, Stephen Juan. 2009. *The New Authoritarianism in the Middle East and North Africa*. Bloomington: Indiana University Press.

Kremer, Michael. 1993. "The O-Ring Theory of Economic Development." *The Quarterly Journal of Economics* 108 (3): 551–75.

Loewe, Markus. 2013. "Industrial Policy in Egypt 2004–2011." DIE Discussion Paper 13/2013, Deutsches Institut fuer Entwicklungspolitik, Bonn.

Malik, Adeel. 2013. "The Economics of the Arab Spring." *World Development* 45: 1–13.

Malouche, Mariem, José-Daniel Reyes, and Amir Fouad. 2013. "New Database of Nontariff Measures Makes Trade Policy More Transparent." Mimeo, World Bank, Washington, DC.

Marotta, Daniela, Christian Ugarte, and Leila Baghdadi. 2014. "Weak Links in Tunisia." Mimeo, World Bank Washington, DC.

Owen, Roger. 2004. "State, Power and Politics in the Making of the Modern Middle East." Routledge.

Rijkers, Bob, Caroline Freund, and Antonio Nucifora. 2014. "All in the Family: State Capture in Tunisia." Working Paper, World Bank, Washington, DC.

Roll, Stephan. 2013. "Egypt's Business Elite after Mubarak: A Powerful Player between Generals and Brotherhood." SWP Research Paper 8 (September), Stiftung Wissenschaft und Politik, Berlin.

Sfakianakis, John. 2004. "The Whales of the Nile: Networks, Businessmen and Bureaucrats during the Era of Privatization in Egypt." In *Networks of Privilege: Rethinking the Politics of Economic Reform in the Middle East*, edited by S. Heydemann. New York: Palgrave Macmillan.

Tlemcani, Rachid. 1999. "Etat, Bazar, et Globalisation: L'Aventure de l'Infitah en Algerie". Algiers: Les Editions El Hikma.

UNIDO. 2010. "Compilation of Energy Statistics for Economic Analysis." Development Policy and Strategic Research Branch Working Paper 01/2010, UNIDO, Vienna.

World Bank. 2009. "From Privilege to Competition: Unlocking the Private-Led Growth in the Middle East and North *Africa*." MENA Development Report. Washington, DC: World Bank.

Implications for Policy

This report shows that the factors holding back formal sector job growth in MENA, such as weak firm entry and exit and low productivity growth, are rooted in a policy environment that favors a few dominant market players and insulates them from competition. The various privileges that such firms capture come at a heavy cost to job creation. Few new firms enter these markets and when they do, they are excluded from these privileges and do not grow. Aggregate job creation is therefore weak, many people stay out of the labor market, or are obliged to find employment in small-scale and low productivity activities.

The roadmap to more jobs in MENA countries cannot therefore stop at a destination that includes only improved supply-side policies—education, wages, job training, and so forth. It must also encompass significant reforms to stimulate labor demand. The findings in this report point to certain critical elements of this roadmap including: (a) removing the costly policies identified in this report; (b) promoting competition, open markets, and equal opportunities for all entrepreneurs; and (c) most critically, ensuring that going forward, policies and the policy administration are aimed at leveling, rather than tilting the playing field. In the rest of this section we discuss these components of the roadmap; however, the specific details will depend on each country case and should include additional policy areas not covered in this report.

First, governments in MENA should reform policies that unduly constrain competition and the ability of entrepreneurs to pursue opportunities on an equal footing. Chapter 1 suggest that if MENA governments want to pursue private sector development programs targeting specific types of firms, they would be well advised to focus on firm age and not firm size as the primer targeting criterion. Chapter 2 identifies a number of policies that lower competition, tilt the playing field and reduce firm entry, productivity growth, and ultimately, job creation in

MENA countries. These policies include energy subsidies to industry; exclusive license requirements to operate in specific sectors; legal barriers to FDI; trade barriers, including nontariff measures; administrative barriers to entry and firm growth; and barriers in access to the judiciary, land, and industrial zones. Moreover, several other policies not analyzed in this report but potentially as important in maintaining a level playing field, should also be considered when dealing with specific country cases, such as barriers to firm entry and exit resulting from restrictive hiring and firing laws, cumbersome bankruptcy laws, and so forth.

Second, policymakers should ensure that state interventions that affect competition and equality of business opportunity for all entrepreneurs are enforced uniformly across firms. The implementation of laws is not consistent for all firms, even when they operate in the same sector. The predominance of not only arbitrary, but predatory decision making in the exercise of administrative discretion discourages entrepreneurship and reduces competition. The even-handed enforcement of laws and regulations demands that public officials have incentives to exercise discretion fairly and transparently, in pursuit of the legitimate aims of public policy. Such incentives are more likely to exist when laws and regulations are clear; policy implementation is simple and predictable; entry and promotions into the administration are based on merit instead of political connections; and when merit is judged on the basis of potential or actual contributions to the legitimate goals of public policy.

Third, if MENA governments want to pursue state-led development policies, they would be wise to avoid past mistakes and ensure that these new industrial policies—and the administrative structure that implements them—minimize the scope for capture, promote competition, and tightly link support to performance. Chapter 3 lists elements of industrial policy design and complementary institutional changes that appear crucial to making industrial policy work. These include far-reaching organizational reforms in the public sector; a focus on correcting market failures and on *new* economic activities where market failures are more likely to have a binding influence; an evaluation system in which the performance of both policies and officials is judged by their effects on economic growth and job creation; and ensuring that all firms and potential entrants in the targeted sector have access to these specific interventions based on their performance.

One critical aspect of this reform agenda is to create the institutions necessary to prevent future capture, thus safeguarding competition and equal opportunities to all entrepreneurs. While several distortive policies could be removed relatively quickly given the political will, the likelihood that other existing or new policies could be captured or serve privileged firms and undermine competition and open markets is high. Faced with external pressure to reform the economy, the Arab Republic of Egypt substantially reduced import tariffs in the early 2000s. However, when one source of privilege disappeared, another emerged: tariffs declined, but nontariff barriers dramatically increased. Table 4.3 showed that these nontariff barriers disproportionally benefitted politically connected firms. To prevent this, policymakers need to build institutions that promote competition and prevent future capture of policies; such institutions include, but are not limited to, a strong, well-organized and highly competent public administration. A strong public administration is necessary to implement the policy changes necessary to build open markets that are resilient to the risk for capture. These policy changes include a strong competition law and an independent competition authority; appropriate procurement laws and implementation; an independent judiciary, and so forth.

Another component, just as important, is to ensure policy making is transparent and open, with processes that allow citizens to participate. Transparency is not a panacea, but it is hard to conceive how institutions that safeguard open markets and competition can emerge without citizen access to information on proposed and ratified laws and regulations; citizen input into policy design and evaluation; citizen knowledge of politicians' stakes in firms that benefit from government policies; and citizen awareness of the beneficiaries of subsidies, procurement tenders, public land transactions, privatizations, and so forth.

Last, this report points to a decision-making guide that summarizes the foregoing, which governments can use as a framework when designing and implementing policies. It is also important when using this framework to recognize that policymaking faces risk and uncertainty as to which policies will work and achieve its objectives. The decision-making guide is aimed to maximize the likelihood of success given inherent uncertainties and maximize the positive impact of policies on growth and jobs by ensuring that they respond to real obstacles to job growth while minimizing the risk for capture. The decision-making guide suggests that any development policy should pass the following questions; a negative response to one of the subsequent questions raises a red flag indicating that the proposed policy could lead to inefficient and inequitable outcomes ultimately failing to create jobs:

1. Does the policy seek to provide a good or service currently not available in the country in an economically efficient and sustainable manner?

2. Do all potential market participants have equal access to the benefits of the policy?

3. Are the benefits of the policy reversible if rigorous performance measures are not met?

4. Will the bureaucracy and courts implement the policy accurately, fairly, transparently?

Policy Making Affecting the Private Sector: Decision-Making Flow Chart

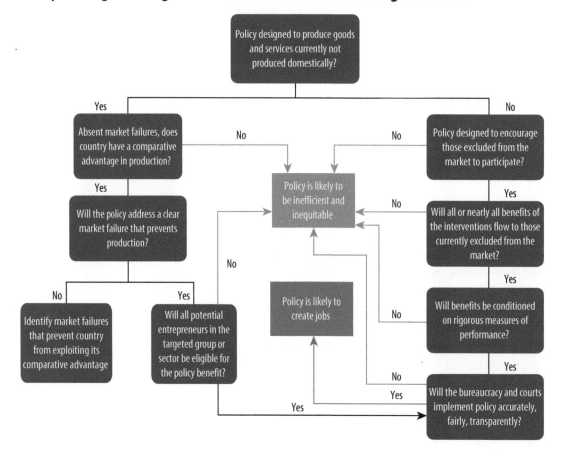

Economic Growth
and Structural Transformation

Our analysis is based on data on employment, value added, and labor productivity by sector for a panel of 35 countries, of which seven countries are from the Middle East and North Africa (MENA) region. Nominal value added is converted to value added in constant purchasing power parity (PPP) terms using the PPP conversation factor from Penn World Tables Revision 7.1. Labor productivity for sector i is calculated as value add in constant PPP terms of sector i divided by employment of sector i. The data set expands data used by Timmer and de Vries (2009) and McMillan and Rodrik (2011), by adding newly compiled statistics for MENA countries.

Our time series on value added, price deflators, and employment by sector for MENA countries is constructed from available statistical sources. We follow the methodology developed by Timmer and de Vries (2009), also used by McMillan and Rodrik (2011), using national data which tends to be harmonized in terms of industry classifications. Gross value added in current and constant prices is taken from the national accounts of the various countries. In recent years, value added series have been compiled according to the 1993 United Nations System of National Accounts (UN SNA, see UN 1993). So, international comparability is, in principle, high. We follow Timmer and de Vries (2009) and McMillan and Rodrik (2011) as closely as possible to construct a data set for the main 9 sectors according to the definition of 2nd revision of the internal standard industrial classification (ISIC, rev. 2). These nine sectors are 1) agriculture, hunting, forestry and fishing; 2) mining and quarrying; 3) manufacturing; 4) public utilities (electricity, gas, and water); 5) construction; 6) wholesale and retail trade, hotels and restaurants; 7) transport, storage and communications; 8) finance, insurance, real estate and business services; and 9) community, social, personal, and government services. We also use data from population censuses as well as labor surveys to estimate sector employment, which captures here all persons employed in a particular sector, independent of their formality status or whether they are self-employed.

We received employment data from the Central Agency for Public Mobilization and Statistics for the Arab Republic of Egypt using the ISIC Rev. 3 classification for 1998, 2006 and 2012 and linearly projected employment data for the periods 1999–2005 and 2007–11. Employment for Morocco comes from the population census, for Tunisia from the National Employment Survey (Enquête Nationale de l'Emploi), and includes public and informal employment. We complement this data with information on the level of education of workers by sector for Tunisia, Morocco, and Jordan.

Labor productivity growth in terms of change in output per worker can be decomposed into within-sector change and changes across sectors, or structural change. Structural change captures the contribution of real-location of labor (or change in sector weights) to growth. This can be written as:

$$\Delta y_t = \sum_N s_{i,t-k} \, \Delta y_{it} + \sum_N y_{i,t} \, \Delta s_{it}$$

where Δy_t is the change in aggregate labor productivity between t and t–k, s_{it} is the employment in sector i at time t and y_{it} is the productivity level in sector i at time t. The first term is the "within" component and the second term the "across" component (figure 1.13). Economy-wide labor productivity is thus decomposed into two parts. The first

FIGURE A.1

Real GDP Per Capita Growth Decomposition

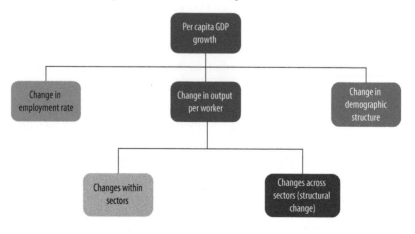

FIGURE A.2

Long-Term Structural Change in Four MENA Countries

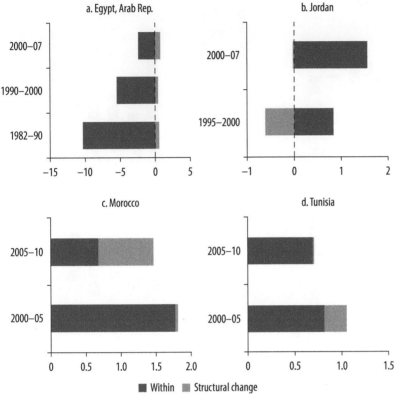

Source: World Bank data.

component measures the change in labor productivity that is due to changes in sectoral labor productivity, and it captures how labor productivity evolved under constant employment shares across sectors. The second component captures the impact of structural change on labor productivity development. It measures the counter-factual productivity level that was reached if sectoral productivity levels remained unchanged and only shifts in labor across sectors change productivity.

Marginal Productivity of Labor

The aforementioned analysis of structural change has been based on average productivity. To pass judgment on whether this change was welfare improving and growth promoting, however, would require a

FIGURE A.3

Structural Change, by Sector, 2000–05

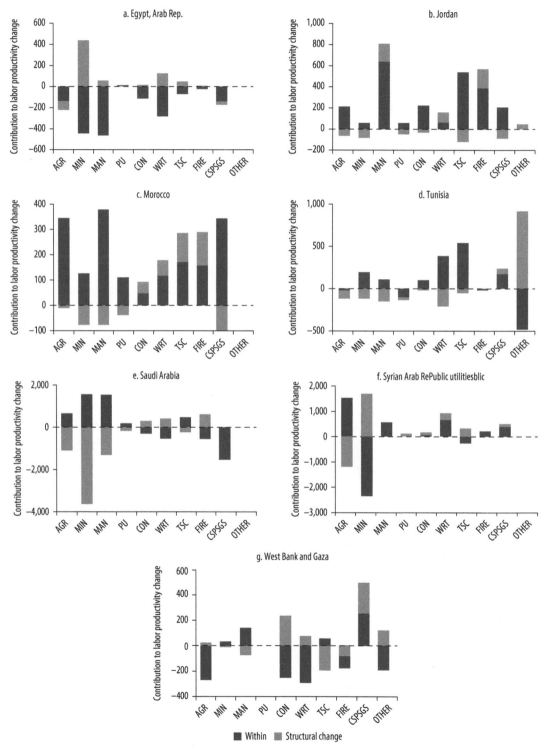

Note: AGR = agriculture; MIN = mining; MAN = manufacturing; PU = public utilities; CON = construction; WRT = wholesale and retail trade; TSC = transports and communication; FIRE = financial and business-oriented services; CSPSGS = community and family-oriented services; OTHER = other sector.

more in-depth analysis.[1] One important step in this direction is to look at marginal productivity across sectors. Under perfect competition, marginal labor productivity—not average productivity—should be equalized across sector. Assuming a constant returns production function, since labor share are not necessarily negatively correlated with average productivity, large gaps in average productivity may reflect large gaps in marginal labor productivity. There are some caveats though. For example, high average labor productivity in capital-intensive sectors, such as mining, may simply reflect that the labor share is low.

The marginal productivity of labor can be calculated by estimating the labor share of income. Using World Bank I2D2 data, we calculated the income share of labor using wage data for Tunisia and Egypt, the only two countries with reliable wage data.[2] In a perfectly competitive market, wages equal the marginal product of labor. Labor markets are often not perfectly competitive, for example, in the presence of unionization or indexed contracts. Moreover, in many developing countries some workers, such as those in the agricultural sector household employees are only paid partially in wages. Using wages to calculate labor's share of income automatically leads to an exclusion of self-employed. To eliminate biases arising from unobserved heterogeneity, the data is narrowed down to a subset of workers. The marginal labor productivities are calculated for single males aged 30–34 years with elementary education. The wage data is adjusted for the rural-urban price differential.

The share of labor force in paid employment is particularly low in agriculture. In Egypt, only 12.1 percent of the agriculture labor force was in paid employment in 2006, declining from 14.3 in 1998 (table A.1). In Tunisia, agriculture is also the sector with the lowest share of the labor force in paid employment, though at 28.2 percent in 2001. The sectors with the highest share of the labor force in paid employment are public utilities and mining.

Gaps in marginal productivities measured by average wages across sectors are smaller than gaps measured by value added per worker, but sectoral differences remain significant. In 1998 in Egypt, the gap between the highest productivity sector (mining) and the lowest productivity sector (community services) was 57, while the difference in raw wages between the minimum (agriculture) and maximum (financial intermediation) wage was only 2.2. The difference becomes even smaller when controlling for individual characteristics, shrinking to 1.5. However, this gap between wages has increased in Egypt. In 2006, an individual with the same characteristics and education would have earned nearly 2.5 half times more if she would have moved from agriculture (the lowest wage sector) to mining (the highest wages sector).

TABLE A.1

Estimates of Labor's Share and Marginal Productivities Using Harmonized Household Survey Data from the World Bank (I2D2)

Country	Year	Sector	Code	Value added per capita		Average wages (raw differences)		Average wages (controlling for individual characteristics)[a]		Average wages (controlling for additional individual characteristics)[b]		Labor force in paid employment, %	Employment share in I2D2, %
				In 2005 PPP dollars	Employment in national accounts share %	In 2005 PPP dollars	Implied labor share (pc), %	In 2005 PPP dollars	Implied labor share (pc), %	In 2005 PPP dollars	Implied labor share (pc), %		
Egypt, Arab Rep.	1998	Agriculture	agr	6,320	29.7	1,447	22.9	1,394	19.3	1,448	19.4	14.3	40.5
		Mining	min	298,623	0.5	2,681	0.9	1,642	0.9	1,694	0.9	95.5	0.2
		Manufacturing	man	12,642	11.5	2,281	18.0	1,837	19.5	1,899	19.5	81.3	11.9
		Public utilities	pu	21,056	0.8	2,737	13.0	1,734	13.7	1,797	13.7	100.0	0.7
		Construction	con	7,888	6.9	2,188	27.7	1,929	29.4	2,002	29.4	87.8	5.3
		Commerce	wrt	19,262	10.5	2,032	10.5	1,835	13.6	1,898	13.6	36.0	11.9
		Transports and communications	tsc	16,908	4.3	2,586	15.3	1,823	16.7	1,882	16.7	81.7	4.5
		Financial and business-oriented services	fire	14,529	1.4	3,247	22.4	1,929	24.3	2,002	24.3	84.2	1.5
		Community and family-oriented services	cspsgs	5,221	34.5	1,856	35.6	1,304	37.8	1,351	37.8	95.3	23.5
	2006	Agriculture	agr	6,166	27.3	1,646	26.7	1,654	22.3	1,712	22.3	12.1	38.4
		Mining	min	229,672	0.8	5,623	2.4	3,935	2.7	4,083	2.7	89.6	0.2
		Manufacturing	man	8,138	12.7	2,631	32.3	2,104	33.6	2,169	33.6	73.2	11.6
		Public utilities	pu	25,656	0.8	3,520	13.7	2,163	14.3	2,235	14.3	98.7	0.7
		Construction	con	6,287	7.8	2,667	42.4	2,294	44.9	2,366	44.9	82.0	6.3
		Commerce	wrt	18,278	11.6	2,397	13.1	2,267	16.9	2,337	16.9	45.3	14.5
		Transports and communications	tsc	16,420	4.7	3,379	20.6	2,592	21.5	2,675	21.5	79.2	5.8
		Financial and business-oriented services	fire	13,978	1.4	3,680	26.3	2,393	29.4	2,475	29.5	77.7	2.2
		Community and family-oriented services	cspsgs	5,137	33.0	2,583	50.3	1,697	53.3	1,754	53.3	96.9	19.6
Tunisia	2001	Agriculture	agr	9,036	21.8	249	2.8	249	2.5	215	2.6	28.2	22.0
		Mining	min	109,239	0.6	782	0.7	406	0.8	353	0.8	95.6	0.5
		Manufacturing	man	12,302	18.2	380	3.1	315	3.4	272	3.4	80.7	20.5
		Public utilities	pu	34,167	0.6	408	1.2	310	1.1	268	1.1	90.3	12.8
		Construction	con	6,158	11.9	468	7.6	283	8.3	245	8.3	54.6	3.4
		Commerce	wrt	12,842	17.3	417	3.3	287	3.5	248	3.5	50.7	14.1
		Transports and communications	tsc	30,666	5.8	610	2.0	342	1.9	296	1.9	64.6	5.4
		Financial and business-oriented services	fire	69,077	0.8	837	1.2	365	1.3	314	1.3	98.0	0.8
		Community and family-oriented services	cspsgs	13,169	18.7	592	4.5	308	4.8	267	4.8	93.5	20.3

Source: I2D2; World Bank calculation.

a. Regression results controlling for urban location, gender, age (6-year intervals), marital status, occupation and education level (no education, primary, secondary and postsecondary).

b. Adds household size and number of working members to the previous controls.

A 30–34 year-old male Tunisian worker with primary education, work-ing in an elementary education and living in 6-person household with three working members would have increased his wage 1.6 fold in 2001 by moving from agriculture (the lowest wage sector) to mining (the highest wage sector).

The Productivity in Modern Formal Sectors Converges but Their Labor Shares Remain Small

The decline of the employment share in manufacturing of several MENA countries could potentially slow down their rate of conver-gence. According to Rodrik (2013), labor productivity in formal manufacturing in poorer countries tends to converge to that in high income countries independent of institutions, education, or other growth determinants. Rodrik (2013) argues that this unconditional convergence in formal manufacturing, however, does not imply unconditional aggregate income convergence because of (a) the lack of unconditional convergence in the rest of the economy; and (b) very small and in some developing countries declining (formal) manufac-turing labor shares.

Manufacturing labor productivity in MENA's formal manufactur-ing sector is converging at the same rate as the rest of the world inde-pendent of MENA policies or institutions. Table A.2 (left panel) reports the results of the two main estimation specifications from Rodrik (2013).[3] It shows a convergence rate of 2.9 percent implying that industries that are a tenth of the way to the technology frontier (roughly the bottom 20 percent of industries in the worldwide sample)

TABLE A.2

Manufacturing Labor Productivity Growth Rates

	Rodrik (2013)			Did the speed of convergence differ in manufacturing productivity in MENA?							
	All countries	Countries	Observations	MENA	Oil-importing	Oil	Jordan	Syrian Arab Republic	Egypt, Arab Rep.	Morocco	Tunisia
Baseline	−0.029**	118	2,122	−0.041	−0.037	−0.044	−0.033	−0.039	−0.064**	−0.005**	0.195**
	(−6.95)			(−1.51)	(−0.75)	(−1.05)	(−0.57)	(−0.56)	(−3.21)	(3.30)	(3.49)
Post-1990	−0.029**	104	1,861	−0.037	−0.039	−0.026	−0.033	−0.144**	−0.064**	−0.005**	
	(−7.14)			(−1.01)	(−0.95)	(0.21)	(−0.58)	(−8.32)	(−3.33)	(3.43)	

Source: World Bank calculation.

Note: Columns 2–4 replicate the baseline finding of Rodrik (2013). Columns 5–12 show the convergence rate in manufacturing labor productivity different MENA countries and MENA country groups. Each cell is based on a regression of growth on initial productivity including year-industry dum-mies and a region dummy as well as the interaction term of the region dummy with initial productivity. The coefficient shows the compound conver-gence coefficient (baseline-coefficient + interaction term). Standard errors are clustered at the country level in all specifications.

Significance level: * = 10%, ** = 5%.

experience a convergence boost in their labor productivity growth of 6.7 percentage points per year. In table A.2, we test whether the convergence rate was different in the MENA region. Therefore, we include a region dummy and its interaction term with log initial labor productivity in the corresponding estimation specifications.[4] The coefficient of the interaction term measures whether the convergence rate was differed from the convergence rate across all other countries. The results show that the convergence rate in the MENA region overall was the same as in the rest of the world. There is some evidence that the pace of convergence is slightly lower in oil-exporting countries. Moreover, unconditional convergence of formal manufacturing labor productivity tended to be faster in Egypt and the Syrian Arab Republic but slower in Morocco and Tunisia; in the latter case it did not converge at all.

Unconditional convergence in formal manufacturing in MENA did not lead to aggregate productivity convergence because of the very small and in some countries declining labor share of formal manufacturing in the region. The average labor share of formal manufacturing was as low as 2 percent in Syria, 5 percent in Morocco, and 7 percent in Egypt and Jordan, respectively. Moreover it was declining in Morocco and Egypt between 1995 and 2005.

Do We Observe Specific Patterns of Specialization in Formal Manufacturing in MENA?

We analyze the pattern of specialization and performance of formal sector manufacturing in MENA countries in more detail through the lens of the product space. The product space illustrates the relatedness between products whereby distances between two products represent the similarity between their production structures. Hidalgo et al. (2007) argue that the assets and capabilities needed to produce one good are imperfect substitutes for those needed to produce other goods; in part because the production processes of two goods require similar technology, (intermediate) inputs, or machinery. The authors derive an empirical measure for the relatedness between every pair of 775 four-digit SITC products and show that countries that manufacture more "connected" goods are better positioned to diversify in new (related) products. Figure A.4 presents the raw product space which is a graphical illustration of this measure of the relatedness between products. It reveals the existence of a densely connected industrial core (center) and peripheral clusters, garments (left), textiles (left), or electronics (lower right).

FIGURE A.4

The Product Space

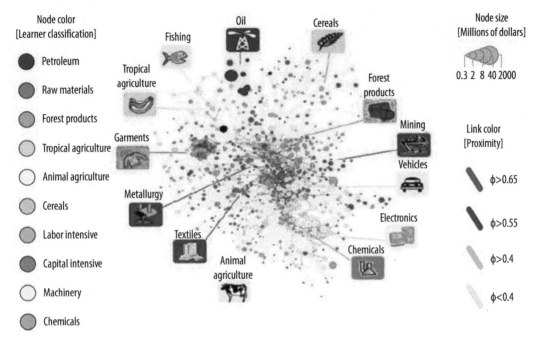

Source: Sahnoun and Schiffbauer 2013.

The comparison with the evolution of the production structures in East Asia reveals a lack of cluster formation among related products or manufacturing subsectors in MENA. Figure A.5 illustrates the product space among lower middle income countries (LMIC) of different regions of the world today and 30 years ago. While the product space itself is the same for all countries (by definition), countries or regions differ in the specialization of products that they successfully export. We follow the authors to use the revealed comparative advantage (RCA) as the measure of export specialization; products in which a country or region has an RCA in exporting are depicted as "black squares." Figure A.5 shows that low middle income countries in MENA had a comparative advantage in exporting oil and agricultural products (upper sparse part of the product space) 30 years ago. Over time, they developed a comparative advantage in processed food (upper left), garments (left), and base metal product clusters (middle left). Thus, MENA (LMIC) countries' prospects to further diversify have improved over the last 30 years. However, a comparison with the evolution of the product spaces among LMICs in East Asia or Latin America reveals that the speed diversification in MENA

FIGURE A.5

Product Space in Selected Regions, 1976–78 and 2007–09

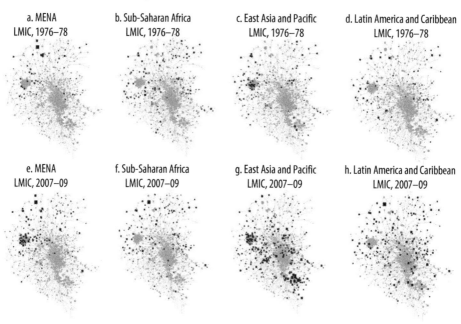

Source: Sahnoun and Schiffbauer 2013.

manufacturing has been lagging. For example, LMICs in East Asia developed export clusters in garments, textiles, electronics, and motor vehicle parts. In contrast, MENA countries did not develop production clusters among related products or manufacturing subsectors (apart from garments).

Notes

1. Not all structural change is good. For example, productivity may be higher in sectors with monopoly power. A reallocation to these sectors would contribute positively to structural change but would not necessarily promote growth or enhance welfare (for a more detailed discussion, see Maloney 2012).

2. See also McMillan (2013) "Measuring the Impact of Structural Change on Labor's Share of Income," unpublished manuscript.

3. We would like to thank Danny Rodrik for sharing the original data and Stata codes of Rodrik (2013) with the authors. We added regression specifications to test for differences in the speed of unconditional manufacturing convergence in Latin America. All potential errors are the responsibility of the authors.

4. Each cell of the table reflects the coefficient (and t-value) of a regression. In all cases, the dependent variable is the (compound annual) growth rate of labor productivity for two-digit manufacturing industries. The explanatory variables are the log of initial labor productivity and industry-year fixed effects. The baseline estimation specification consists of a pooled sample that combines the latest 10-year period for each country with data maximizing the number of countries covered (118). Because each country enters with around 20 industries, the total number of observations is 2,122. The second specification restricts the sample to post-1990 10-year periods while the third is a pure cross section for 1995–2005.

Firm Censuses and Surveys: Countries, Time, and Sector Coverage

The Arab Republic of Egypt: establishment census; all nonagricultural sectors; no size restrictions in repeated cross sections, 1996, 2006; manufacturing establishment census for firms with at least 10 employees, panel 2007–11.

We use two main establishment census data sets. The data are obtained from the department of statistics in Egypt (Central Agency for Public Mobilization and Statistics). First, the establishment census covers information on employment and firm characteristics of over 2,000,000 and 2,400,000 (nonfarm) economic establishments for the repeated cross-sections in 1996 and 2006, respectively. It covers all economic establishments with a fixed location independent of their size; it includes self-employed. Second, we use the annual industrial production survey between 2007 and 2011 also obtained from the Central Agency for Public Mobilization and Statistics. It includes all surviving establishments with at least 10 employees in manufacturing and mining as well as a sample of smaller establishments. The data are in panel format so that we are able to follow individual firms over time. However, given that we only observe firm exit in 2011, we cannot compute firm turnover between 2007 and 2010. The industrial production survey includes various production variables such as value added and capital (fixed assets) allowing us to compute firm productivity. We used two-digit sector output and added value price indices to deflate production and added value. For more details, see Hussain and Schiffbauer (2014).

Jordan: establishment census; all nonagricultural sectors; no size restrictions; repeated cross section, 2006, 2011; panel data with sampling weights available for 15,470 establishments.

The establishment census data are obtained from the Department of Statistics in Jordan. The census covers information on employment, capital, and firm characteristics of about 150,000 (nonfarm) economic establishments in 1996 and 2006. Information on establishments' output (revenues) is not available (establishments only report if their revenues are within a certain range). The census covers all nonagricultural economic establishments with a fixed location independent of their size; it includes self-employed. Panel data are available for a subsample of 15,470 establishments which are observed in both years. Thus, we do not observe firm exit. Sampling weights are available for these firms allowing us to compute changes in the variables between 2006 and 2011 representing all establishments (operating in both years). We used two-digit sector output and added value price indices to deflate production and added value. For more details, see Al-Kadi (2014).

Lebanon: firm census; all nonagricultural sectors formal firms with a unique tax identifier; no size restrictions; panel 2005–10.

The firm census data are obtained from the department of statistics in Lebanon. It includes only firms that to valid tax identifier with the federal tax administration. The census covers information on employment, value added, capital, wages, and firm characteristics of about 150,000 (nonfarm) economic establishments from 2005–10; it includes private sector establishments with a fixed location independent of their size (including self-employed). We used two-digit sector output and added value price indices to deflate production and added value.

Morocco: manufacturing firm census, mostly firms with at least 10 employees; panel 1996–2006.

The database used originates from the yearly survey conducted by the Ministry of Industry and Trade. This survey covers all manufacturing firms with at least 10 employees or with an annual turnover that exceeds 100,000 MAD (about US$11,000). It collects firm level data on a set of variables such as turnover, output, value added, exports, gross labor cost, and the number of permanent and temporary employees. It does not include capital (fixed assets). The survey has almost universal coverage of manufacturing firms across all sectors and areas of the country, with approximately 90% of firms responding.[1] On average 7,082 firms were interviewed each year during the sample period of which 536 were new firms and 412 had exited. We used two-digit sector output and added value price indices to deflate production and added value. For more details, see Sy (2013).

Tunisia: firm census; all nonagricultural sectors; no size restrictions; panel 1997–2012.

We use two main firm census data sets. First, the Tunisian registry of firms, the Répertoire National des Entreprises, 1996–2010 collected by the Tunisian Institut National de la Statistique. The Répertoirc National des Entreprises draws on information from a host of constituent administrative databases including from the social security fund (Caisse Nationale de la Sécurité Sociale—CNSS), which is the source for the employment data, as well as from Tunisian Customs, the Tunisian Ministry of Finance, and the Tunisian Investment Promotion Agency (l'Agence de Promotion de l'Industrie et de l'Innovation), containing data on all firms registered with the tax authorities (see Institut National de la Statistique 2012) for detailed information on its construction). It has information on inter alia the employment, age and main activity of all registered private nonagricultural firms, except cooperatives. The census covers all nonagricultural private sector firms with a fixed location independent of their size; it includes self-employed. In 2010, the census data contained information on 102,660 firms with employees and an additional 501,746 firms without paid employees (the registered self-employed). Second, the Répertoire National des Entreprises was merged with confidential profit and turnover data from the Tunisian Ministry of Finance including private firm tax records for the period 2006 through 2010. The smaller sample of merged data includes production variables such as value added and profits but not capital (fixed assets). We used two-digit sector output and added value price indices to deflate production and added value. For more details, see Rijkers et al. (2014).

West Bank and Gaza: establishment census; all nonagricultural sectors; no size restrictions in repeated cross sections, 2004, 2007, 2012; manufacturing establishment census for firms with at least 10 employees, panel 2004–12.

We use two main establishment census data sets. The data are obtained from the department of statistics in the West Bank (Palestinian Central Bureau of Statistics). First, the establishment census covers information on employment and firm characteristics of over 80,000 (nonfarm) economic establishments in 2003, 2007, and 2012. Information on establishment age (i.e., year of creation) is not available. It covers all economic establishments with a fixed location independent of their size; it includes self-employed. Second, we use the annual industrial production survey between 2004 and 2012. The data are in panel format so that we are able to follow individual firms over time. The industrial production survey includes various production variables such as value added and capital (fixed assets) allowing us to compute firm productivity. We used two-digit sector output and added value price indices to deflate production and added value.

Turkey: employment and firm characteristics for all firms; no size restrictions in repeated cross sections 2005–10; annual panel 2005–10 with production variables for all firms with at least 20 employees.

The Annual Industry and Service Statistics (AISS) provides detailed information on revenue, costs, employment, investment, sector of activity, and the region of location. The census covers more than 2,400,000 nonagricultural private sector firms with a fixed location independent of their size; it includes self-employed. The AISS does not cover the following sectors: Agriculture, hunting and forestry (A), Fishing (B), Financial Intermediation (J), Public administration and defense; compulsory social security (L), Other community, social and personal service activities (O), Activities of households (P), Extraterritorial organizations and bodies (Q). The AISS data set covers production variables for all firms with 20 or more employees, and a representative sample of small firms with 1–19 employees (AISS provides sampling weights). However, all firms with more than one plant (regardless of number of employees) are covered if they are in one of the following sectors: mining and quarrying (C), electricity, gas and water supply (E) and transport, storage and communications (I). The AISS data set does not contain information on physical capital stocks. We use depreciation allowances to impute capital stocks at the firm level. We used two-digit sector output and added value price indices to deflate production and added value. For more details, see Atiyas and Bakis (2014).

Note

1.　The high response rate can be attributed to the rigorous manner in which the survey is conducted. Each year, firms are sent (via post) a questionnaire to complete. Firms failing to complete this questionnaire are then visited by officials from the Ministry of Industry, Commerce and Productivity (MICP) in order to conduct a face-to-face interview.

Share of Employment in Large Firms among State-Owned Enterprises and Foreign Firms

Jordan's, and to a lesser extent Tunisia's, relatively high concentration of employment in large firms is in part explained by higher inflows of foreign direct investment. That is, 19 percent of all large firms in Jordan and Tunisia are foreign owned (figure C.1).[1] These firms account for 30 and 19 percent of employment generated by large establishment in both countries, respectively.[2]

The contribution of large domestic private sector firms to total employment in economic establishments in the Arab Republic of Egypt

FIGURE C.1

Number of Firms and Jobs in Foreign, Domestic Private, or Public Establishments

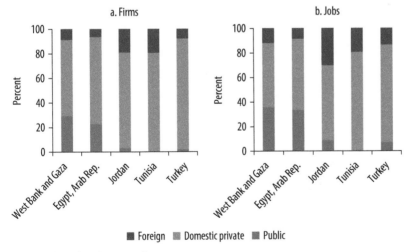

Source: Calculation based on census data.

Note: Large firms have at least 100 employees. Establishments are defined as public or foreign if at least 10 percent of the capital was owned by the state or foreign owners, respectively. In the Arab Republic of Egypt, we added establishments that are foreign branches according to their legal status. In West Bank and Gaza, we added establishments with a legal status of a domestic nongovernmental organization to public establishments; these are the majority of public establishments in West Bank and Gaza.

and West Bank and Gaza is marginal even by regional standards. These firms accounted for less than 10 percent of total employment in Egypt and West Bank and Gaza in the late 2000s (figure C.1). Figure C.1 shows that among the few large establishments in Egypt in 2006 only about half were domestic private sector firms. Furthermore, state-owned enterprises in Egypt still accounted for 29 percent of total employment in large establishments with at least 100 employees. In West Bank and Gaza, almost all employment attributed to the public sector is in nongovernmental organizations. Taken together, figure 1.6 and figure C.1 reveal that the share of jobs in large domestic private sector establishments in Egypt and West Bank and Gaza is small compared with regional peers.

Notes

1. SOEs in Tunisia are excluded; they are, however, relatively few in number. Establishments are defined as public or foreign if at least 10 percent of the capital was owned by the state or foreign owners, respectively. In Egypt, we added establishments that are foreign branches according to their legal status. In West Bank and Gaza, establishments with the legal status of an nongovernmental organization are tallied with the number of public establishments (which are the majority of public establishments in West Bank and Gaza).
2. The evolution of foreign direct investment in Jordan and its effect on domestic employment is analyzed in detail in Chapter 2.

Employment Growth over Firms' Life Cycles: Manufacturing Sector

FIGURE D.1

Manufacturing: Employment Growth over the Life Cycle

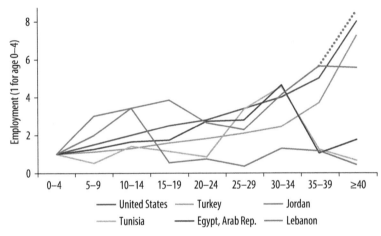

Source: Calculations based on census data.
Note: The figure shows the average number of employees for different age-cohorts across establishments in manufacturing (weighted by employment share of 4-digit sectors following Hsieh and Klenow (2012). The average number of employees in each age cohort has been normalized to 1 for the youngest age category (age 0–4 years). The analysis for Turkey, the Arab Republic of Egypt, and Lebanon is based on census data in 2006, for Tunisia in 2009, for Jordan in 2011, and for the United States in 2002. Results for Jordan and Tunisia are similar for other years (2006, 2010, or 2012). We excluded the two largest firms in the oldest age category in Jordan (the dotted line shows the average size of firms when including these outliers).

FDI Inflow and Employment in Jordan: Regression Analysis

TABLE E.1

Employment Spillovers from FDI, by Firm Characteristics

Variable	(1) All	(2) Manufacturing	(3) Services	(4) Small	(5) Large	(6) Old	(7) Young	(8) All	(9) Manufacturing	(10) Services
Foreign share 06	0.000	0.000	−0.001	−0.001*	−0.001	−0.002	0	0.000	0.000	−0.001
	−0.001	−0.001	−0.001	−0.001	−0.001	−0.001	−0.001	−0.001	−0.001	−0.001
Horizontal 06	−0.148**	−0.048	−0.157	−0.157**	−0.331*	−0.338**	−0.087	−0.117	−0.053	−0.171
	−0.073	−0.093	−0.127	−0.077	−0.188	−0.158	−0.083	−0.073	−0.094	−0.126
Backward 06	0.111	−0.057	0.400**	0.078	0.157	0.006	0.163*			
	−0.075	−0.086	−0.166	−0.079	−0.205	−0.162	−0.084			
Forward 06	0.023	−0.13	0.623**	0.027	−0.033	0.149	−0.033			
	−0.08	−0.097	−0.224	−0.084	−0.217	−0.187	−0.088			
Backward services 06								0.171**	−0.022	0.605**
								−0.086	−0.135	−0.239
Forward services 06								0.714**	0.347	1.076**
								−0.251	−0.736	−0.301
Backward manufacturing 06								−0.07	−0.079	1.282*
								−0.092	−0.096	−0.704
Forward manufacturing 06								−0.084	−0.142	1.120*
								−0.084	−0.099	−0.596
Constant	0.315**	0.264	−0.932**	0.204**	−0.119	−0.107	0.068	0.276**	0.230	−1.132**
	−0.069	−0.196	−0.217	−0.061	−0.219	−0.163	−0.08	−0.070	−0.200	−0.262
Observations	15,465	2,637	12,828	14,605	860	3,464	12,001	15,465	2,637	12,828
R^2	0.01	0.019	0.013	0.011	0.085	0.023	0.012	0.012	0.019	0.013
Industry fixed effects	Yes	Yes		Yes	Yes	Yes	Yes	Yes	Yes	Yes
Region fixed effects	Yes	Yes		Yes	Yes	Yes	Yes	Yes	Yes	Yes

Significance level: * = 10%, ** = 5%.

Quality of Business Environment and Jobs in Morocco: Data, Methods, and Main Findings

The data used in this paper derive from two sources: the Moroccan Annual Census, and detailed surveys conducted by the World Bank. The Moroccan Annual Census of Manufacturing covers the period 1997–2004. This annual census covers all manufacturing firms with no size limitation. It contains information on sales, value added, output, exports, employment, date of creation, location, investment, and four-digit industry code using the Moroccan Nomenclature of Economic Activities (NMAE). For a subset of firms we also have access to three much more detailed data sets: (1) FACS which contains production data for the years 1998 and 1999 (with some data for 1997), and business environment data for 1998, (2) Investment Climate Assessment (ICA)-2004 which contains production data for the years 2000–02 and business environment data for 2000 and (3) ICA-2007 which contains production and business environment data for 2002 and 2005. The firms included in FACS, ICA-2004 or ICA-2007 are all contained in the Census. In order to correct for the possible over or underrepresentation of firms in the ICA and FACTS samples, we weight each firm surveyed in the FACS and ICA by the share of the corresponding firm type in the census. The weights are defined on the basis of the 10 NMAE industries, 10 regions, and three size classes used in the regressions. Thus, the results can be interpreted as benign representative for the manufacturing sector in Morocco.

The FACS and ICA surveys cover food, textiles, garment, leather, chemicals, wood & paper including publishing, rubber & plastics, metals & mechanical, and electrical & electronic industries. The surveys include firm location with seven distinct geographical areas identified.[1] The data contains considerable detail on production variables, firm characteristics, and features of the business environment. We use two-digit NMAE production price index and investment price index to deflate production, value-added, and investment. The capital stock is available only for years 1997–2002 and 2005 in the FACS and ICA databases and for 2003–04 in the Census.

To obtain the stock of capital for the remaining years of the sample, we use the available data on investment and apply the perpetual inventory method taking a depreciation rate of physical capital of 5 percent. After cleaning of the data set we end up with an unbalanced panel containing 35,534 observations and 6,119 firms.[2] Each firm appears in the sample for at least three consecutive years and at most 9 years (see Table F.1).

The estimation function is based on the theoretical model of firm growth proposed by Evans (1987). We model plant growth as a function of age and size. For employment growth we employ the job creation rate following Davis, Haltiwanger, and Schuh (1996), which accounts for the employment growth that occurs in the year that a firm was created, and the employment destruction that occurred when a firm exits. Given the aim of our analysis, in addition to age and size, we control also for trade orientation adding the average firm export share, a dummy variable capturing whether the firm has any foreign ownership, the productivity level and the level of competition at the four digit level. The core regression equation therefore takes the following form:

$$JCR_{i(t,\ t+n)} = \beta_1 + \beta_2 \ln S_i + \beta_3 Age_i + \beta_4 AgeSQ_i + \beta_5 Trade_i$$
$$+ \beta_6 ForeignOwn_i + \beta_7 TFP_i + \beta_8 Herf_i + d_r + d_s + u_{i_i}$$

where JCR is the computed job creation rate; ln_S and Age refer to the logarithms of beginning-of-the period total employment and age; AgeSq is the squared age and captures the nonlinear relation between this variable and firm growth. Trade is computed as the average firm export share (exp_share) over the time period and ForeignOwn is a dummy variable which is equal to 1 if the firm reports a positive share of foreign capital at the beginning of the period. Estimates of total factor productivity (TFP) are derived at the firm level in the presence of endogenous input choices and selection issues using investment as a proxy for unobservable firm productivity. The estimates are based on both the semi-parametric method developed by Olley and Pakes (1996, henceforth OP), as well as the improvements suggested by Ackerberg, Caves, and Frazer (2007, henceforth ACF). For the degree of competition (Herf) we use the Moroccan census to compute Herfindahl indices at both the three digit and four digit level and explore the sensitivity of the results to these alternatives. Industry (d_s) and regional (d_r) dummies are added.

We then consider the role of the financial, policy and business constraints and competition variables, and this is done in two ways. In a first stage, we run a series of regressions where we sequentially and separately include each of the finance, policy, business, and competition variables in order to assess whether in aggregate these appear to be correlated with employment growth. In a second stage, we again take each of these variables, and consider whether different "types" of firms show a different relationship between each variable and employment growth. Here we divide firms into different types in various ways: by size, by age, by export-share intensity; by foreign ownership status, by level of productivity, and by the degree of competition in Morocco as measured by the Herfindahl index. (Table F.2 summarizes the main findings; it only reports the actual coefficients of the interaction terms if they are significantly different from zero [statistically.])

TABLE F.1

List of Regulatory Policy Variables

Name	Description		Type	Source
Long-term credit cost	The interest rate on long-term domestic debt	440	C	FACS
Access to bank credit	To what extent is this an obstacle to the growth of your firm?	684	0–4	ICA
Equivalent fiscal treatment	Do firms in your sector face equivalent fiscal treatment?	668	0–1	FACS
Dispute resolution	To what extent is this an obstacle to the growth of your firm?	830	0–4	ICA
Judicial system	To what extent is this an obstacle to the growth of your firm?	684	0–4	ICA
Wait permit	What is the average time taken to obtain a construction permit?	660	C	ICA
No. of permits for enterprise creation	If firm was set up in 1999 how many permits were needed?	575	C	FACS
Admin constraints	No of permits needed each year to operate?	488	C	FACS
Corruption	To what extent is this an obstacle to the growth of your firm?	822	0–4	ICA
Unfair informal sector competitors	To what extent is this an obstacle to the growth of your firm?	684	0–4	ICA
No. of competitors	For your principal product how many competitors do you have?	640	C	FACS
Extent of foreign competitors	Are there any foreign firms among your competitors on Morocco?	667	0–1	FACS

Note: C = continuous.

TABLE F.2

Job Growth Regression with Coefficients of the Policy and Environment Variables

Dependent variable: Job growth	Coefficient without interaction	Small firms (<=15)	Medium (10–100)	Large firms (>100)	Startups (<=3)	Young firms (4–10)	Old firms (>10)
Regulatory constraints							
Equivalent fiscal treatment	0.024				0.311**	−0.132**	
Dispute resolution	0.010			0.053**	0.260**	−0.173**	
Judicial system	−0.005				0.275**	−0.193**	−0.048**
Wait permit	−0.047**	−0.050**	−0.048**	−0.041**		−0.083**	−0.063**
No. of permits firm creation	−0.011				0.088**	−0.066**	−0.033*
Admin constraints	0.010		0.019*		−0.069**	0.088**	
Corruption	−0.001	−0.059**		0.058**	0.238**	−0.207**	
Competition							
Unfair informal comp	−0.004	0.031**	−0.030**		0.134**	−0.112**	
No. of domestic competitors	0.001	0.012**			0.012**	−0.002*	
Extent of foreign comp	−0.058**	0.027*	−0.086**	−0.110***		−0.055**	−0.086**
Finance constraints							
Long-term credit cost	−1.66**	−0.958**	−1.81**	−2.26**	0.487*	−2.16**	−2.42**
Access to bank credit	−0.020	0.067**	−0.044**	−0.039**	0.152**	−0.121**	−0.061**

Note: Coefficients of all variables are shown in the first column. However, coefficients of the interaction terms in subsequent columns are only shown if significant.
Significance level: * = 10%, ** = 5%, *** = 1%.

Notes

1. Grand Casablanca, Tanger-Tetouan, Rabat-Sale-Zemmour, Fes-Boulmane-Meknes, Oriental, Chaouia-Ouardigha, and Agadir.

2. The procedure used is close to Fernandes' one (2008) but less restrictive. Our cleaning has been realized in two steps. In a first one, we have eliminated from the sample (a) firms that have never reported any sales or material costs (costs of raw materials), (b) observations when exports are bigger than sales, and (c) observations with year-to-year growth rates in any of 3 ratios (sales to total workers, material costs to total workers and capital to total workers) larger (smaller) than 500% (–500%). These year-to-year growth rates are calculated with the constant variables. In a second step, we have always kept the firms who exist at less three consecutive years and we have dropped observations when we have one isolated year.

Political Connections and Private Sector Growth in the Arab Republic of Egypt

We use this macroeconomic quasi-experimental setting, to test whether aggregate employment growth over a 10-year period between 1996 and 2006 declined after the entry of politically connected firms into initially unconnected (open) sectors. Therefore, we use the following difference-in-difference estimation specification, whereby ΔY_{st} measures employment growth of the four-digit sector s between 1996 and 2006, PCEntry indicates the entry of politically connected firms between 1997 and 2007, NPC are sectors without connected firms before 1997, X is a matrix of control variable (employment and age), and S a matrix of sector dummies:

$$\Delta Y_{s,2006-1996} = \beta_E PCEntry_{s,1997-2006} + \beta_N NPC_{s,1996}$$
$$+ \beta_{EN}(PCEntry_{s,1997-2006} * NPC_{s,1996})$$
$$+ \beta_X X_{s,1996} + S + \varepsilon_{s,2006} \qquad (G.1)$$

Holding all else constant, entry always increases employment in the sector regardless of the fact that the entrant is connected or not. Thus, we expect that the entry of connected firms leads to sector employment growth, unless the adverse impact of connected firms on the growth opportunities of their unconnected peers leads to their exit or shrinkage. In contrast, we do not expect to observe the latter adverse effect (or at least expect it to be less pronounced) when connected firms enter into sectors which were already dominated by connected firms in previous years. Therefore, negative aggregate employment growth after the entry of connected firms into previously unconnected sectors implies that the decline in employment in unconnected firms (which cannot compete) outweighs any positive job creation of the connected firm(s).[1] Table G.2 shows that several sectors across the economy that previously had no connected firms have experienced the entry of connected firms in the time period of interest.

Table G.1 summarizes the findings of the difference-in-difference estimation. Columns 2 and 3 show the results for our most conservative

TABLE G.1

Employment Growth Declines after Politically Connected Firms Enter Initially Unconnected Sectors

| | Employment growth, 1996–2006 | | | | | |
	CEO		Owner		Broad	
Entry PC	32.2*	36.1**	7.15	10.3	4.83	4.40
	(1.95)	(2.09)	(0.84)	(1.24)	(0.99)	(0.77)
Not connected before 1996		−6.32		15.1		−10.5
		(−0.58)		(0.82)		(−0.67)
(Entry PC)*		−24.8**		−18.7**		−14.96
(not connected before 1996)		(−2.17)		(−3.47)		(−0.97)
ln(empl)	−.418**	−.401**	−.420**	−.382**	−.420**	−.376**
	(−2.44)	(−2.17)	(−2.37)	(−2.16)	(−2.34)	(−2.62)
Age	12.5	12.6	12.4	12.3	12.4	12.9
	(1.57)	(1.56)	(1.51)	(1.53)	(1.51)	(1.55)
No. of sectors	224	224	224	224	224	224
R^2	0.161	0.163	0.155	0.159	0.048	0.160
Sector dummies	1-dig	1-dig	1-dig	1-dig	1-dig	1-dig

Significance level: * = 10%, ** = 5%.

TABLE G.2

Entry of Connected Firms into Initially Unconnected Sectors, 1997–2006

Sector name 2-digit	ISIC Rev. 3.1 4-digit	Sector name 4-digit
Other mining and quarrying	1410	Quarrying of stone, sand, and clay
	1429	Other mining and quarrying n.e.c.
Manufacture of food products and beverages	1551	Distilling, rectifying, blending of spirits
	1552	Manufacture of wines
	1553	Manufacture of malt liquors and malt
	1554	Manufacture of soft drinks and mineral water
Manufacture of chemicals and chemical products	2412	Manufacture of fertilizers
Manufacture of basic metals	2720	Manufacture of basic precious metals
Manufacture of electrical machinery	3140	Manufacture of primary cells and batteries
Manufacture of radio, TV, and communication equ.	3230	Manufacture of television and radio receivers
Manufacture of furniture	3691	Manufacture of jewellery and related articles
Recycling	3710	Recycling of metal waste and scrap
	3720	Recycling of nonmetal waste and scrap
Electricity, gas, steam, and hot water supply	4010	Electricity production, transmission, and distribution
	4020	Manufacture and distribution of gas
Collection, purification, and distribution of water	4100	Collection, purification, and distribution of water
Wholesale trade and commission trade	5131	Wholesale of textiles, clothing, and footwear
	5141	Wholesale of solid, liquid, and gaseous fuels
	5152	Wholesale of electronic and telecommunications parts
Retail trade	5211	Retail sale in nonspecialized stores with food
Water transport	6120	Inland water transport
Insurance and pension funding	6601	Life insurance
Renting of machinery and equipment	7111	Renting of land transport equipment
Other business activities	7411	Legal activities
	7430	Advertising

measure, firms managed by a political connected CEO. We find that entry of connected firms into initially already connected sector increased employment growth, potentially because of the direct positive employment impact of the new connected entrant. Most important, however, we find that aggregate employment growth declines once connected firms enter new, initially unconnected sectors; the corresponding coefficient is significant at the 5 percent level. The economic impact is large. The magnitude of the corresponding coefficient suggests that aggregate employment in these sectors shrinks by 25 percent over the 10-year period 1996–2006. Note that the connected firms did not necessarily enter directly in 1997 so that employment growth might have been positive in earlier years but then declined substantially because of the sudden presence of the connected firm with access to policy privileges guaranteeing a large cost advantage over the existing competitors or potential new (unconnected) entrants. The negative aggregate employment growth effect after the entry of connected firms into new unconnected sectors is comparably large and significant at the 5 percent level when we restrict our definition of cronyism to firms owned by politically connected businessmen (column 5). For the broadest measure of connectedness, which also includes firms that received investments from connected private equity funds, the relevant coefficient of the interaction term is still negative and of comparable magnitudes but not significant at conventional levels.

Note

1. We do typically not observe if other first-tier politically connected firms operated in these "unconnected" sectors but exited before 2006. Thus, we have to assume in this macroeconomic quasi-experiment that, if unobserved first-tier connected firms which were forced to exit before 2006 existed, they did not operate in these "unconnected" sectors. All available evidence, however, suggests that policy privileges granted to the private sector expanded rather than declined between 1996 and 2006 (see Demmelhuber and Roll, 2007; Roll, 2013) making the exit of unconnected firms less likely.